Ambrotype by Samuel G. Alschuler, Urbana, Illinois, taken the day before Lincoln had replaced Judge David Davis at the Champaign Circuit Court. Probable date April 25, 1855. (Courtesy of The Lincoln Museum, Ft. Wayne, Indiana, a part of the Lincoln National Corporation)

Lincoln as a Lawyer:
An Annotated Bibliography

Elizabeth W. Matthews

With a Foreword by Cullom Davis

Southern Illinois University Press
Carbondale and Edwardsville

94 93 92 91   4 3 2 1

Library of Congress Cataloging-in-Publication Data

Matthews, Elizabeth W., 1927-
    Lincoln as a lawyer : an annotated bibliography / Elizabeth W.
Matthews ; with a foreword by Cullom Davis.
        p.   cm.
    Includes index.
    1. Lincoln, Abraham, 1809-1865--Career in law--Bibliography.
2. Lawyers--Illinois--Bibliography. 3. Practice of law--Illinois--
History--Bibliography. I. Title.
KF368.L52M37   1991
016.34973'092--dc20
[016.34730092]   90-39143
ISBN 0-8093-1644-7   CIP

The paper used in this publication meets the minimum requirements of American National Standard for Information Sciences--Permanence of Paper for Printed Library Materials, ANSI Z39.48-1984. ∞

Contents

Illustrations

Foreword

Abraham Lincoln practiced law for nearly twenty-four years. Except for part-time service in the Illinois legislature, a term in Congress, and extended political campaigning in 1858 and 1860, this was his full-time occupation and professional identity throughout his adult years in Springfield. Through three partnerships, a substantial and diverse caseload, extensive practice on the Eighth Judicial Circuit, and ample work before the Illinois Supreme Court and United States district and circuit courts, Lincoln fashioned both an outstanding reputation and a comfortable income. Law was his life for nearly half his fifty-six years. It provided a prosperous upper-middle-income livelihood, shaped consequential habits of analytical thought and logical rhetoric, exposed a provincial western figure to the larger world of developing corporations and professions, gained him stature among the era's public leaders, and produced invaluable political contacts and experiences. Also, it mirrored and thus epitomized the nineteenth-century evolution of American common law, from simple frontier-stage litigation to a hierarchical jurisprudence based on precedent.

To answer a famous historian's rhetorical question, the "Lincoln theme" is not and never will be exhausted. Interest in this complex and extraordinarily important figure is as lively in the 1990s as it ever was. His life and work carry a message to each generation of Americans, and to admirers around the world. How else could one explain why the eight-volume *Collected Works of Abraham Lincoln* is back in print thirty-seven years (and forty thousand copies) after it was first released? Or why Lincoln remains an arresting subject for attention by serious biographers?

However meritorious the best of modern scholarship on Lincoln may be, all of it suffers from insufficient attention to the law practice. Among the specialized studies the best known (John J. Duff, *A. Lincoln: Prairie Lawyer*) is uneven and unreliable. There are several dated book-length studies that offer useful information based either on reminiscences or incomplete examination of the cases. *Lincoln as a Lawyer*, by John P. Frank, offers the most sophisticated interpretation, but it is too broad for detailed understanding.

Given such limitations, biographers have perhaps unwittingly devoted scant attention to Lincoln's legal career. Among the best general biographies of the past fifty years, none apportions more than five percent of its text to the law practice, and most are well under that amount. The tendency is to describe his three partnerships, recount the rigors and rewards of his Eighth Circuit practice, and summarize a handful of noteworthy or entertaining cases. By direct statement or inference, all acknowledge Lincoln's success and satisfaction as a lawyer, but they fail to explore this with anything like the detail or analysis accorded other topics.

Promising steps are under way to redress this relative neglect. One is a long-term effort to locate, edit, and publish all of the estimated fifty thousand documents associated with Lincoln's law practice. When completed, The Lincoln Legal Papers will finally provide historians and biographers with the full documentary record they need to assess accurately his legal career.

This timely annotated bibliography is another such achievement. Elizabeth W. Matthews has carefully surveyed the extensive Lincoln literature, identifying over five hundred monographs, journal articles, sections of books, and pamphlets that devote reasonable attention to Lincoln as a lawyer. She covers the familiar and the rare published sources, and thereby reveals the extent to which modern authors either borrowed from their predecessors or broke new ground. During the one hundred years that historians have written about Lincoln as a lawyer, there has been a noticeable ebb and flow of published attention. These and other insights qualify Matthews' study for the select group of indispensable reference guides in Lincolniana.

The author brings to her task the library scientist's bibliographic precision and the historian's respect for context. Since 1974, Elizabeth W. Matthews has been a law librarian at Southern Illinois University, and also a regular contributor to library literature. This latest of her achievements began as an in-house reference project three years ago. Favorable response from colleagues and Lincoln specialists encouraged her to expand and publish the work. Students of both Lincoln and legal history are in her debt.

Cullom Davis

Preface

It has been suggested that more has been written about Abraham Lincoln than any other historical figure with the exception of biblical personages. There is voluminous material on this one man, as Monaghan's general bibliography covering the century 1839-1939 will attest. He stated that there was a morsel for the lawyer in his volumes, and he was correct in that there are few citations to the legal phase of Lincoln's career. As yet, there are only six full-length books on the topic. The definitive study has yet to be done. Several of the articles included in this bibliography decry the little factual information on Lincoln's career as a lawyer.

The purpose of this book has been to survey the literature, identify and bring together in a bibliography material on Lincoln as a lawyer, including bibliographic description, with summary annotations. The material includes journal articles, books, as well as significant portions of monographs, and pamphlets on Lincoln as a practicing attorney. It includes neither brochures nor newspaper articles, with the exception of a few outstanding newspaper magazine section treatments of the topic. It excludes *belles lettres*, audiovisual material, and foreign imprints. Annotations, which are descriptive rather than critical, emphasize the professional law aspect of any item listed, and Lincoln's preparation for his career.

The time frame of Lincoln's law practice was from 1837 when he became an attorney until 1861 when he departed from his law office in Springfield for Washington, D.C., indicating to his partner that he planned to practice again upon his return. The political aspects of Lincoln's life are not within the scope of this bibliography. A companion publication could conceivably be entitled "Lincoln as a Politician: An Annotated Bibliography." Therefore, political speeches and debates have not been included. For interested persons, the speeches would be in his *Collected Works*, or collections of speeches, as described within the bibliography; however, neither books nor journal articles have been scanned for Lincoln's political life, nor has Lincoln's family life been included during these years of law practice. One must admit that family and politics certainly had some bearing on his life during those twenty-four years, yet it is the purpose of this book to emphasize only the lawyer, the professional man, the career. Without question his years as a lawyer influenced his presidency; nevertheless, the content of the book does not extend to that aspect, unless there is incidental mention of it in an overall description of any particular item.

Certainly every known full-length book on the topic of Lincoln the lawyer has been included, which accounted for no more than six books, Whitney (1892), Hill (1906), Richards (1916), Woldman (1936), Duff (1960), and Frank (1961). There are a number of shorter items that deal with the subject, such as a monograph contributed by Moores, appearing in serial format, as well. Pamphlets, defined as less than fifty pages, brought several items on point. A number of volumes contained significant portions of books, although such selection has been judgmental. What is "a significant section"? Generally volumes including entire chapters devoted to the topic have been included, and occasionally a subsection, although there were a few instances when a chapter with an enticing heading, such as "At the Bar," included no more than a few sentences, and was therefore omitted. Several volumes with but little information have been included because of uniqueness, and a number have been included with larger amounts of topical material that was not separated into a chapter or subsection.

Information on the legal aspect of his career was almost nonexistent for a number of years following his death. An early campaign biography (Howells 1860) was corrected by Lincoln himself, and although it included only a few sentences regarding his preparation and career, has been included. The first full-length biography (Raymond 1865), and a volume respected by some later authors (Holland 1866), as well as general biographies with career information by his contemporaries, have been included because of the scarcity of any information on Lincoln's life as a lawyer at that time. This material, very nearly hidden in these larger general biographies, was the foundation upon which other biographers have built. First publishing efforts on the legal aspect began in the 1880s, with seven monographs containing some information, and three articles, increasing in the 1890s to a dozen articles, and ten monographs, including Whitney's book on circuit life. As the century turned, some twenty-four monographs, one a full-length book, appeared and very nearly the same number of articles. The greatest amount of publishing activity took place during the 1930s, with thirty-three monographs including Woldman, one of the best full-length books on the subject; forty-eight journal articles appeared. The 1940s were also productive, with twenty-six monographs and forty-three journal articles. The 1950s brought forth sixteen monographs and forty-two articles. The 1960s and 1980s were productive for journal articles, with twenty and thirty-five respectively; two full-length books were among the twelve monographs published in the sixties. In contrast only a few monographs that contained any legal career information had appeared between 1860 and 1869, and no journal articles as such, although the death proceedings by his fellow members of the bar in the Illinois Supreme Court accounted for a single 1869 entry.

Early works on the lawyer aspect follow the publishing pattern of general biographies, with the first material following Lincoln's death being laudatory, including the works emanating from his private secretaries. The Robert Todd

Lincoln papers were not immediately available to the public and hindered publishing efforts. Little factual material was available. Even court records were sometimes missing, trial court records being notably hard to track. Reminiscences were useful, most often laudatory and not always reliable, depending for accuracy on the memories of his friends. Later, critical material was introduced by Lamon, with Black, and by Herndon, whose works have remained controversial. Angle's *A Shelf of Lincoln Books* identified books that he considered of permanent value, although not all bibliophiles agreed with his list. Generally, historians appreciated his selected list and critical comments.

Authors contributing to the story of Lincoln's legal career have included lawyers and historians, for the book-length material. There are few articles by historians, with the exception of Illinois historians, particularly those in Springfield, where the executive secretaries and others furnished lengthy articles through the Abraham Lincoln Association, and earlier Lincoln Centennial Association; the *Journal of the Illinois State Historical Society* was a vehicle for the lawyer aspect of Lincoln's life as well. Contemporaries of Lincoln wrote articles also; many of the journal articles were contributed by the legal community through law reviews. Although emanating from schools of law and aimed at the legal community, they are quite readable. Of course, popular articles, several by journalists, some by laymen, appeared about this man of national prominence.

The most notable cases, of which there were four, were reported by numerous authors, each with his own interpretation. Of all the cases, one sparked the interest of nearly every author who discussed cases and several who discussed only this one case. The Duff Armstrong case was without equal in any description of Lincoln's legal cases. The story of his persuasion of the jury by using an almanac to prove that there was not enough moonlight for witnesses to have seen a murder has been told and retold. One author has even written an entire article, on the position of the moon on the meridian after gathering data from university astronomers. The story is not without controversy; there are those who have hinted that the almanac was not genuine, or published for another period in time, as opposed to others who have determined exactly which almanac was used, even to title and year. Other cases that were frequently described included *McCormick v. Manny*; *Hurd v. Rock Island Bridge Co.*, known as "Effie Afton"; and *Illinois Central Railroad v. County of McLean.*

Other conflicts appear in the literature, often over the smallest point. There was great discussion of Lincoln's obtaining Blackstone's *Commentaries.* Almost every author agreed that he had a copy and read it, but the issue was where he had obtained it. There was a full-length article dealing with the "barrel" theory as opposed to the "auction" theory. There were variant spellings of the names of parties to the cases. Differences in details, such as dates of events, have generally been reported in the summaries as the authors have stated them.

Lincoln's law practice was the practice of the frontier. Cases were often small, such as the $3.00 damage suit dealing with a single pig, which he appealed to the state supreme court. Unusual court sessions on the circuit took place in log cabin courthouses, where he led the proceedings out of the building in one instance to determine ownership of a colt, which went to its mother, thereby disputing the testimony of thirty-odd witnesses, and supporting the testimony of thirty others. Lincoln's practice involved more than these small cases, extending to corporation practice for the railroads, some of those cases setting precedents.

Authors generally agreed that Lincoln enjoyed the congeniality of life on the circuit and many of them depicted circuit life in detail, so that the reader could envision the muddy roads, travel by horse, the inns and accommodations of the day, and the excitement of court day in the fourteen counties of the old Illinois Eighth Judicial Circuit.

This compilation of books and journals on the topic has been intriguing and an outgrowth of a routine in-house bibliography compiled from materials in the library of Southern Illinois University School of Law for local clientele in 1987. Dissemination of that information brought an expressed need for such a bibliography. This author was unable to locate any bibliography on the topic of Lincoln as a lawyer, although thousands of books and articles have been written on very nearly every aspect of his life. Therefore the search began first at the local level, Morris Library, Southern Illinois University, where the Clint Clay Tilton Collection was located, and where numerous indexes were located. The university library also had microfilm of Lincoln Memorial University, Harrogate, Tennessee. An on-site visit to the library and museum of that institution was worthwhile, as was an examination of The Louis A. Warren Lincoln Library, Ft. Wayne, Indiana. The University of Illinois Lincoln Collection had a wealth of information, as did the Chicago Historical Society, and Lincoln College, in the town named for Abraham Lincoln while he was a practicing attorney. Visits to the Illinois State Historical Library in Springfield were essential, from the initiation of the project until its completion.

Utilization of catalogs and indexes was the key to finding and locating books and articles. Indexes included the old and reliable *Readers' Guide to Periodical Literature*, *Poole's Index to Periodical Literature*, and *Nineteenth Century Readers' Guide to Periodical Literature*, as well as *Essay and General Literature Index*, *Annual Bibliography of English Language and Literature*, *Social Science Abstracts*, *Biography Index*, *American History and Life*, and *Historical Abstracts*. Kermit Hall's *A Comprehensive Bibliography of American Constitution and Legal History* listed some fifty articles on Lincoln as a lawyer that were useful for verification and cross-checking. For legal material, particularly the law review articles, indexes included *Index to Legal Periodical Literature*, *Index to Legal Periodicals*, *Current Law Index*, *Legal Resource Index*, computerized LegalTrac, and LEXIS. The statewide LCS system, a link of ILLINET Online, provided an index for collections within the state of Illinois, and the Online Computer Library Center (Dayton, Ohio), for entries throughout the nation, with locations of material. In fact, with few exceptions, items listed can be located through OCLC by means of the "display holdings" screen for any given title in libraries. Journals, although not the specific articles, can be located by the same method. Some cases, such as Lincoln's United States Supreme Court cases, were viewed on LEXIS in full text, as were federal cases of district and circuit courts. Unfortunately Illinois cases in this early time of reference have to be viewed in the traditional printed *Illinois Reports*, as they have not yet been entered into the computerized database. There are numerous Lincoln cases that were cited in later cases online. It has been intriguing to consider the computerized reports in comparison with the early handwritten records.

While this bibliography indicates the state of published material on Lincoln as a lawyer at this point in time, it is anticipated that there will be extensive publishing after the Lincoln Legal Papers project has been completed some five years hence in Springfield, with filming of the courthouse records and other documents pertaining to Lincoln's legal career.

For monographic items in this bibliography, Monaghan numbers have been included for convenience of the reader. An effort has been made to include a listing of other editions with American imprints, especially those that have appeared following the Monaghan bibliography, published in 1943. This does not extend to unrevised printings. In addition, microform editions have been noted, as original items have long been out of print. Items within the bibliography have been organized into two parts, Monographs and Journal Articles. When an item has appeared as a journal article and also in separately published monograph form, generally a single annotation has been given, with cross-reference to the entry. Lincoln's published works are entered under his name as author, with cross-references from compilers or editors.

This bibliography, although not exhaustive, has been as complete as possible for American imprints. There must be the caveat, however, that a bibliography is never complete.

I am indebted to curators in several museums, and to librarians in all of the libraries mentioned above, as well as in several small public libraries, where an occasional older volume was retrieved. Computerized resource sharing through interlibrary loan has brought in a great deal of material. Without it, there would have been numerous other field trips for the purpose of data gathering. I wish to express my gratitude to the School of Law interlibrary loan personnel, particularly Sharon Oas, for persistence in obtaining this voluminous material, to my research assistant in the initial stages of the project, Joseph Vargo, and to student assistant Debby Nelson for help along the way, also to Pamela Graham for her computer expertise during the final phase. Sabbatical leave from Southern Illinois University School of Law has permitted the time necessary for completion of this bibliography. I appreciate William Beard's time and effort in reading parts of the manuscript, and for his suggestions. And a special thank you to Cullom Davis, director of The Lincoln Legal Papers, for his interest, encouragement, and support for the project.

List of Journals

Abraham Lincoln Quarterly
Albany Law Journal
American Bar Association Journal
American City
American Heritage
American History Illustrated
American Journal of Jurisprudence
American Journal of Legal History
American Law Review
Annals of Iowa Magazine of History With Notes and Queries
Association News
Atlantic Monthly

Bar Association of the State of Kansas Report
Bar Examiner
Biography: A Digest Magazine
Brief
Brooklyn Barrister
Buick Magazine
Bulletin of the Abraham Lincoln Association
Bulletin of the California State Society Sons of the Revolution
Bulletin of the Historical and Philosophical Society of Ohio
Bulletin of the Louisville Bar Association

California State Bar Association and State Bar Journal
Case and Comment
Central Law Journal
Century Magazine
Chicago Bar Record
Chicago Daily Law Bulletin
Chicago Legal News
Chicago Sunday Tribune Graphic Magazine
Chicago Tribune
Classmate
Commercial Law Journal

Connecticut Bar Journal
Cornhill Magazine
Courier Journal Magazine

Daughters of the American Revolution Magazine
Detroit Lawyer
Dickinson Law Review
Docket

Eastern Illinois University Bulletin

Farm and Fireside
Federal Bar Journal
Florida Bar Journal
Forum
Foxboro Recorder
Front Rank

Green Bag

Harper's Magazine
Harvard Law School Bulletin
Historic Illinois
Hobbies
Holborn Review
Homiletic Review

I.C.C. Practitioners Journal
Illiniwek
Illinois Bar Journal
Illinois Central Magazine
Illinois Historical Society Journal
Illinois History
Illinois Law Review
Illinois Libraries
Illinois Magazine
Illinois Quest
Illinois Reports
Illinois Representative
Illinois State Bar Association Annual Report
Illinois Times
Indiana Historical Society Publications
Iowa Law Review
Irish Law Times and Solicitors' Journal

Journal of the Illinois State Historical Society
Journal of the Missouri Bar
Journal of the National Association of Referees in Bankruptcy
Journal of the Patent Society

Kansas State Bar Association
Kentucky Bench and Bar
Kentucky State Bar Journal

Law Notes
Law Society Journal
Law Student
Law Student's Helper
Lawyer and Banker
Life
Lincoln Centennial Association Addresses
Lincoln Centennial Association Bulletin
Lincoln Fellowship of Wisconsin Historical Bulletin
Lincoln Group Papers
Lincoln Herald
Lincoln Lore
Lincoln News
Lincoln Newsletter
Litigation
Los Angeles Bar Bulletin
Los Angeles Daily Journal

McClure's Magazine
Manuscripts
Michigan State Bar Journal
Midland Monthly
Minnesota Law Review
Mississippi Valley Historical Association Proceedings
Month at Goodspeed's Book Shop

National Electric Light Association Bulletin
National Law Journal
National Magazine
National Republic
Nevada State Bar Journal
New Colophon
New Jersey Law Journal
New York Central Lines Magazine
New York Law Journal

New York Times
New York University Law Quarterly Review
North American Review
Notre Dame Lawyer

Ohio State Bar Association Report
Oregon Law Review
Outlook

Palimpsest
Papers of the Lincoln Centennial Association
Pennsylvania Bar Association
Pennsylvania Law Journal-Reporter
Philomathen Monthly
Prairie Farmer

Railroad Progress
Reader's Digest
Reports of the American Bar Association
Rough Notes

St. John's Law Review
Science and Society
Sohioan
Solicitors' Journal and Weekly Reporter
South African Law Times
State Bar Journal of the State Bar of California
Summons

Temple Law Quarterly
Texas Bar Journal
Transactions of the Illinois State Historical Society
Tyler's Quarterly Historical and Genealogical Magazine

United States Law Review

Virginia Bar Register

Washington State Bar Association Report of Proceedings
West Virginia Bar
Wisconsin Magazine of History

Youth's Companion

Monographs

Monographs

1

A. Lincoln, the Circuit Lawyer, 1839-1859. McLean County, Illinois. [Bloomington, Ill.: Lincoln Sculpture Committee, available from McLean County Historical Society, 1977.]
34 p. illus.

A life-size bronze statute of Abraham Lincoln as a circuit rider is located in the McLean County Law and Justice Center in downtown Bloomington, Illinois. "Budd" Fairfield's history classes at Bloomington High School in McLean County, Illinois conceived the idea and raised the funds to commission the statue. This pamphlet gives a history of the work from January 1975 to its dedication in August 1977, explaining in particular how sculptor Keith Knoblock constructed it.

Some history of Lincoln in McLean County reveals that Lincoln spent about two weeks per year in the county as he rode the Eighth Judicial Circuit, "The Mud Circuit." Travel was rigorous and conditions often terrible, with poor food and lodging. Yet it was said of Lincoln, he was "happy in no other place." "Lincoln was among the two or three most sought-out lawyers in the state." Courts in those days were of relaxed procedures, an almost carnival-like atmosphere. Lincoln's first McLean County case was in 1837; he was dismissed by his client. By 1853 "Lincoln handled a great deal of litigation for the Illinois Central Railroad" including the famous case of the railroad in a dispute with McLean County over taxes. Lincoln prevailed and later sued to collect his fee. The booklet includes brief discussion of Lincoln as a prosecuting attorney in a McLean County murder trial, and notes various friendships he made while in the county.

2

Abraham Lincoln as Attorney for the Illinois Central Railroad Company. Chicago: Ginthorp Warren, 1905.
[13] p. illus., port., facsim.

This little booklet contains facsimiles of handwritten Lincoln documents, including documents Lincoln wrote in suing to collect a fee from the Illinois Central Railroad. "Soon after the incorporation of the Illinois Central Railroad Company . . . Lincoln . . . was appointed one of its attorneys." He was consulted upon the construction of the charter of the company. This pamphlet includes discussion of several cases Lincoln tried on behalf of the railroad for livestock damage and taxation. Perhaps his most important case for the railroad involved an attempt by McLean County to tax the railroad, even though it was exempt from such taxes by charter. The corporation refused to pay Lincoln's fee, saying "the payment of so large a fee to a western country lawyer without protest would embarrass the general counsel with the board of directors. . . ." Lincoln then sued and collected his fee, representing himself.
Monaghan 1447

----. Microfilm. New Haven, Conn.: Yale University Library, 1988.
----. Chicago: Ginthorp Warren. December 1905. 25 leaves.
----. Microfilm. New Haven, Conn.: Yale University Library, 1989.

3
Abraham Lincoln: Tributes From His Associates: Reminiscences of Soldiers, Statesmen and Citizens. With introduction by the Rev. William Hayes Ward. New York: Thomas Y. Crowell, 1895.
xiii, 295 p.

Two of the tributes deal with the lawyer Lincoln:

Herndon, W. H., Esq. (p. 17-21). This tribute includes an unpublished letter from Lincoln's law partner. In this piece, there is discussion dealing with Lincoln on education and his view of women's rights.
Weldon, Hon. Lawrence (p. 237-255). "Reminiscences of Lincoln as a Lawyer" includes incidents of his practice in Illinois; an interesting case; and a notable address to a jury.
Monaghan 2988

4
Abraham Lincoln's Last Case in Chicago. Chicago: Barnard & Miller "Briefs," ©1933.
12 p. illus.

The last important case Lincoln ever tried was *Johnston v. Jones and Marsh*, the famous Sand-Bar case in United States Circuit Court, March 23, 1860. The case involved title to land of great value formed by waves along the shore of

Lake Michigan near the Illinois Central right of way. Little has been known about the case; official records went up in smoke in October of 1871.

5
Anderson, David D.
Abraham Lincoln. New York: Twayne Publishers, 1970.
205 p. (Twayne's United States Authors; 153)

A chronology includes Lincoln's admission to practice, move to Springfield, and practice of law, among other aspects of his life. Chapter headings in the form of quotations include one entitled, "... He ... removed to Springfield, and commenced the practice ..."; and another chapter, "... He went to the practice of law with greater earnestness than ever before. ..." In discussion of his education, Anderson indicated that the reasoned analysis and prose of Blackstone's *Commentaries on the Laws of England* gave impetus to order and clarity in Lincoln's own writing. An example of his forthrightness is provided in a statement that is "legalistic and rational in thought and execution."

The author points out that mature actions and professional statements were a contrast with Lincoln's immature emotional life. John T. Stuart, law partner, who also acted as personal and political friend, was particularly knowledgeable about this phase of his life.

A Lincoln letter to friend Joshua Speed reveals incidents pertaining to the Trailor case. There was some indication that Lincoln minimized his role as defense attorney. The author taps Lincoln's "Essay on the Trailor Case" for information that appeared anonymously in the *Quincy Whig*.

--- ----. Microfilm. New York: AMS Press, 1970.

6
Angle, Paul M. ed.
Abraham Lincoln by Some Men Who Knew Him: Being Personal Recollections by Judge Owen T. Reeves, Hon. James S. Ewing, Col. Richard P. Morgan, Judge Franklin Blades, John W. Bunn. With Introd. by Isaac N. Phillips. Edited with notes and foreword by Paul M. Angle. Bloomington, Ill.: Pantagraph Printing, 1910.
167 p.

Reeves, Owen T., attorney and later city attorney and clerk of Bloomington, came to Bloomington in 1854 to practice law. He said that Lincoln was an individual with a different personality. Reeves met Lincoln often, when he attended all of the sessions of the McLean County Circuit Court from March 1855 until Spring 1860. He recalled the variety of his cases, such as his assisting the state's attorney in prosecution of Wyatt for murder. He saw Lincoln for the plaintiff in a case to set aside sale of the Pike Hotel; he defended a chancery suit; and represented the Illinois Central Railroad Company in the McLean County tax case.

Ewing James S., who later practiced law in Bloomington, was but a boy when Lincoln was on the circuit. He met him among guests at his father's old National Hotel. The youngster attended court, where many suits were trivial. He saw Lincoln as a "jury lawyer" with the power of clean and logical statements. Members of the jury felt that Lincoln was a friend; he used pertinent illustrations and anecdotes and was masterful in his legal arguments. He had knowledge of general principles of law and a clear and logical mind.

--- ----. Chicago: Americana House, 1950.
--- ----. Freeport, N.Y.: Books for Libraries Press, 1969.

7
Angle, Paul M.
Lincoln 1854-1861: Being the Day-by-Day Activities of Abraham Lincoln From January 1, 1854 to March 4, 1861. Springfield, Ill.: Abraham Lincoln Association, 1933.
xxx, 400 p. maps.
On cover: Lincoln day by day, 1854-1861.

The Association published seven day-by-day accounts of Lincoln, each covering one of the years from 1854 to 1861. These volumes were revised and reissued in one volume.
Monaghan 3368

See **Angle,** below, for individual volumes, and annotation.

8
Angle, Paul M.
Lincoln in the Year 1854: Being the Day-by-Day Activities of Abraham Lincoln During That Year. Springfield, Ill.: Lincoln Centennial Association, 1928.
57 p.

This is one of a series of seven volumes each covering Lincoln's daily activities during a particular year, intended to give a "graphic account of the most important period in Lincoln's pre-presidential career."

There is a brief description of each day for which there is a record of Lincoln's activities. It gives an account of Lincoln's courtroom activities, indicating court and case. The information was obtained from county court records that were available to the author. As Lincoln's fame grew, relevant records and newspaper accounts make it easier to track Lincoln's daily activities.

Although a daily synopsis does not go into depth, it gives the reader an idea about Lincoln's daily schedule on any given day during this time period.
Monaghan 2988

--- ----. Microfilm. New Haven, Conn.: Yale University Library, 1988.

Other volumes in the series are listed below:

9
Angle, Paul M.
Lincoln in the Year 1855: Being the Day-by-Day Activities of Abraham Lincoln During That Year. Springfield, Ill.: Abraham Lincoln Association, 1929.
57 p.
Monaghan 3076

--- ----. Microfilm. New Haven, Conn.: Yale University Library, 1988.

10
Angle, Paul M.
Lincoln in the Year 1856: Being the Day-By-Day Activities of Abraham Lincoln During That Year. Springfield, Ill.: Abraham Lincoln Association, 1930.
57 p.
Monaghan 3165

11
Angle, Paul M.
Lincoln in the Year 1857: Being the Day-By-Day Activities of Abraham Lincoln During That Year. Springfield, Ill.: Abraham Lincoln Association, 1930.
57 p.
Monaghan 3166

12
Angle, Paul M.
Lincoln in the Year 1858: Being the Day-By-Day Activities of Abraham Lincoln During That Year. Springfield, Ill.: Lincoln Centennial Association, 1926.
56 p.
Monaghan 2830

13
Angle, Paul M.
Lincoln in the Year 1859: Being the Day-By-Day Activities of Abraham Lincoln
During That Year. Springfield, Ill.: Lincoln Centennial Association, 1927.
56 p.
Monaghan 2900

14
Angle, Paul M.
Lincoln in the Year 1860 and as President-Elect: Being the Day-By-Day
Activities of Abraham Lincoln from January 1, 1860 to March 5, 1861.
Springfield, Ill.: Lincoln Centennial Association, 1927.
66 p.
Monaghan 2901

--- ----. Microfilm. New Haven Conn: Yale University Library, 1988.

15
Angle, Paul M., ed.
The Lincoln Reader. Edited, with an introduction, by Paul M. Angle. New
Brunswick, N.J.: Rutgers University Press, 1947.
xii, 564 p. illus.

This biographical collection on Abe Lincoln, was written by sixty-five authors
from 179 of their writings. The editor, Librarian of the Illinois State Historical
Library, compiled the works of Carl Sandburg, Lord Charnwood, William H.
Herndon, John Hay, himself and others into a comprehensive study of the life
of Abraham Lincoln. He structures the discussion using the narrative of various
authors for the text of the book. It provides a full overall picture of Lincoln.

A separate chapter regards Lincoln's life as a lawyer: "Attorney and
Counsellor-at-Law," by Woldman, Angle, Nicolay and Hay, and Beveridge. In
addition to reviewing his education, it explains how the law became his
absorbing interest. It tells of his borrowing law books from Squire Bowling
Green, and his reading of law books during travel from Springfield to New
Salem. Lincoln drafted some legal instruments before acquiring his license to
practice, and his experience in the justice of the peace courts was an
"apprenticeship" for him.

There is information regarding Linocln's partnership with Stuart, and later,
Logan. His selection of Herndon as partner is explored, as well as riding the
Circuit of the Eighth Judicial District. The reader can see a facsimile of his
professional card from the *Sangamo Journal*, and typical entries from his
account book.

A chapter entitled, "Leader of the Illinois Bar," by Benjamin P. Thomas, Henry C. Whitney, Jesse W. Weik, Albert A. Woldman, Harry E. Pratt, John H. Littlefield, and Thomas Drummond, deals with his resumption of practice after his return from Washington.

Description of life on the circuit follows. Pleadings in Lincoln's handwriting have been located in courthouses comprising the Eighth Circuit. Several of his cases are discussed, such as *Hildreth v. Turner*, a patent case; the Duff Armstrong case; the Illinois Central Railroad; and Lincolns' suit against the railroad to collect his fee.

Includes bibliography.

--- ----. Westport, Conn.: Greenwood Press, 1981, ©1947.
--- ----. New York: Da Capo Press, 1990, ©1947. In press.

Angle, Paul M., comp.
New Letters and Papers of Lincoln.
See **Lincoln**, Abraham.

16
Angle, Paul M.
One Hundred Fifty Years of Law: An Account of the Law Office Which John T. Stuart Founded in Springfield, Illinois, a Century and a Half Ago. By Paul M. Angle and Robert P. Howard. Springfield, Ill.: Brown, Hay, and Stephens, 1978.
84 p. [16] leaves of plates.

This book is an enlargement of Angle's *One Hundred Years of Law*. In addition to the history of the first one hundred years, another fifty years of the law firm are included. Material beyond the original brings the history of the firm up to 1978. Robert P. Howard is author of the updated part of the volume.

Portraits of members of the firm, including Lincoln, appear. The summary page of firm members shows "Stuart and Lincoln, 1837-1841."

17
Angle, Paul M.
One Hundred Years of Law: An Account of the Law Office Which John T. Stuart Founded in Springfield, Illinois, a Century Ago. Springfield, Ill.: Brown, Hay, and Stephens, 1928.
53 p.

This volume marks the one hundred year anniversary of the opening of a law office by John T. Stuart, a twenty-one-year-old lawyer in Springfield, Illinois,

on October 25, 1828. The firm had continuously operated for a century at the time the book was written. Abraham Lincoln got his start in the law profession through a partnership with Stuart; four years later the partnership was to dissolve. There is description of the law offices, as to location and furnishings, and the account book with typical entries.
Monaghan 2989

--- ----. Microfiche. Littleton Colo.: Fred B. Rothman, [1989]. (Law Books Recommended for Law Libraries--Biography; No. 89)

18
Appleman, Roy Edgar, ed.
Abraham Lincoln: From His Own Words and Contemporary Accounts. Edited by Roy Edgar Appleman.   Washington: United States Dept. of the Interior, National Park Service, 1942.
viii, 55 p.   illus.   (Source book series; no. 2)

The editor attempts to bring together some of the more "important and significant passages of Lincoln's letters, speeches, and state documents," with observation from those who knew Lincoln. Forty different subjects are covered, many with illustrations.
Lincoln's brief autobiography showed that he studied law during his legislative period, and from 1849-1854 he "practiced law more assiduously than ever before." Other subjects include: Lincoln's befriending a revolutionary soldier's widow in a suit to obtain a pension wrongfully withdrawn; Lincoln in his law office, as told by his longtime law partner, William H. Herndon. The editor uses a speech by Judge David Davis to describe Lincoln's professional traits and talents as a lawyer. Lincoln had tried hundreds of cases before Judge Davis on the Eighth Illinois Judicial Circuit.
Other subjects, although not directly on point as Lincoln the lawyer, illustrate some of his traits, such as "Advice to a Young Friend"; "Power of Memory"; "Lincoln, the Speaker"; "Lincoln Interprets the Declaration of Independence"; "Mr. Herndon's Lincoln."
Includes bibliography.

--- ----. Rev. ed. Washington: Government Printing Office, 1946.
--- ----. Washington, D.C.: WANT Pub. Co., 1985.
--- ----. London: United States Information Service, 1959.

19
Arnold, Isaac N.
Abraham Lincoln: A Paper Read Before the Royal Historical Society, London, June 16th 1881. Chicago: Fergus Printing Co., 1881.

38 p.
Reprinted from Transactions of the Royal Historical Society, 10.

In this paper, Arnold, who had been a contemporary of Lincoln, discusses "a lawyer." He mentions how Lincoln's beginnings in the practice of law in rude log courthouses contrasted with proceedings in Westminster Hall. He states simply that Lincoln was a great lawyer, convincing his juries by application of principle rather than by citation of authorities. He was stronger before a jury than court, suggesting that there has not been a greater advocate before the jury when he was on the right side, requiring his faith in a case to bring out his best. He was almost intuitive in reading of a person's character, and he had direct, candid methods. Not only did he excell in statement of a case, but was skillful in cross examination. He did not misrepresent an opponent's case, nor misstate evidence. He was in active practice until his nomination for the presidency, May 18, 1860.
Monaghan 971

--- ----. Microfiche. Sanford, N.C.: Microfilming Corp. of America, 1983. (Pamphlets in American History: Civil War: CW 673)
--- ----. Microfilm. New Haven, Conn. Micrographic Systems of Connecticut, 1986.
--- ----. Chicago: Fergus Printing Co., 1883. 45 p.
--- ----. [With] Stephen A. Douglas; An Eulogy Delivered before the Chicago University, July 3rd, 1861, by James Sheahan. Chicago: Fergus Printing Co., 1881.
--- ----. Microfiche. Ann Arbor, Mich.: University Microfilms International, 1989. (Genealogy and Local History; LH 5494)

20
Arnold, Isaac N.
The Life of Abraham Lincoln. 3rd ed. Chicago: A. C. McClurg, 1885. 471 p.

The great depth and detail of this volume are devoted to politics and the presidency; nevertheless, Arnold devotes considerable attention to Lincoln's life as a lawyer. Arnold was a contemporary and a close personal friend of Lincoln's. Later he was a confidant and trusted advisor to Lincoln the president. Both of these men had practiced law in Illinois and both of them were associated and opposed each other in litigation. The author pens a book about Lincoln's life based on research and his vantage point of knowing and watching Lincoln.
Monaghan 1010

--- ----. 4th ed. Chicago: A.C. McClurg, 1887. Other "editions," i.e., printings: 5th, 1891; 6th, 1893; 7th, 1896; 8th, 1898; 10th, 1906; 11th, 1909; 12th, 1916. 471 p.
--- ----. Chicago: Jansen, McClurg, 1885, ©1884. 462 p.
--- ----. Microfilm. New Haven, Conn: Micrographic Systems of Connecticut., 1986.

21
Arnold, Isaac N.
Reminiscences of the Illinois Bar Forty Years Ago: Lincoln and Douglas as Orators and Lawyers. Chicago: Fergus Printing Co., 1881.
29 p.
Monaghan 969

--- ----. [S.l.: s.n., 1881] 18 p.
--- ----. Microfiche. Woodbridge, Conn.: Research Publications, 1985. (19th-Century Legal Treatises; no. 6844)

For annotation, see **Arnold,** Journal Articles. Reminiscences of the Illinois Bar: 1840. 47 ILLINOIS BAR JOURNAL (February 1959), 572-578.

22
Arnold, Isaac N.
Sketch of the Life of Abraham Lincoln. Compiled in most part from the History of Abraham Lincoln, and the Overthrow of Slavery. New York: John B. Bachelder, 1869.
75 p. port.

According to the preface, this volume contains subject matter never before made public. Arnold, a contemporary, and member of Congress from Illinois, provides a glimpse of Lincoln as a lawyer within a few pages: his admission to the bar, practice at the bar, the fact that he was admitted to the bar of the Supreme Court of Illinois, Autumn 1836, and his name first appears on the roll of attorneys in 1837. In April he moved to Springfield and entered into partnership with John T. "Stewart" [*sic*], i.e., Stuart. As a lawyer, he manifested the power of simplification and clarification. There is information regarding circuit practice, "riding the circuit," where few books could be obtained, except for an odd volume in a saddlebag. Arnold points out that ordinarily a mere case lawyer was helpless before intellectual giants. He lists several books which Lincoln studied, Blackstone, Kent, Chitty and Starkie's Evidence.

Leading members of the bar followed judges to log courthouses where Lincoln was surrounded by friends. He was popular with judges, lawyers, juries, and spectators. He was known for his wit and humor, and he aided and counseled young members of the bar.

His manner of conducting jury trials was effective; he used conversational language and gave the impression of addressing individual jurymen. Treating witnesses with respect, his examination of them was effective. No one questioned his truthfulness and honesty. As a jury lawyer, on the right side, he probably never had a superior; on the wrong side he was comparatively weak. Monaghan 912

23
Barker, H. E. (Harry Ellsworth)
Abraham Lincoln, His Life in Illinois: Being Year by Year Incidents from 1830 to 1865 Written and Compiled by H. E. Barker. New York: M. Barrows, 1940. 64 p. illus.

Issued by the Lincoln Fellowship of Southern California, where Barker was Curator, this short book tracks Lincoln in Illinois year by year, chronologically from 1830 to 1865. Short on text, numerous photographs are from the film "Abe Lincoln in Illinois," by Robert E. Sherwood.

Several pages pertain to the lawyer Lincoln:

"Lincoln studies law--elected to legislature, 1834" (p. 17-19).
Describes his finding a set of Blackstone's *Commentaries on the Law*, which he studied since he had determined that law and politics should be his occupation and avocation. He is quoted as having said of the Blackstone volumes," The more I read the more intensely interested I become. Never in my whole life was my mind so thoroughly absorbed. I read until I devoured them."

"Lincoln's plea for law observance, 1837" [*sic*] (p. 22).
While still a resident of New Salem, Lincoln gave an address on this topic January 27, 1838, in Springfield. He advised the people never to violate in the least particular laws of the county nor to tolerate violation of them by other persons.

"Lincoln defends a friend, 1840" (p. 27-28).
This piece describes Lincoln looking down into the courtroom from a hole in the ceiling from his law offices above. As he heard his friend E. D. Baker, making a speech, confusion followed if not the beginnings of a riot when there was disagreement among the audience. Lincoln entered the scene by way of the "scuttlehole" and urged that Baker had a right to speak.

"Lincoln's legal acumen, 1841" (p. 28-29).
Four years after practicing law with John T. Stuart, Lincoln became a law partner of Stephen T. Logan. During his three years association with Logan, he

adopted Logan's methodology of keen analytical search into both sides of a case before taking it into court. He learned to weigh both sides of an issue.

"Lincoln's advice to lawyers, 1850" (p. 43).

Lincoln outlined several basics for lawyers, the first of which was diligence, followed by doing work promptly, and accomplishing all that could be done for business at hand. He urged them to discourage litigation, and encourage compromise, to be a peacemaker, rather than to stir up litigation. He stated that exorbitant fees should not be charged and advised them not to take the entire fee in advance. He believed that they would have more interest in a case if prior fees were not collected in their entirety. He urged them to be honest.

24

Barondess, Benjamin.
The Adventure of the Missing Briefs. New York: Civil War Round Table of New York, 1955.
[12] p. facsims.

Reprinted from 8 *Manuscripts* (Fall 1955), 20-24, 64.

The author relates the story of his search for Abraham Lincoln's briefs concerning two cases in which Lincoln appeared before the United States Supreme Court. The briefs had been presumed stolen. The cases were *Lewis v. Lewis* decided in the January 1849 term and *Forsyth v. Reynolds* decided in 1853. At the Supreme Court the author found the records on appeal but was unable to locate the briefs by Abe Lincoln. It was a requirement that briefs be submitted to the court plus one served on opponent, so it was obvious the briefs existed at one time. The author contends the lost, stolen, or destroyed briefs if they could be recovered would be of great value in measuring his abilities as an attorney "at his professional best."

Includes photocopy of handwritten *Lewis v. Lewis* record.

25

Barrett, Joseph Hartwell.
Life of Abraham Lincoln: Presenting His Early History, Political Career, and Speeches In and Out of Congress; Also, a General View of His Policy as President of the United States; With His Messages, Proclamations, Letters, etcs.: and a History of His Eventful Administration, and of the Scenes Attendant Upon His Tragic and Lamented Demise. Cincinnati: Moore, Wilstach & Baldwin, 1865.
x, 842 p. illus.

Based on public and private documents.

Chapter 6 of this volume addresses several aspects of Lincoln the lawyer, very briefly: his law studies, his license to practice; progress in his profession, his qualities as an advocate; and incidents in his practice. The author includes discussion of the Armstrong case in some detail.
Monaghan 22

--- ----. Ultrafiche. Dayton, O.: National Cash Register, 1970. (PCMI Library Collection)
--- ----. New York: Loomis National Library Association, 1888.
--- ----. New York: William L. Allison, 1889.
--- ----. New York: International Book Co., [1894?]
See also Monaghan 20, 21, 23.

26
Barrett, Oliver Roger.
The Immortal Autograph Letters, Documents, Manuscripts, Portraits, Personal Relics and other Lincolniana, collected by the late Oliver R. Barrett. New York: Parke-Bernet Galleries, 1952.
264 p. illus., facsims.

The book concerns the Public Auction Sale, February 1952, of Oliver R. Barrett's collection of Lincolniana, sold by order of the executors of his estate. A foreword by Carl Sandburg quotes Benjamin P. Thomas, "The Barrett Collection is so full and basic that a pretty good life of Lincoln could be written from it alone, whereas no present-day life could be written without it. Barrett's generosity has enriched the Lincoln story." The book gives a good description of each of the 842 items to be auctioned: letters, notes, photos, paintings, sculptures, documents, personal items, with numerous illustrations.
Many of the items pertain to Lincoln as a lawyer, such as "One of the Earliest Legal Documents Drawn by Lincoln," in 1833 before he began his law practice; "Stuart & Lincoln for Plffs," 1837, a praecipe on behalf of Herndon; an excerpt from the Stuart & Lincoln fee book, 1837-38; agreement on contingency fee; complaint of plaintiff in a suit; holographic manuscript, "The court instructs the jury. . . ." A book listed for sale: Sir William Blackstone, *Commentaries on the Laws of England*, vol. 1 only, with imprint New York, 1845. The name of the firm Lincoln & Herndon is inscribed. Also, Lincoln and Herndon's copy of George T. Curtis, *Digest of the Decisions of the Courts of Common Law and Admiralty in the United States*, vol. 3, 1848.
From the firm of Lincoln and Herndon, W. H. Herndon's "Law Commonplace Book," recording authorities of cases, briefs, etc., without entries by Lincoln. Other documents include detainers, complainants' bills, chancery

cases, letters concerning real property cases, notes for an argument before the Supreme Court of Illinois, and others.
[Catalog 1315]

27
Barton, William E. (Eleazar)
The Influence of Chicago Upon Abraham Lincoln: An Address Delivered Before the Chicago Historical Society on February 10, 1922.   Chicago: University of Chicago Press, 1923.
54 p. port.

This address, by the pastor of a Congregational church, includes information on the Rock Island Bridge case, known as the "Effie Afton" case, tried in Chicago in 1857, with Lincoln on the side of the defendant. The "Sand-Bar" case, or *Johnston v. Jones*, United States District Court, was the last case in which Lincoln appeared in Chicago.
Monaghan 2549

--- ----. Microfilm. New Haven, Conn.: Yale University Library, 1988.

28
Barton, William E. (Eleazar)
The Life of Abraham Lincoln. Indianapolis: Bobbs-Merrill, 1925.
2 v. illus., facsims., ports.

Volume one deals with Lincoln's life before his election to the presidency. The author traveled as a circuit preacher, much as Lincoln traveled as a lawyer on the circuit. Barton traveled and lived in Illinois and Kentucky, following the footsteps of Lincoln. Some time after Lincoln's death, he was able to talk with and live among people who knew Lincoln or who were from his time. This extensive work covers the events and people who were involved in Lincoln's life.
    The early years of his practice are covered in a chapter entitled, "Lawyer and Lover, 1836-1839." Concerning Lincoln as a lawyer, there is brief mention of his preparation, the disputed stories about how he acquired Blackstone's *Commentaries*, and how he borrowed books from John T. Stuart. Lincoln did not suppose his education for law to have been great, and referred to himself as a "mast-fed lawyer." He proved to be a lenient bar examiner.
    Chapter 21, entitled "Lincoln as a Lawyer, 1848-1860." explains the dissolving of the Logan and Lincoln firm, and how the Lincoln and Herndon firm was established the same day. When with Logan, Lincoln was left largely in charge of the office, paying attention to the details of legal practice.
    In either office, Lincoln as the younger partner was more likely to be sent out on unimportant cases in other counties. However, he liked it better than the

office work. Lincoln had a method of becoming associate counsel with local lawyers in the county seats within the judicial district. A law student, Milton Hay, who knew Lincoln well, described the legal practice of those days.

Routine cases in central Illinois in that day were petty. Although Lincoln was offered a partnership in Chicago, he remained Herndon's partner. There is description of the lawyers traveling by horseback or buggy from county to county on the circuit.

The sizable number of cases in which he appeared as counsel in the Supreme Court of Illinois is recorded, with the notation that he appeared before the Supreme Court of the United States. Several of his well-known cases are discussed.

Monaghan 2758

--- ----. [Indianapolis]: Bobbs, Merrill for The Educational Press, 1925.
--- ----. Boston: Books, Inc., 1943, ©1925.

Basler, Roy P., ed.
Abraham Lincoln: His Speeches and Writings.
See **Lincoln**, Abraham.

Basler, Roy P., ed.
The Collected Works of Abraham Lincoln.
See **Lincoln**, Abraham.

29
Bateman, Newton.
Abraham Lincoln: An Address, by Hon. Newton Bateman.   Galesburg, Ill.:
Cadmus Club, 1899.
46 p.

Newton Bateman, had an office that was in a room adjoining the one used by "Mr. Lincoln." One of his favorite places was a little consulting room, south of and adjoining the Supreme Court Library in the old State House. Bateman knew him from the Secretary of State's office in the same building. He saw much of Lincoln in the State House, in the courtroom, and elsewhere.

Bateman explains that Lincoln was often pitted at the bar against a very eminent lawyer, who was careless in dress. Once, Lincoln in addressing the jury, pointed out this carelessness to his advantage. Bateman tells of a murder trial in a crowded courtroom, where Lincoln made a calm, clear, plain, and forcible speech. His opponent said that Lincoln had not believed in the case and wore a "mask" to conceal the fact that he was merely acting. "Honest Abe Lincoln" arose and said that not a word of that could be applied to him. Then the senior counsel took back all of his words, and there was applause.

Bateman tells the story of a poor and simple elderly lady who brought Lincoln a parcel amid distinguished guests, and indicates how gracious Lincoln was in receiving it. He uses incidents of character to illustrate that Lincoln was extremely careful and cautious in statements, using fact aimed at exact truth. When mere opinion was involved, he was known for the expression, "It seems to me," or "It appears to me."
Monaghan 1238

--- ----. Microfilm. New Haven, Conn.: Micrographic Systems of Connecticut, 1985.
--- ----. 2nd ed. Gardena, Calif.: Privately printed by H. E. Barker, Spanish American Institute, 1932.
Monaghan 1239

30
Beard, William.
Barret v. Alton and Sangamon Railroad Company. Illinois Supreme Court, December Term 1851. Springfield: The Lincoln Legal Papers, 1989.
30 p.

A sample transportation case with commentary and annotated documents gives the Lincoln scholar a preview of a representative selection of cases as they will appear in the Lincoln Legal Papers. The *Barret v. Alton and Sangamon Railroad* includes: Lincoln to William Martin; Declaration and Praecipe; Copy of Subscription Book; Deposition of Isaac Gibson; Lincoln to William Martin; and Opinion of the Court by Chief Justice Samuel H. Treat. In the latter document, Justice Treat's written opinion could not be located, therefore the text is from the *Journal and Opinion Record, I-SC, Central Grand Division*, including the final court order which is not printed in the *Illinois Reports*.

31
Beveridge, Albert Jeremiah.
Abraham Lincoln, 1809-1858. Boston: Houghton Mifflin, 1928.
4 v. illus., ports.

This comprehensive four-volume work by historian, scholar, and former Senator Beveridge, deals with the life of Abraham Lincoln from his birth in 1809 until 1858. The author had planned a complete work of Lincoln's life to end in 1861 with a later work on the presidential phase, but his death halted the work on Lincoln at the 1858 date.

Volume 2 contains most of the material involving Lincoln's career as a lawyer. Chapter 4, "Law: Life: Growth," includes information on the law office of Lincoln and Herndon, riding the circuit, David Davis, Swett and Lamon, Lincoln's reading, Lincoln's associates on circuit; acts as judge; and cases in which Lincoln appeared. Chapter 5 entitled, "Last Years at the Bar," includes: Lincoln's fees; description of certain cases, such as, the Wright pension case, Duff Armstrong murder trial, railroad litigation, Illinois Central Railroad Company tax case, Rock Island Bridge Company's case, a slander case, the McCormick Reaper case, and others.

The work is authoritative and documented.

Volume 1 includes bibliography.

Monaghan 2999 (Standard Library edition; Manuscript edition)

--- ----. Microfilm. New Haven, Conn.: Yale University Library, 1988.
--- ----. Boston: Houghton Mifflin, 1928. 2 v.
--- ----. St. Clair Shores, Mich.: Scholarly Press, 1971. 2 v.

32
Binns, Henry Bryan.
Abraham Lincoln. London: J. M. Dent; New York: E. P. Dutton, 1907.
xiii, 379 p. illus. ports., maps, facsims. (Temple Biographies)

This book, by a British author, published in London and New York, has a chapter "Becomes a Lawyer," with information on preparation for Lincoln's legal life. The following chapter includes: Stuart and Lincoln; Logan and Lincoln. Chapter 5, "On the Eighth Circuit," contains: Lincoln & Herndon; Lincoln on the circuit; as a lawyer; important cases; view of the law; appearance and habits. Includes his notes for a law lecture.

Binns notes that the majority of Lincoln's cases dealt with minor matters. Yet he had a number of more difficult cases, for which he depended upon his powers of analysis.

Monaghan 1520

--- ----. Microfilm. New Haven, Conn.: Yale University Library, 1988.
---. The Life of Abraham Lincoln. London: Dent; New York: Dutton, 1927. (Everyman's Library. Biography. [no. 783])
--- ----. Microfilm. New Haven, Conn.: Yale University Library, 1988.

33
The **Bollinger** Lincoln Lectures. Addresses Given at the Dedication of the Lincoln Library. Collected by James W. Bollinger Lincoln Foundation, November 19, 1951. Edited by Clyde C. Walton, Jr. With a preface by Virgil M.

Hancher. [Iowa City]: State University of Iowa Libraries, Bollinger Lincoln
Foundation, 1953.
x, 80 p. port.

Includes "Lincoln and the Effie Afton Bridge Case," by Charles J. Lynch, Jr., p.
46-67.

This collection of speeches was edited by Clyde C. Walton, Jr., rare-book
curator, and formerly Illinois State historian. Speakers included Paul M. Angle,
Harry Pratt, Benjamin P. Thomas, Charles J. Lynch, Jr., and Louis A. Warren
on the occasion of the dedication ceremony of Judge James W. Bollinger's 4,000
volume Lincoln collection at the State University of Iowa.

Charles J. Lynch, Jr., discussed Judge Bollinger's great interest in "Lincoln's
most celebrated case" the "Effie Afton" bridge case. This was the first bridge
constructed over the Mississippi River and "the legality of its construction was
the subject of one of Lincoln's most important cases." The case pitted the
railroad interests against those of river and barge traffic with Lincoln
representing the railroad. Lynch explores the background of the case, the case
itself, and the effect of Lincoln's forceful argument on the jury. A hung jury was
discharged by the judge, thus, a victory for Lincoln and railroad.
Includes footnotes.

34
Brooks, Noah.
Abraham Lincoln and the Downfall of American Slavery. [New ed.] New York:
G. P. Putnam's Sons, 1894.
xv, 471 p. illus., facsims. ports.

Brooks, resident of Dixon, Illinois, knew Lincoln with some degree of
intimacy through politics, beginning in 1856. Later he was with the *Sacramento
Union*, in Washington, D.C.

Chapter 9, entitled "Lincoln the Lawyer," presents: an honest advocate and
counsellor; the Snow Boys and Old Man Case; famous lawsuits about Negroes;
Jack Armstrong's son on trial for murder; Lincoln's vindication of his old friend;
how the attorney looked and spoke.

This work is a reissue of the author's *A. Lincoln: A Biography for Young
People*, 1888. The author based his work on information published by Ward H.
Lamon, Isaac N. Arnold, J. G. Holland, John G. Nicolay, and John Hay.
Monaghan 1040

--- ----. New York: G. P. Putnam's Sons, 1896. (Heroes of the Nations)
--- ----. Microfilm. New Haven, Conn.: Micrographic Systems of Connecticut,
1986.

--- ----. New York: AMS Press, 1978.
--- ----. With varying subtitle: Abraham Lincoln: The Nation's Leader in the Great Struggle . . . New York: Putnam's, 1888; Washington: National Tribune,1909; and Microfilm. New Haven, Conn: Yale University Library, 1988.

----. The Life of Lincoln. In **The Writings** of Abraham Lincoln, edited by Arthur Brooks **Lapsley**. With an Introduction by Theodore Roosevelt, together with the Essay on Lincoln by Carl Schurz; The Address on Lincoln by Joseph H. Choate; and the Life of Lincoln by Noah Brooks. Constitutional edition. New York: G. P. Putnam's Sons, 1923. (8 v.) Vol. 8, 467 p. Chapter 9, p. 121-130, "Lincoln the Lawyer." Monaghan 1466.

35
Browne, Francis F., comp.
The Every-day Life of Abraham Lincoln: A Biography of the Great American President From an Entirely New Standpoint, With Fresh and Invaluable Material. Lincoln's Life and Character Portrayed by Those Who Knew Him. . . . Prepared and arranged by Francis F. Browne. New York: N. D. Thompson, 1886.
xxvii, 747 p. illus., ports.

Former editor of *The Dial*, Francis F. Browne brought together reminiscences by people who had known Lincoln. The collection has been organized to provide some continuity in portrayal of his personality. Anecdotes are taken from well-known biographers, as well as from obscure writers. Acknowledgment is made to the biographers, but exact citation is wanting.
Part 2 includes "Lincoln as Lawyer and Politician." "Lincoln's Law Practice" includes the following: appearance in court; reminiscences of a law-student in Lincoln's office; novel way of keeping partnership accounts; charges for legal services; trial of Bill Armstrong; kindness toward unfortunate clients; refusing to defend a guilty man; wanted to wash his hands; couldn't take pay for doing his duty; better make six hundred dollars some other way; a small crop of fight for an acre of ground; fixing a plug for his gallus; taking up tackling before a jury; a man who hadn't sense enough to put on his shirt; Lincoln as a horse trader; some striking opinions of Lincoln as a lawyer.
Monaghan 1019

--- ----. Boston: Mason & Fowler, 1886.
--- ----. Minneapolis: Northwestern Pub. Co., 1887, ©1886.
--- ----. St. Louis: Wm. G. Hills, 1896, ©1886.
--- ----. (subtitle varies) New and thoroughly rev. ed. Chicago: Browne & Howell, 1913. 2 v. (Integration of the material has been revised.)

36
Carter, Orrin N. (Nelson)
Lincoln and Douglas as Lawyers. An Address Given Before the Mississippi
Valley Historical Association, Chicago, Illinois. [Cedar Rapids, Iowa, 1911].
28 p.

Reprinted from Proceedings of the Mississippi Valley Historical Association,
1910-1911. 4 MISSISSIPPI VALLEY HISTORICAL ASSOCIATION
PROCEEDINGS (1912) 213-240.

Carter contends that perhaps "no other two men in our history, both
reaching such eminence in national affairs, were so closely associated in many
things as were Douglas and Lincoln." They began the practice of law about the
same time (Douglas 1834, Lincoln 1836), Lincoln practiced law before Supreme
Court of Illinois, and Douglas was a judge. They were in the Illinois legislature
together, courted the same woman, and were rivals for both the United States
Senate and the presidency.

The author notes each was very different from the other yet both were
"above reproach in private life" and "both were of extraordinary ability." They
were self-made men. A history of both legal careers is included, showing
Douglas' appointment to the Illinois Supreme Court bench at twenty-seven years
of age. Douglas resigned from the court some two years later to run for
Congress. Lincoln's rise to prominence as a lawyer, though not as rapid as
Douglas' was equally as brillant, Lincoln being recognized as the leading trial
lawyer in Illinois in the 1850s.

Isaac N. Arnold, a friend to both, claimed that they were strong jury lawyers.
"Lincoln was the stronger in a case when he believed he was on the right side.
On the wrong side Douglas was the stronger."
Includes bibliography.
Monaghan 1973

37
Cartwright, James H.
Lincoln the Lawyer. In **Addresses** Delivered at the Memorial Exercises Held at
Springfield, Illinois, February 12, 1909. Commemorating the One-Hundredth
Birthday of Abraham Lincoln. Springfield: The Illinois Centennial Commission,
1909.
226 p. port.
p. 166-173.

Cartwright refers to the memorial service held in the Supreme Court of
Illinois soon after the death of Abraham Lincoln. While other people speak of
him as a chosen ruler or orator, professional brethren speak of him as a lawyer.

For nearly thirty years, he was a member of the bar of the Supreme Court of Illinois, and for a quarter century he engaged in active practice in that court and in the trial court. It was his early ambition to be a lawyer. Perseverence permitted him to achieve that goal. He was devoted to law and had reverence for principles. He referred to an address in Springfield in 1837 in which Lincoln exhorted listeners never to violate the laws, nor to tolerate their violation.

Law books were few in number at that time in history, but there were fundamental rules under which justice was administered. Practically Lincoln's whole education was gained from law books; they molded his intellect and character. He learned the principles of law and had the common sense to apply them. His ability, integrity, and devotion won for him an exalted place at the bar.

At this memorial service, a bronze tablet was dedicated as a marker for the site of the first law office of Abraham Lincoln.

38
Charnwood, Lord (Godfrey Rathbone Benson)
Abraham Lincoln. By Lord Charnwood. 3rd ed. New York: H. Holt, 1917.
482 p. (Makers of the Nineteenth Century)

According to the preface, this book was a "first considered attempt by an Englishman to give a picture of Lincoln." Against the backdrop of the growth of the nation, Charnwood, of the English peerage, delineates the personal traits forming the character of Lincoln. The author describes his going very nearly to the extreme in legal practice, refusing to take cases if he did not approve of them as "honest." He describes and analyzes a few of his interesting cases. Charnwood scrutinizes the reasons for Lincoln's cunning actions, with some attempt at interpretation.
Monaghan 2229

--- ----. London: Constable, 1916;
--- ----. London: Constable, 2nd ed., 1917.
--- ----. Microfilm. Annapolis, Md.: USNA Library, 1979.
--- ----. New York: Holt, 1916.
--- ----. Garden City, N.Y.: Garden City Pub. Co., 1917.
--- ----. [S.l.] Independent Press, 1924, ©1927.
--- ----. 2nd ed. New York: Holt, 1917
--- ----. Garden City, N.Y.: Garden City Pub. Co., 1938.
--- ----. New York: Pocket Books, 1939.
--- ----. New York: Pocket Books, 1952, ©1917. 501 p.

39
Chittenden, L. E. (Lucius Eugene)
Personal Reminiscences 1840-1890, Including Some Not Hitherto Published of
Lincoln and the War. New York: Richmond, Croscup, 1893.
ix, 434 p.

Chapter 34 includes: Abraham Lincoln: his successes; the lawyer; the advocate;
the popular man.

　　Lincoln created the conditions of his own success. He was honest, with
rugged integrity; he cultivated his storytelling, and was popular, without rivals
in his profession. The author describes an incident of Lincoln's extricating
himself from a case when the client had deceived him. He includes the dramatic
almanac scene with details from the Armstrong case, and quotes the *Cleveland
Leader* regarding the swift acquittal.
Monaghan 1116

--- ----. Microfiche. Chicago: Library Resources, 1970. (Library of American
Civilization, 12432)
--- ----. Freeport, N.Y.: Books for Libraries Press. 1971, 1893.

40
Choate, Joseph H. (Hodges)
The Career and Character of Abraham Lincoln. An address delivered by Joseph
H. Choate, Ambassador to Great Britain at the Philosophical Institution of
Edinburgh, November 13, 1900. Chicago: Chicago, Milwaukee, and St. Paul
Railway [1902?]
30 p. port. (Chicago, Milwaukee, and St. Paul Railway Series; no. 22)

　　Year after year Lincoln's knowledge, power, experience, and reputation were
extended. His mental faculties and power of persuasion developed to an
extraordinary degree. Little by little he rose to prominence at the bar during
twenty-three years from the time of his establishment as a lawyer. His
professional brethren asked how by random reading of a few miscellaneous law
books he could become a learned and accomplished lawyer. Books and libraries
were scarce in Illinois; life was crude and so were the courts and administration
of justice. Lawsuits were extremely simple. They relied on principles of natural
justice, without resort to technical learning. It was by constant contact with
educated and powerful men at the bar in Illinois that Lincoln acquired
professional strength and skill. The speaker laid great stress on Lincoln's career
as a lawyer, much more than his biographers.

--- ----. Microfilm. New Haven, Conn.: Yale University Library, 1988.
---. Abraham Lincoln. New York: Thomas Y. Crowell, 1901. 38 p.

41
Chrisman, Herring.
Memoirs of Lincoln. [Mapleton, Iowa]: Published by his son, William Herring
Chrisman, 1930.
97 p.

The chapter "Lincoln Before He Was Great" describes how the author saw
Lincoln in his dark and dingy law office in Springfield in 1856, where the
attorney sat low in his chair reading law. He consulted him regarding the
purchase of land. When the client returned two weeks later for advice, Lincoln
told him that he could not purchase said land. The man, concerned then about
the legal fee, was relieved to learn that it was only five dollars.
Monaghan 3179

--- ----. [Mapleton, Iowa: Mapleton Press for William Chrisman, 1927] 22 p.

42
Coffin, Charles Carleton.
Abraham Lincoln. New York: Harper, 1893.
xiii, 542 p. illus., ports., maps.

The author knew Lincoln from the time he was nominated for president. He
gathered data for his book from those who knew him, as well as by on-site visits.
In his chapter entitled "Riding the Circuit," Coffin describes the judicial
district, circuit judges, and Abraham Lincoln as a young lawyer, not yet a leading
member of the bar. He relates the background in the case of Nancy, the slave
girl sold to Bailey by Cromwell. Bailey gave his note and had not paid it. The
case came to Lincoln; he argued that the Ordinance of 1787 prohibited slavery
in the Northwest Territory, so she could not be held as a slave. Neither
Cromwell nor Bailey could hold her and Cromwell was not entitled to the
money Bailey had promised to pay. The court decided in Lincoln's favor.
The author tells of several other cases such as one involving ownership of
a colt, Lincoln moving the case to the courthouse lawn, and the animals
deciding, with the colt going to its mother, more reliable that the thirty witnesses
on one side and thirty-four on the other.
He mentions several cases including: the Revolutionary War widow's pension
case; *The State v. Mr. Whiskey*; and the Snow boys.
Monaghan 1117

--- ----. Ultrafiche. Dayton, Ohio: National Cash Register, 1970. (PCMI Library
Collection 000064)

43
Coleman, Charles Hubert.
Abraham Lincoln and Coles County, Illinois. New Brunswick, N.J.: Scarecrow Press, 1955.
xii, 268 p. illus.

A chapter of this book by Coleman, social science professor, describes Abraham Lincoln's Coles County law practice, largely from 1841 to 1847, and occasionally thereafter. He practiced law in Charleston, the county seat of Coles County, although it was not in the Eighth Circuit. There are incomplete case files in Coles County Circuit Court in which Lincoln appeared as attorney. The author concluded it was unlikely that a complete list could be made, and provides a selective list. There is some discussion of the Matson slave case. Includes bibliography.

44
Current, Richard N.
Lincoln and the Eighth Circuit. Delivered at the Lincoln Colloquium, October 11, 1987, Springfield, Illinois. Cosponsored by Lincoln Home National Historic Site and the Sangamon County Historical Society. Springfield, 1987.
p. 11-20.

(On cover: "Delivered at the 1986 Lincoln Colloquium.")

Historian Current quotes Judge Davis in saying that Abraham Lincoln was happy on the Eighth Judicial Circuit, which originated in 1839, and by 1850 had fourteen counties, reduced to five by 1857.

Traveling the circuit took three months, twice annually. In spring and fall, Lincoln covered the whole circuit, whereas some twenty-five or thirty other lawyers made only part of the trip. Lincoln rode in his buggy or with Judge David Davis. Current describes life on the circuit, including inns, taverns, and food.

While Lincoln enjoyed social life, the main business was practice of law. People came to watch proceedings, sometimes with Lincoln substituting on the bench for Judge Davis. Several memorable cases are mentioned, such as the Rock Island Bridge case and the Duff Armstrong "almanac" case. A few lesser known cases are described, such as one for child support, and one concerning the defense of twenty-one women, reported as *The State v. Mr. Whisky*, and the Peachy Harrison case. Lincoln defended more often than he prosecuted and did not always win a case; nevertheless he was sought after as an attorney.

45
Curtis, William Eleroy.
Abraham Lincoln, 1809-1865. In **Great** American Lawyers, edited by William
Draper **Lewis**. Philadelphia: John C. Winston Co., 1908. Vol. 5.
p. 461-500.

--- ----. South Hackensack, N.J.: Rothman Reprints, 1971.

Curtis' *Abraham Lincoln* appeared originally in *The True Abraham Lincoln*.
Philadelphia: J. B. Lippincott, 1893.
Monaghan 1370

For Annotation, see **Curtis** below.

46
Curtis, William Eleroy.
The True Abraham Lincoln. Philadelphia: Lippincott, 1903.
409 p.

This biographical essay, first published as *Abraham Lincoln*, begins with his
becoming inspired to become a lawyer from the accidental access to the *Revised
Statutes of Indiana*. The author draws on Lincoln's own brief autobiography in
indicating what a short period of formal schooling he had, and listing books
which Lincoln read in his youth, including the aforementioned Statutes. He
expresses surprise that Lincoln found them interesting enough to read and very
nearly memorize, being able to provide the actual citations. He mentions
Lincoln's striving to understand language and meanings.

Curtis quotes information which Lincoln furnished in his own handwriting
to Charles Lanman, editor of the *Congressional Directory*, in which he states that
his education was "defective" and his profession was "lawyer." Curtis also tells of
John T. Stuart's encouraging Lincoln to study law, and of his reading law books
while traveling. Includes a list of books that Lincoln recommended to a young
man wanting to know how to become a lawyer.

The author notes dates of his admission to the bar, his listing in the
published list of attorneys, and his first case, *Hawthorne v. Wooldridge*. He
comments on Lincoln's small fees, life on the Eighth Judicial Circuit, and his
skill with juries. He describes, as well, Lincoln's action regarding the licensing
of a theatrical company in Springfield. There is some description of the familiar
cases, Duff Armstrong, McCormick, and Illinois Central Railroad. Some of his
characteristics and traits are catalogued.
See Monaghan 1370

--- ----. 3rd ed., 1903; 4th ed., 1904; 5th ed.,1905; 7th ed, 1907; 8th ed.,1909.
Same pagination.

--- ----. Microfilm. Hew Haven, Conn.: Yale University Library, 1988.
---. Abraham Lincoln. Philadelphia: Lippincott, 1902.

47
Davis, Cullom.
Crucible of Statesmanship: The Law Practice of Abraham Lincoln. [Address] International Conference on Abraham Lincoln, Taipei, Taiwan, Republic of China, November 12-15, 1989. Springfield, 1989.
20 p.

Davis, director and senior editor of the Lincoln Legal Papers, calls the attention of the conference attendees to the fact that little attention has been paid to Lincoln's quarter-century career as a practicing attorney. The essay addresses the scant and imperfect information that is available about this important phase of his life.

The author offers two different cases as examples that dispel the view of Lincoln as a small-town lawyer with routine and unrewarding case work. The cases, *Barret v. Alton and Sangamon Railroad* and *People v. Peachy Quinn Harrison*, exemplify the types of litigation that were a formative influence in his steps toward mature statesmanship.

Includes bibliographic notes.

(A copy of a recently located hand-written transcript of the Harrison case, comprised of nearly 100 pages, has been furnished to the Lincoln Legal Papers, *New York Times*, 10 February 1989, Sect. 2, p. 7)

48
DeBoice, Benjamin S.
A New Look at Lincoln, the Lawyer.
[Address] given before The Sangamon County Bar Association, February 12, 1954, at Lincoln's Tomb. [Springfield, Ill: 1954?]
8 leaves.
Typescript. Illinois State Historical Library.

DeBoice mentions voluminous material written on the life, character, and service of Lincoln, including every phase of his career exhaustively studied-- books written to preserve for posterity every little incident in his life's story. Yet, he points out, there is misunderstanding and misinformation concerning Abraham Lincoln the lawyer. Part of the misconception stems from the fact that his biographers stressed the meagerness of his formal education, unable to grasp the possibility that any man surmounted such a handicap, becoming a great lawyer. Frequently biographers brushed over this phase of his career, ignoring the fact that it was the training and education he received in practice of law which fitted him to cope with the great problems of the presidency. Exactly when he took up the study of law was not clearly established. Some biographers record that when he was in the grocery business, he bought a box of household goods from an immigrant; at the bottom of the box he found a four-volume set of Blackstone's *Commentaries*. The official records disclose that he took his first formal step toward admission to the bar on March 24, 1836. The orator believes serious study of law as a career started after his election to the legislature in 1834.

49
Dedication of the Bronze Statue, "Lincoln the Lawyer." Harrogate, Tenn.: Lincoln Memorial University, 1949.
16 p.

For annotation, see **Dedication**, Journal Articles.

50
Donald, David Herbert.
Herndon: Lincoln's Law Partner. [Champaign, Ill.: The Author], 1947.
321 p.

Dissertation (Ph.D.), University of Illinois, 1946.

Donald's dissertation is based on Herndon's published writings, such as *Herndon's Lincoln*, printed sources as listed in Monaghan, Springfield newspapers, court records, land deeds, and legal documents; the Herndon-Weik collection and other individual letters. While the major thrust of the study is about Herndon, it reveals much about Lincoln. One learns here of the beginning of their partnership, how Herndon studied in the office of Logan and Lincoln. Upon the dissolving of that partnership, Lincoln offered Herndon a partnership. Although he became a competent partner, he served somewhat as an apprentice, carrying books and searching for authorities. After Lincoln's term in Congress, he returned to practice with Herndon. Generally in their office, Lincoln welcomed clients, heard stories, gave advice, and appeared in court, while Herndon did research, checked facts, drew up briefs, cited authorities, and managed the office. Lincoln spent long months on the circuit, while Herndon seldom was outside of Springfield. Here, too, is information on Lincoln and the Kansas-Nebraska Act, and the Lincoln-Douglas campaign.

--- ----. Abstract. Urbana, Ill., 1946.
13 p.

51
Donald, David Herbert.
Lincoln's Herndon. Introduction by Carl Sandburg. [1st ed.] New York: Alfred
A. Knopf, 1948.
xv, 392, xxiii p. illus., ports.

Historian Donald produced a first book about the life of William H.
Herndon, Lincoln's law partner. Herndon is known, as well, for writing the
controversial Lincoln biography, *Herndon's Lincoln*. Through his long law
partnership with Lincoln, Herndon knew him as well or better than any other
man. His life is interesting in itself, regardless of his association with an
American hero. Herndon fell on hard times after the death of Lincoln, but
found the time and inspiration to write a Lincoln biography. He also possessed
a large collection of Lincoln materials that he eventually gave away or sold. His
biography and various lectures concerning Lincoln were often controversial in
that he portrayed him as an average and common man, whereas the general
public had made him into a hero.
Includes a chapter on Lincoln.
Includes bibliography.

--- ----. Microfiche. Littleton, Colo.: Fred B. Rothman, 1989. (Law Books
Recommended for Libraries. Biography no. 101)
--- ----. Lincoln's Herndon: A Biography. New York: Da Capo Press, 1988,
©1948.
392 p.
A Da Capo paperback. Includes a new introduction by the author.

52
Duff, John J.
A. Lincoln: Prairie Lawyer. New York: Bramhall House, 1960.
viii, 433 p. illus.

The author, a New York lawyer, gathered the facts for his book by following
Lincoln's legal trail, touring the old Eighth Judicial Circuit, and studying cases.
Afterward, he published this extensive work dealing exclusively with Lincoln's
life as he practiced law, starting in March of 1837 when he was sworn in to the
bar until the year when he became president. He describes Lincoln as a lawyer,
and discusses various cases that he handled. Includes an Appendix listing all of
the lawyers who were associated with Lincoln on the Eighth Circuit and the
judges of the Supreme Court of Illinois before whom Lincoln practiced.
Includes bibliography.

--- ----. lst ed. New York: Rinehart, 1960.
viii, 433 p. illus.

53
East, Ernest E.
Abraham Lincoln Sees Peoria: An Historical and Pictorial Record of Seventeen
Visits from 1832 to 1858. Peoria: [Record Pub. Co.], 1939.
37 p. illus., ports., facsims.

This item deals with Lincoln's associations with Peoria. Prior to East's
research, historians had recorded only five visits of Lincoln to Peoria. While the
pamphlet deals with occasions other than law, such as his return from the Black
Hawk War, debates, conventions, and travel, there is information on his law
career. There is a summary of the sensational divorce case *Wren v. Wren* in
"Defends an Accused Wife Who Fights Divorce Suit," records of which are in
Peoria County Circuit Court. And there is a sequel in which the wife tried, after
her husband's death, to secure her right of dower in her husband's real estate.
He describes another case, "In Court for a Creditor Against Peoria Merchants."
where Logan and Lincoln were attorneys for Adam W. Spies, a New York City
merchant against Neal [et al.], retail merchants.
Monaghan 3672

54
Emerson, Ralph.
Mr. & Mrs. Ralph Emerson's Personal Recollections of Abraham Lincoln.
Rockford, Ill.: Wilson Brothers, Printers, 1909.
18 p. illus., ports.

Includes "An Intimate View of Abe Lincoln," by Ralph Emerson, p. 5-12.
These recollections are important for Emerson's explanation of Lincoln's
contribution to the *McCormick v. Manny* case in Cincinnati. He explains "we"
became involved in important litigation. Emerson paid him the largest retaining
fee he had ever received up to that time. The litigation was important, therefore
a number of lawyers were engaged on each side, including Senator Douglas,
William H. Seward, and others. The important point that Emerson makes is that
when the case came on hearing in Cincinnati, "As Lincoln had not had sufficient
time to prepare, he did not speak, but he was present through the whole
hearing, which consumed several days. We were limited to two lawyers on a
side." Edward M. Stanton spoke for "us." Lincoln was intensely interested, and
stood at rapt attention or walked back and forth listening. Afterward, he walked
and talked with Emerson, remaining silent and dejected, and said he was going
home to "study law," that college-trained men were coming west now.
Monaghan 1716

55
Enos, Z. A.
The Early Surveyors and Surveying in Illinois. Before the Illinois Society of
Engineers, January 29, 1891. Springfield: Springfield Printing Co., 1891.
7 p. [2 facsims.]

Contains an opinion by A. Lincoln on congressional regulation of surveying.

During a convention of surveyors, a committee agreed to submit a question
regarding the authority for land surveying to some able lawyer for his decision.
"In the selection of the attorney, the convention chose Mr. Lincoln, on account
of his being a practical surveyor as well as a recognized leading member of the
bar, on the principle that a good lawyer could better interpret and apply the law
to a subject with which he was thoroughly conversant."
    They obtained a written opinion, settling the question in the Convention as
to the controlling authority of the law of 1805, 11th Section of the Act of
Congress (approved February 11, 1805) prescribing rules for the subdivision of
sections of land within the United States system of surveys.
    A facsimile shows the opinion in Lincoln's handwriting, with the signature
A. Lincoln, dated January 6, 1858.
Monaghan 1082

56
Evans, Henry Oliver.
Abraham Lincoln as a Lawyer. [Pittsburgh: Smith Brothers Co., 1927?]
17 p.

The author tracks the law career of Abraham Lincoln, who on March 24,
1836, became licensed to practice law. He notes Lincoln's inadequate schooling,
lack of cultural background, influential family or friends, and meager
professional preparation. Yet this man had climbed to the leadership of the
Illinois bar by the time he tried his last important case, known as the Sand-Bar
case.
    Lincoln became interested in the law when a complaint was filed against him
for infringing on a ferry franchise. Evans divides Lincoln's law career into three
parts, the first being his law partnership with John T. Stuart where Lincoln "was
immediately thrown on his own resources in handling an active practice." He
identifies the second as his partnership with Stephen T. Logan, where Lincoln
learned how to study and prepare for a case. And the third was Lincoln's
partnership with William H. Herndon who relieved Lincoln of the office work,
which permitted him to travel the circuit and engage in public life.
    The writer depicts Lincoln's life on the circuit, the men with whom he
associated, and his trial tactics and mannerisms. He discusses several of
Lincoln's noted cases including *Bailey v. Cromwell*, the Duff Armstrong murder

case, the McCormick Reaper patent case, and the Rock Island Bridge case. He discusses briefly Lincoln's legal position on the war powers under the Constitution. The author concludes "that the 24 years of Lincoln's work as a lawyer was the training ground which produced our greatest American. . . ." Includes bibliographical references.
Monaghan 2920

Fehrenbacher, Don, ed.
Abraham Lincoln: Speeches and Writings.
See **Lincoln, Abraham.**

57
Frank, John Paul
Lincoln as a Lawyer. Urbana: University of Illinois Press, 1961.
x, 190 p.

Lawyer John Paul Frank believes that no one can understand Lincoln as a public figure, which accounted for twenty percent of his life, without understanding the other eighty percent. He portrays Lincoln as "a litigation man." Frank goes into depth describing Lincoln's law practice and how he practiced law, especially how he handled various legal problems as a trial attorney. The author uses Lincoln's cases to illustrate his methodology in solving these problems.

The author reminds his readers that Lincoln learned the law by practicing it, rather than by formal training. He poses five qualities invaluable to Lincoln, as well as to lawyers generally: personality, succinct organization of material, effective verbal expression, retentive mind, and capacity for hard work. A section is included on "The Practitioner in Public Life" relating Lincoln's law training and experience to his accomplishments as a politican and public office holder.

The author concludes with a thumbnail sketch of Lincoln's law skills and an appendix, "A Sampling of Lincoln's Cases." It does not give so much an historical account of Lincoln's cases as most Lincoln works do, but rather an analysis, providing insight into how he operated as a practitioner.
Includes bibliographical references.

58
Friend, Henry C.
Abraham Lincoln's Commercial Practice: A Series of Articles. [Chicago]: Commercial Law Foundation, 1970.
28 p. ports.

This collection is comprised of a series of short articles by the author concerning Lincoln's practice of commercial law. He notes that a substantial part of Lincoln's practice involved collection of debts, bankruptcy, and work on behalf of the railroads. The author saw an analogy between the pattern and procedure Lincoln used in collecting debts with the way he handled his generals later in life.

Friend includes a short article on Lincoln's style in collecting a debt against the *National Intelligencer*, and another short piece on the trust account used by Lincoln for keeping his clients' money separated from his personal funds.

The author tells the story of Logan and Lincoln being asked by Joshua Speed to collect a debt from Judge Thomas C. Browne, Illinois Supreme Court judge. Speed, against Lincoln's wishes, refused to bring suit. Another article concerns Lincoln's returning claims. He was not always prompt because he was frequently out of town and had an inadequate filing system (often his hat). The last article involves the case of *Kelly v. Blackledge*. Kelly had sold a mill in Ohio, the transaction financed by promissory notes executed by Harris with Blackledge as security. When Harris could not pay, Blackledge fled to Logan County where Lincoln was employed to collect the debt, a judgment having been rendered in Ohio. The article discusses how Lincoln proceeded, and his correspondence with the interested parties.

See also **Friend**, Journal Articles for the individual journal articles:

"Abraham Lincoln and a Missing Promisory Note"
"Abraham Lincoln and Commercial Law: Returning Claims"
"Abraham Lincoln and the National Intelligencer: The Lawyer's Dilemma"
"Abraham Lincoln as a Receiving Attorney: Kelly vs. Blackledge"
"Abraham Lincoln's Trust Account"

59
Gernon, Blaine Brooks.
The Lincolns in Chicago. Chicago: [s.n.], 1934.
64 p.

This chronological arrangement shows Lincoln first in Chicago in 1847. By 1850 he was out of politics and bent on becoming a good lawyer. His reputation as a lawyer was growing. There is mention of a lawsuit by Parker in United States District Court, Chicago. In 1855, *McCormick v. John H. Manny* was scheduled in Rockford before Judge Drummond in federal court. Lincoln of Springfield was recommended as attorney. The year 1857 saw the Illinois Central Railroad fee case, and two cases in federal court, the Rock Island Bridge case and an ejectment case, *Peter S. Hoes v. James Barclay*.

Part I was published in 27 *Journal of the Illinois State Historical Society* (October 1934).
Monaghan 3426

60
Gridley, James Norman.
Lincoln's Defense of Duff Armstrong; The Story of the Trial and the Celebrated Almanac. Springfield: Illinois State Historical Society, [1910?].
23 p.
For annotation see **Gridley**, Journal Articles.

61
Gross, Anthony, ed.
Lincoln's Own Stories. Collected and edited by Anthony Gross. New York: Harper, 1912.
vii, 223 p. port.

The author has selected and consecutively arranged stories that "embody truth" omitting dubious tales attributed to Abraham Lincoln.
Part II, entitled "The Lawyer," includes incidents and stories. There is one regarding notification of a client concerning real estate: "We cannot attend to it. We are not real estate agents, we are lawyers." There are stories from the circuit, some quoted from Whitney. The selections include a trial suit involving infringement of a waterwheel patent, the Snow Brothers, the Armstrong case. The collection shows how Lincoln used laughter to literally "laugh a case out of court."
Monaghan 2024

--- ----. Garden City, N.Y.: Garden City Pub. Co., 1912.
--- ----. Microfilm. New Haven, Conn.: Yale University Library, 1988.
--- ----. New York: Sun Dial Press, 1940.

Gunderson Robert Gray.
"Stoutly Argufy": Lincoln's Legal Speaking. Address.
See **Gunderson**, Journal Articles.

62
Hapgood, Norman.
Abraham Lincoln: The Man of the People. New York: Macmillan, 1899.
xiii, 433 p. illus. facsims., ports.

The chapter entitled "Lincoln as a Lawyer" tells how Lincoln settled into circuit practice in Springfield. He was offered a partnership in Chicago by Grant Goodrich, but he declined the offer. In his partnership with Herndon, he spent half of the year at Springfield, and the other half on the circuit.

Lincoln enjoyed reading, but did not neglect the law when a case was at hand. His reputation grew for legal arguments, particularly for jury trials, where he used familiar language. He did not care for technicalities, but was a strong advocate when the case was in the right.

Hapgood discusses his characteristics, quoting at times from Judge Davis. The reader learns of Lincoln's high degree of intelligence, and kindness to young lawyers. The author comments on his reasonable fees. Stories illustrating his traits are intermingled with description. Neither the informality of his office is overlooked, nor his clothing and appearance.

He describes scenes from life on the circuit, and tells of the *McCormick v. Manny* case in Cincinnati.
Monaghan 1250

--- ----. Microfilm. New York: Macmillan, 1901 reprint; New Haven, Conn.: Yale University Library, 1988.
--- ----. New ed. New York: Macmillan, 1906, ©1899.
--- ----. Microfilm. New ed. New Haven, Conn.: Yale University Library, 1988.
--- ----. New ed. New York: Christian Herald Bible House, 1914.

63
Harman, Jerome.
Abraham Lincoln's Advice to Young Lawyers. [Topeka, Kans.: 1972?]
[4] p.

Lincolns' advice, "If you are resolutely determined to make a lawyer of yourself the thing is half done already. Get a license, go to practice and still keep reading. The leading rule is diligence. Your own resolution to succeed is more important than any other one thing. Leave nothing to tomorrow which can be done today." He added a postscript, "If I went west, I think I would go to Kansas."

Harnsbarger, Caroline Thomas, comp.
The Lincoln Treasury
See **Lincoln**, Abraham.

64

Hasbrouck, Jacob Louis.
Lincoln in Some of His Unheroic Hours. Paper by Jacob Louis Hasbrouck
Before the Rotary Club of Bloomington, Illinois, February 10, 1938.
[Bloomington, Ill.]: McLean County Historical Society, Printed by cooperation
of The Daily Pantagraph, 1938.
16 p.

A subsection of this paper is entitled "As Bloomington Lawyer." After
returning from Congress, Lincoln concentrated on hard work in his profession.
He practiced law in Bloomington, where life was hard. When there on the
circuit, he stayed in barren boarding houses or the old Phoenix Hotel.
Hasbrouck was unable to find the smallest scrap of paper with Lincoln's
signature or handwriting in the courthouse. He had actually scanned charred
boxes after a fire destroyed records in the attic of the third courthouse on the
site.
    He quoted Judge Lawrence Weldon, contemporary of Lincoln and Jesse
Fell, in saying that the famous autobiography had its inception in the
Bloomington courthouse. At the insistence of Fell, Lincoln wrote it while sitting
at a desk in the old courtroom. Hasbrouck acknowledges that Paul Angle
disagrees with this account. Then he tells of seeing the actual copy of Lincoln's
autobiography, which Alice and Fannie Fell of Normal, Illinois, kept in their
safe.
Monaghan 3622

65

Herndon, William Henry.
Herndon's Life of Lincoln: The History and Personal Recollections of Abraham
Lincoln. As originally written by William H. Herndon and Jesse W. Weik.
With introduction and notes by Paul M. Angle, new introduction by Henry
Steele Commager. New York: Da Capo Press, 1983.
x, xlvi, 511 p. illus.

The author was Lincoln's law partner for many years, also his friend,
companion, and confidant. He probably knew Lincoln as a person as well or
better than any other person. In his book, Herndon writes of "the subjective
Lincoln . . . to portray him in his passions, appetites . . . perceptions . . . just as
he lived, breathed, ate, and laughed." He portrays Lincoln as the ordinary man,
rather than the hero often found in the works of other biographers. He wants
the reader to see the man in human terms as citizen, lawyer, and statesman. The
reader can very nearly visualize Lincoln in his law office. The book was
extremely controversial when it was first published in 1888 and still is to some
extent today. Because of his personal association with Lincoln, some of
Herndon's material was the first to be put in print. His purpose in the book was

to present a truthful account of Lincoln's life as he knew it. The editor's preface briefly sketches Herndon's own life.

Herndon covers the following topics: Abe reads his first law book; law student; licensed to practice law; in partnership with John T. Stuart; early practice; bar of Springfield; address to the "Young Men's Lyceum"; partnerships with Stuart, Logan, and Herndon; settling down to practice law when on the circuit; habits as a lawyer and methods; law office of Lincoln and Herndon; Lincoln's first appearance in the Supreme Court of Illinois; the juror in the divorce case; a glimpse into the law office; how Lincoln kept accounts and divided fees with his partners; Lincoln in argument of a case; tribute of David Davis; characteristics as a lawyer; one of Lincoln's briefs; the Wright case; reminiscences of the circuit; suit against Illinois Central Railroad; the Manny case; defense of Armstrong; last lawsuit in Illinois; includes a number of Lincoln letters.
See Monaghan 1053

Without introduction:
--- ----. New York: Boni, 1892. 2 v.
--- ----. Springfield: Herndon's Lincoln Pub. Co., 1921. 3v.
--- ----. With introduction and notes by Paul M. Angle. New York: A. & C. Boni, 1930. M1053
--- ----. Cleveland: World Pub. Co., 1942, ©1930.
--- ----. Microfilm. New Haven, Conn.: Yale Universtiy Library, 1988.
--- ----. Fine Editions Press, 1949.
--- ----. Greenwich, Conn.: Fawcett Publications, 1961.

Also published as Herndon's Lincoln: The True Story of a Great Life. Monaghan 1049.
--- ----. Chicago, New York: Belford, Clarke, 1889. 3 v.
--- ----. New York: D. Appleton, 1892 2 v.
--- ----. New York: D. Appleton, 1920. 2 v.
--- ----. Microfilm. New Haven, Conn.: Yale University Library, 1988.

See also Monaghan 1951. Abraham Lincoln: The True Story of a Great Life.

66
Herndon, William Henry.
The Hidden Lincoln From the Letters and Papers of William H. Herndon. Edited by Emanuel Hertz. New York: Viking Press, 1938.
461 p. illus., ports., facsims.

The editor collected letters from and letters written to William Herndon concerning Lincoln. He also included statements collected by Herndon, as well as notes and monographs taken from the Herndon collection. "[T]he Lincoln documents gathered and prepared by William H. Herndon in the sixties of the last century have been used for seventy years as the foundation stones of later biographies." Herndon, after the assassination of his friend Lincoln, recorded his recollections of Lincoln. He actively interviewed and wrote to people associated with Lincoln in an effort collect data. "Herndon stands alone as a biographical authority" on Lincoln's life before he left for Washington in 1861.

A number of pages address "Lincoln the Lawyer" in particular. For instance, there is information on "Lincoln's First Appearance in the Supreme Court of Illinois," "The Stolen Horse - A Lincoln Story." Letters to Herndon include one from Beardstown, dated 1866, with information on the Duff Armstrong case, and on the almanac. Herndon uses his notes on topics such as Beardstown, in court, in the law office, in the Trailor case, on the circuit, and regarding the *Mason v. Slidell* case.

--- ----. New York: Blue Ribbon Books, 1940, ©1938.

67
Hertz, Emanuel.
Abraham Lincoln: A New Portrait. Foreword by Nicholas Murray Butler. New York: Liveright, 1931.
2 v. illus., ports., facsims.

Three chapters pertain to Lincoln's life as a lawyer.
Chapter 5, The Legal Phase of the "First American."
Chapter 6, Lincoln More Than a Country Lawyer.
Chapter 7, Lincoln's Law Partners, Clerks and Office Boys.
Monaghan 3264
For Annotations of Chapters published as separates, See **Hertz** 69, 70, 71.

68
Hertz, Emanuel.
Abraham Lincoln: As to His Kindness and Mercy--Let Women Testify. Delivered Before the Women's National Republican Club, February 11, 1929. [S.l.: s.n., 1929?]
17 p. facsim., port.

Hertz selects two cases as typical of those in which women were Lincoln's clients. The first, concerned a Revolutionary War widow who had been charged one-half of her $400 compensation for getting her claim allowed. Lincoln's appeal notes for the jury show: "No contract. Not professional services. Unreasonable charge. Money retained by Def't not given by Pl'ff. Revolutionary War, Describe Valley Forge privations. Ice. Soldiers bleeding feet. Pl'ffs husband. Soldier leaving home. Skin Def't. Close."

In the second case, without pay he saved the inherited farm of a young woman, Rebecca Daimwood. She and her husband William M. Dorman lost in trial court, but Lincoln was retained on appeal to the supreme court. The court in a long opinion reversed the decree of the trial court.
Monaghan 3090

--- ----. Microfilm. New Haven, Conn.: Yale University Library, 1988.

69
Hertz, Emanuel.
Abraham Lincoln: His Law Partners, Clerks, and Office Boys. [S.l.: s.n., 1930]
22 p. illus., port., facsims.

The author notes that Lincoln's three law partners, Stuart, Logan, and Herndon were well known and much has been written about their associations. However, little has been written about Lincoln's local partners, particularly those on the Eighth Circuit. Lincoln had a partnership with Ward Hill Lamon of Danville, which was advertised in the local paper. Also the court records make clear that when Lincoln, or Lincoln and Herndon, were specially retained or associated with other counsel, it was noted in the record. Hertz says that a series of cases cite Lincoln's appearance as that of a member of a firm, often in Lincoln's own handwriting. Hertz discusses briefly some of these "temporary partners." Lincoln's many associations brought him into contact with a wide variety of legal topics. Although these partnerships were not exclusive or continuous for long periods, the author feels they were partnerships none the less, brought on by need to associate with local legal counsel as Lincoln traveled the circuit. Hertz also discusses Lincoln's office boys and students. The author concludes "Lincoln might well be proud of all his partners, all his clerks, all his secretaries both permanent and temporary."
Monaghan 3283

--- ----. 44 THE MAGAZINE OF HISTORY WITH NOTES AND QUERIES (1931) Extra Number 173 Rare Lincolniana (no. 42) 11-26.

See also **Hertz**, Abraham Lincoln: A New Portrait.

70
Hertz, Emanuel.
Abraham Lincoln: More than a Country Lawyer. Delivered at the Bronx County Bar Association, February 8, 1928. [New York: s.n., 1928]
30 p. illus., ports., facsims.

Hertz agrees with Beveridge in comparing Lincoln with the legal instincts of Chief Justice John Marshall. Hertz claims "almost every paper Lincoln put his hand to, comes out a perfect legal document."

The author dispels the notion that Lincoln was always "perfectly angelic" with his clients and litigants. He does this by way of illustration, a stinging letter to a client suggesting that he take his business elsewhere.

He suggests Lincoln was a "conscientious lawyer at all times," "punctilious as to his charges," and "absolutely fearless as a lawyer."

He discusses a case whereby Lincoln defended Father Chiniquy of Kankakee in Urbana. Chiniquy gives heaping praise to Lincoln in his book *Fifty Years in the Church of Rome*, for not only defending him against false charges, but also for being "the most devoted and noblest friend. . . ."

Hertz concludes that Lincoln "was not simply the country lawyer" but a lawyer involved in "practically every phase of law and manifestation of the operation of law as it comes into the lives of the people."
Includes the reproduction of several documents to which the author had referred in his speech.
Monaghan 3025

See also **Hertz**, Abraham Lincoln: A New Portrait.

71
Hertz, Emanuel.
Abraham Lincoln: the Legal Phase of the "First American." [Address delivered over radio station WRNY February 12, 1927 under auspices of the Committee on Citizenshp of the New York County Lawyers Association.] [New York, 1927] 8p.

Lincoln practiced law on the Illinois circuit, preferring it to being general counsel for the New York Central Railroad. The lure of Springfield and the Eighth Judicial Circuit was great. He tried his own cases, and collaborated with legal talent of the day. Hertz quotes Lincoln in speaking on the Dred Scott decision. The same hand that wrote the individual legal forms and documents of his practice wrote monumental documents, drafting the legal document that was the title deed of freedom.
Monaghan 2933

See also **Hertz**, Abraham Lincoln: A New Portrait.

72
Hertz, Emanuel.

Lawyer Lincoln [A Review] by Albert A. Woldman. Boston: Houghton Mifflin, 1936.
6 p.

Hertz gives an excellent review of Woldman's *Lawyer Lincoln*. He is grateful that such a volume is available, noting that it has taken at least seventy-one years for such a book on the topic to be produced. Hertz calls attention to the lack of interest by biographers and historians in this important phase of Lincoln's activities. He says that Woldman has destroyed some of the myths associated with his practice of law. He draws attention to the many types of legal activity, virtually every phase of law in which Lincoln participated. Hertz appreciates the chapter by Woldman dealing with "Judge" Lincoln, showing Lincoln actually acting as judge, substituting for Judge Davis in the courtroom, a fact ignored by some biographers. Hertz points out that Woldman clearly defines Lincoln's role as the railroad and big-business lawyer.

He writes of Woldman's belief that Lincoln was able to cope with legal and constitutional problems later in his presidential life just as he solved ordinary legal problems earlier while he was a lawyer.
See Monaghan 3568.

73
Hertz, Emanuel.
Lincoln Talks: A Biography in Anecdote. Collected, collated and edited by Emanuel Hertz. New York: Viking, 1939.
xiii, 698 p. port.

The editor has used the words of a thousand contemporaries, collected from other works, such as newspaper files, magazines, out-of-print books, government documents and manuscripts. He notes the sources utilized for each anecdote.

This book includes a chapter entitled "Lawyer." There are stories of law cases, dealing with commonplace subjects, such as colts, oxen, cowhides, and hogs. Lincoln talks about court, witnesses, judges and juries, customs and law, disbarment, slander, legal advice, compromise, peacemaking, settlement, fees and payment.
Includes bibliography.
Monaghan 3980

--- ----. New York: Halcyon House, 1939.

74
Hertz, Emanuel.

Lincoln the Lawyer: An Article by Emanuel Hertz, published in the *New York Times*, February 7, 1937. Washington, D.C.: United States Government Printing Office, 1937.
7 p.

Printed in *The Congressional Record*, February 11, 1937, App. 192-194.

For Annotation, see **Hertz**, Journal Articles.

75
Hill, Frederick Trevor.
Lincoln the Lawyer. New York: Century Co., 1906.
xviii, 332 p. illus., ports., facsims.

This early work is devoted strictly to Lincoln's career as a lawyer. The author justifies his book by the lack of attention given Lincoln's twenty-three years of law practice even though it is obvious that many of his most momentous actions can be traced to his training and legal skills.

The work traces Lincoln's early interest in the law, his legal apprenticeship, cases and competitors, his law partnerships, life on the Eighth Judicial Circuit, and how Lincoln operated as a lawyer. It shows Lincoln's growth and evolution into one of the most renowned lawyers in Illinois at that time. "It is conceded by all his contemporaries that Lincoln was the best all-round jury lawyer of his day in Illinois."

The Appendix includes the Illinois Supreme Court Memorial, Lincoln's case against the Illinois Central Railroad, and a list of Lincoln's cases in the Supreme Court of Illinois "a record rarely, if ever equaled in his day."
This book was published serially in *The Century Magazine*, 1905-1906.
Monaghan 1502

--- ----. New York: Century, 1912, [©1906] 334 p.
--- ----. New York: Century, 1913, [©1905, 1906] Special limited edition for Lincoln Centennial Association.
--- ----. Albuquerque, N.M.: American Classical College Press, [1985?, 1906] 2 v. (310 p.) illus., ports.
--- ----. Littleton, Colo.: F. B. Rothman, 1986, ©1906.
--- ----. Microfilm. New York: Century. New Haven Conn.: Yale University Library, 1988.

76
Hill, Frederick Trevor.
Lincoln's Legacy of Inspiration. New York: Frederick A. Stokes, 1909.
60 p.

The chapter entitled, "For Those Who Strive for Ideals in Their Work," indicates that Lincoln was not immediately famous in the ranks of his chosen profession. He hated drudgery and technicalities and despised the tricks of the trade. He believed that honesty was compatible with his profession and advised those who did not have the resolve to be honest to choose some other occupation. He had no reverence for the law merely because it was law, refusing to invoke statutes at the expense of justice. The author provides several examples of Lincoln's dealing with dishonest clients. He advised the discouragement of litigation. Lincoln was not a scholar; instead, he relied on truth and persuasion. He supported himself and his family from his earnings as a lawyer for very nearly a quarter century.

Originally, series in *New York Times*, 1-7 February 1909.
Monaghan 1745

77
Hill, John Wesley.
America Needs Today a Reincarnation of the Spirit and Principles of Lincoln: [Lincoln the Lawyer] Address, July 8, 1933. Washington: U.S. Government Printing Office, 1934.
8 p.

Address delivered July 8, 1933, Cedar Point, Ohio, at a session of the Ohio Bar Association, and printed in the *Congressional Record* (January 26, 1934), 1384-1387, as "Abraham Lincoln."

For annotation, see **Hill**, "Lincoln the Lawyer," below.

78
Hill, John Wesley.
Lincoln the Lawyer. (Address) Delivered Before Annual Meeting of the Ohio State Bar Association, Cedar Point, July 1933. Columbus, Ohio: F. J. Heer Printing Co., 1933.
8 p.

An address by the Chancellor of Lincoln Memorial University to the Ohio Bar Association describing Lincoln as springing from the pioneer environment. Lincoln was uneducated by college, yet through "long and lonely hours of wearisome struggle" Lincoln prepared for the law. He tells about Lincoln's career at the bar, and the great lawyers of his day with whom Lincoln crossed swords. He summarizes statistics of his cases thus: "While in the Supreme Court of Illinois he appeared as counsel in fifty-one cases, winning verdicts in thirty-one, and appearing as associate counsel in one hundred and twenty-four cases in which the parties in whose behalf he appeared were successful in sixty-five. In twenty-three cases he appeared alone for the appellant or plaintiff in error, and he was successful in fourteen, while in seventy-one cases taken to the Supreme Court of Illinois by parties represented by him in which other counsel was associated, his clients were successful in thirty-seven, and of nineteen cases taken to the same court on appeal by Lincoln reversals in decisions of the trial court were secured in ten cases."

Hill describes Lincoln's high moral standards and his regard for the Constitution. He concludes by a call for the return of Lincoln, the return of his ideals, morals, and vision to guide the United States in its times of trouble. Monaghan 3388

--- ----. 6 OHIO STATE BAR ASSOCIATION REPORT (July 24, 1933), 241-246.

79
Hobson, J. T. (Jonathan Todd)
Footprints of Abraham Lincoln: Presenting Many Interesting Facts, Reminiscences and Illustrations Never Before Published. Dayton, Ohio: Otterbein Press, 1909.
114 p. illus., ports.

Chapter 6, entitled "Lincoln and the Armstrong Case," includes the following subsections: famous law cases (mentions the *Illinois Central Railroad Company v. McLean County*, and McCormick Reaper patent case); the Clary Grove Boys; the Wrestling contest; Jack and Hannah Armstrong; trial of their son for murder; Lincoln's tact and the acquittal; letters from the surviving attorney in the case; more tangled history untangled; unpublished facts connected with parties in the case.
Monaghan 1746

--- ----. Microfilm. New Haven, Conn.: Yale University Library, 1988.

80
Holland, J. G. (Josiah Gilbert)
Life of Abraham Lincoln. Springfield, Mass.: Gurdon Bill, 1866.
544 p. illus.

Includes chapter "Mr. Lincoln As a Lawyer."

Holland, novelist, contemporary, and later editor of the *Springfield Republican*, contributed a eulogy. In his history of Lincoln's life he describes graphically the private and public life of Lincoln as a citizen, successful lawyer, politician, statesman, philanthropist, and civil magistrate. He describes riding the circuit and relates some incidents of life along the way. Lincoln was not regarded by professional associates as profoundly versed in principles of law, but was looked upon as a remarkable advocate. He had great power before a jury as he presented both sides of a case in simplest terms. With a sense of justice, he took cases in which he believed. Considered cunning, he knew which illustrations to use, and how to bring his arguments to bear on a case. He never made his practice into a lucrative one, and was known for his honesty. The author provides some incidents illustrating his practice, and information on several cases. He quotes David Davis and Judge Breese in regarding Lincoln as the finest lawyer they ever knew.

Later reviews have revealed some errors in this first full-length laudatory biography. Holland, as biographer, did not have access to information available to later scholars. Nevertheless, it was considered a noteworthy contribution at the time. Lamon in his *Life* spoke of it with respect. Angle considered it by far the best of the writings following Lincoln's death.

(Charles Morrissey, "The Perils of Instant History," 7 *The Journal of Popular Culture* [1973], 347-350, discusses Holland's portrayal of Lincoln.)
Monaghan 856

--- ----. Microfilm. Ann Arbor, Mich.: Xerox University Microfilms, 1972. (American Culture Series, reel 535.8)
--- ----. New York: Dodd, Mead, 1887.
--- ----. Microfiche. Louisville Ky.: Lost Cause Press, 1978.
--- ----. New York: Paperback Library, 1961. 447 p.

81
Holmes, Frederick L. (Lionel)
Abraham Lincoln Traveled This Way: The Log Book of a Pilgrim to the Lincoln Country. Foreword by Glenn Frank. Boston: L. C. Page, 1930.
xviii, 350 p. illus., ports., map.

A chapter entitled "Three Law Offices in Springfield" describes those offices and partners. Another, "Abraham Lincoln Traveled This Way 1847-1857," describes circuit practice, with each judge presiding over court in a dozen or more counties for six months of each year. There are illustrations of the trail markers as marked by the Lincoln Circuit tablets, and an illustration of a statue, "Lincoln the Lawyer." Holmes describes Lincoln's two-period legal career, divided by a term in Congress in 1847.

The author writes in a popular tone, including several incidents, such as a mock tribunal, which tried Lincoln for his small fees. He tells of three celebrated cases, "Effie Afton," McCormick Reaper case, and the Sand-Bar case.
Monaghan 3204

--- ----. Microopaque. Louisville, Ky.: Lost Cause Press, 1966.

82
Hopkins, Richard J.
Abraham Lincoln--Lawyer; The Legion of Honor; Charge to a Grand Jury; Stepping Stones. Girard, Kans.: Haldeman-Julius Publications [1937?]. 63 p. [p. 5-22] port. (Little Blue Book; no. 1759)

The first item in this work is an address by Judge Hopkins before the joint session of the Kansas Legislature, February 12, 1937. As he praises Lincoln, he notes how often great men come from lowly, common people and poverty. He said that Lincoln's education was from the "university of nature."

Lincoln's interest in speech making and law was influenced at age seventeen when he heard "one of the famous Breckenridges of Kentucky . . . speak at the courthouse in defense of a man on trial for murder."

Lincoln began the practice of law when admitted to the bar March 1, 1837. The author states that Lincoln became a "successful trial lawyer" largely because "he took great pains to make himself understood by persons, speaking directly and exclusively to them. His sentences were short, compact, and distinct. His words were plain and familiar. The context, clear and simple. His was the language of the juryman, the speech of the people." Hopkins says Lincoln possessed "a wonderfully logical mind." He claims that Lincoln's best work was in the court where "his briefs and addresses to the court were well reasoned and strongly supported by authorities."

The other selections in this volume do not pertain to Lincoln.

83
Houser, M. L. (Martin Luther)
Abraham Lincoln, Student: His Books. [Peoria, Ill.]: Printed by Edward J. Jacob, 1932. 47 p. illus., ports., facsims.

This pamphlet is "virtually a revision of *The Books That Lincoln Read* published by Edward J. Jacob," with several new titles, and one discarded. Lincoln first studied "law" at New Salem with the intention of adopting it as a profession. He had already studied *The Revised Laws of Indiana* in 1824 at the home of David Turnham. During his first winter in Illinois he read *The Revised Code of Laws of Illinois*, and secured a set of Blackstone's *Commentaries*, then devoted himself to its study. The author had firsthand information from a relative who remembered seeing Lincoln lying under a tree studying that work. In addition to Lincoln's study of the Illinois Code, he added Greenleaf's *Evidence*; Story's *Equity*; and Chitty's *Pleadings*. His law library grew to two-hundred volumes and these law books are preserved in various collections.

There are descriptive paragraphs on: textbooks, biography, history, prose, poetry, law, religion, natural sciences, philosophy, politics and government, and miscellaneous. Illustrations of several title pages accompany the text, as well as a list of the books that Lincoln and his family members withdrew from the Library of Congress while he was president.

Includes an alphabetical list by author of books Lincoln studied.
See Monaghan 3328

84
Houser, M. L. (Martin Luther)
Some Books That Lincoln Loved. An Address Before the Lincoln Memorial University, Harrogate, Tennessee on the occasion of the 40th Anniversary of the University, February 12, 1937. Peoria, Ill.. [Harrogate, Tenn.?: s.n., 1937]
16 p.

Among the books that Lincoln loved was Blackstone's *Commentaries*. Houser explains that there were many stories of his studying it. He explains further Lincoln's study of *The Revised Statutes of Indiana*, and *The Revised Code of Laws of Illinois*.
Monaghan 3572

85
Howard, James Quay.
The Life of Abraham Lincoln with Extracts from His Speeches. Cincinnati: Anderson, Gates and Wright, 1860.
102 p.

This campaign biography was written by James Q. Howard as a result of his assignment to gather information for William Dean Howells. Using the biographical material furnished to him by Lincoln, and interviewing techniques, with perusal of *Sangamo Journal* files, and *Journal of the General Assembly*, he published his own biography of Lincoln.
He states that Lincoln bought a copy of Blackstone at an auction in Springfield, and became absorbed in the study of the law. In mentioning his career, Howard states that Lincoln kept busy with labors of his profession, and he tells of the Duff Armstrong trial.
Monaghan 42

--- ----. Columbus, Ohio: Follett, Foster, 1960.
--- ----. Microfiche. Ann Arbor, Mich.: University Microfilms International, 1980.
(Presidential Election Campaign Biographies, PE 150)

86

Howells, William Dean.
Life of Abraham Lincoln, by W. D. Howells. This Campaign Biography
Corrected by the Hand of Abraham Lincoln in the Summer of 1860 is
Reproduced Here With Careful Attention to the Appearance to the Original
Volume. Springfield: Abraham Lincoln Association, 1938.
xvii, facsim. (2), xi-xii, 17-94 p. port.

Includes a facsimile of a part of Samuel C. Park's copy of the original
edition, which has title: Lives and Speeches of Abraham Lincoln and Hannibal
Hamlin. Columbus, Ohio: Follett, Foster, 1860.
A note in manuscript appears on verso of a portrait. "This life of Lincoln
was corrected by him for me, at my request, in the summer of 1860, by notes
in his hand writing in pencil, on the margin." (Signed by Samuel C. Parks, May
22, 1901.)
Howells was commissioned by Follett, Foster & Co. to write a life of
Lincoln. He sent a young law student, J. Q. Howard, to Springfield to gather the
information. Lincoln gave him a copy of the biographical material he had
prepared for John Lock Scripps, *Chicago Press & Tribune*. Howard interviewed
people, looked at *Sangamo Journal files*, and the *Journal of the General
Assembly*. He also wrote his own book.
This volume is important in that it gives an "approved" version of incidents.
Lincoln corrected the biography himself. He let stand the few statements
pertaining to his study and career in law, particularly the statement that he
acquired Blackstone's *Commentaries* at auction, a point which has been argued
by biographers.
Monaghan 45

--- ----. Bloomington: Indiana University Press, 1960.

87

Hunt, H. Draper (Harry Draper)
Lincoln the President: Learner and Mentor, 1854-1865. [Portland, Maine]:
University of Southern Maine, 1984.
[20] p.
Walter E. Russell Endowed Chair in Philosophy and Education Lecture, 1984.

The initial part of this lecture deals with how Lincoln grew as a lawyer, as
well as in politics, during the decade of the 1850s. The lecturer mentions the
famous cases, the Duff Armstrong murder case, and the McCormick-Manny
reaper case. He explains how Lincoln developed an understanding of national
transportation and trade, noting his railroad cases, and the "Effie Afton" case.
He reminds the listener how powerful he was before a jury, and persuasive in
appeal. He quotes Judge Breese in saying that he was "the finest lawyer." There

is a word about Lincoln's clear prose, and discussion of his fees. The latter section of the lecture dealt with Lincoln's opinion of the Dred Scott decision, Lincoln-Douglas, and his political life.

88
Illinois. Supreme Court.
Abraham Lincoln. Proceedings Commemorative of the One Hundredth Anniversary of the Birth of Abraham Lincoln, February 11, 1909. Bloomington, Ill: The Court, 1909.
p. [9]-21.

238 Illinois Reports 9

Includes speeches by Nathan William MacChesney, Justice Hand [et al.] Col. Nathan William **MacChesney** spoke about Lincoln as a lawyer. He stood for highest standards in the profession. As a constant advocate before the court, his name frequently appears in the volumes of the Supreme Court from December term 1840 to January term 1860.

Justice John P. **Hand** told of Lincoln's law partners during his professional career. He described law practice when the country was new, the people poor, and there were few law books. Litigation usually involved small amounts. Civil cases involved promissory notes and accounts and actions of tort for recovery of damages; criminal cases involved personal violence. Most lawyers divided their time between law and politics. Lincoln's first case, 1840, was *Scammon v. Cline* in which he was defeated. (2 Scam. 436).
Monaghan 1650

--- ----. Proceedings in the Supreme Court of Illinois, Commemorating the 100th Anniversary of His Birth. [S.l.: s.n., 1909].
13 p.

Kerner, Fred, comp.
A Treasury of Lincoln Quotations.
see **Lincoln,** Abraham.

89
Ketcham, Henry.
Abraham Lincoln. New York: University Society, 1905, ©1901.
xi, 435 p. (Makers of American History)

A chapter entitled "Entering the Law" provides some information on Lincoln's early life in the law. "On the Circuit" gives an account of his

professional duties on the Eighth Judicial Circuit, comprised of "fifteen" counties, over an area 150 miles long and nearly as wide. Travel was burdensome when the entire company of lawyers was traveling from one county seat to another. The court was the center of interest in the counties. Lincoln's anecdotes were popular, and his fees were low. He had professional kindness for the poor and unfortunate. His practice was as large as that of any other lawyer on the circuit, and he had his share of important cases. His most important case was *McCormick v. Manny* at Cincinnati. Lincoln was known for giving away all points but the pivotal point of any case. His conscience was his guide, preventing him from taking any unfair advantage.
See Monaghan 1344 and note.

--- ----. New York: J. A. Hill, 1904, 1901.
---. The Life of Abraham Lincoln. New York: A. L. Burt, 1901.
---. The Life of Abraham Lincoln. New York: Perkins Book Co., 1901.

90
Kidd, Thomas W. S.
"Lawyer Lincoln," by the Crier of the Court. In Proceedings of the Sangamon County Bar Association from Its Organization to January 1st, 1906. [Springfield, 1906?]
pp. 85-100.

Captain Thomas W. S. Kidd of Springfield, Illinois, delivered the address before the Sangamon County Bar Association at its regular meeting, April 25, 1903. It was for the purpose of giving a court officer's relationship to the attorney, a sketch of an honest man's private life as a lawyer, his going in and coming out before a court, his walk and conversation, the little things of a great man's life that develop the characteristics the world sees. The courtroom is one of the finest fields for study.

Lincoln was not classed with the first of his profession. Others of the bar could credit a greater number of legal attainments, more comprehensive knowledge of particular branches of the law than he; nevertheless he was a good lawyer. Judge Davis had said that he was a great lawyer, both at *nisi prius* and before an appellate tribunal. It was generally thought that his strength was most apparent when standing before a jury, with his careless, earnest style. He talked as though he were having a neighborly chat. His ability as a case lawyer was acknowledged. Lincoln made no pretensions of superiority, mental, moral or physical. His was a mind at work, absorbed in thought. He enjoyed a joke or story with a point, possessing an inexhaustible fund of both.

91
Kincaid, Robert L.
Joshua Fry Speed, Lincoln's Most Intimate Friend. Harrogate, Tenn.: Dept. of
Lincolniana, Lincoln Memorial University, 1943.
70 p.

This item about Lincoln's friend includes a letter from Lincoln to Speed,
June 19, 1841, about the Trailor case, in which victim Fisher was missing,
supposedly murdered, until the doctor told of finding Fisher at his home in bed.

92
King, Willard L.
Lincoln's Manager: David Davis. Cambridge: Harvard University Press, 1960.
xiii, 383 p. illus.

Although this volume is primarily about Judge David Davis, Lincoln's
political manager, information on Lincoln is interspersed within the text.
Chapters entitled "Around the Circuit, 1849-1852" and "Circuit Riders by Rail,
1853-1861" are particularly descriptive of Lincoln's law career. It is a source for
information on Lincoln's sitting as judge for Davis.
      One learns that it was Davis' influence that cut the old Eighth Judicial
Circuit by six counties, so Lincoln had to abandon law practice in those counties,
and later lost an additional county. However, increased practice in the smaller
Eighth Circuit made up for his loss.
      The author of this book based his material on ten years of research, some
10,000 documents and unpublished letters.

--- ----. Chicago: University of Chicago Press, 1976. (Midway Reprint)

93
Knapp, George E.
Lincoln the Lawyer by George E. Knapp, of the Iowa Bar. [S.l.: n.d.]
4 p.

Lincoln's place in history is based upon his political activities and
statesmanship. Even members of the bar are apt to forget his standing and
ability as a lawyer, which influenced his later career. He was able and astute as
an advocate, and a sound counsellor, engaged in some of the most important
litigation in the state. He resolved to take his profession seriously at the close
of his one term in the national House of Representatives in 1849. Herndon had
said that Lincoln preferred trial practice, and did not like office routine. He was
the only lawyer to ride the entire Eighth Circuit. He associated himself with
local attorneys establishing something of a partnership, and participating in
nearly every important case. He followed Judges Davis and Treat around the

circuit, seemingly unaware of physical discomforts and primitive conditions, going home only at the end of the term.

Crowds came to the courthouses when Lincoln was on a case. He was one of the plain people, popular with juries, known for refusing cases that were not on the right side. There are references to several cases, including the Illinois Central case, the Reaper case in Cincinnati, the "Effie Afton" case, and the Sand-Bar case. His conduct was criticized in the notable almanac case. Some persons disagree over the almanac used, but best evidence says that it was *Ayers American Almanac*.

He had a highly credible record from 1849 to 1860.

Monaghan 3106

94

Kranz, Henry B.

Abraham Lincoln: A New Portrait. New York: Putnam, 1959.

252 p. port.

The book is a collection of analytical essays by distinguished Lincoln historians, each writing on a different aspect of Lincoln's personality. "The volume is designed to display the enormous range of Lincoln's arresting personality and interpret some of its puzzling, paradoxical features." Among the twenty-two essays by different authors, there is a chapter on Lincoln as his contemporaries saw him, including David Davis, and William Herndon. Essays of literary contemporaries Walt Whitman and Ralph Waldo Emerson appear, among others. There are samples of Lincoln's addresses and writings, a chronology of Abraham Lincoln, and a bibliography. A selection by Townsend:

Townsend, William H. "Lincoln, The Lawyer," tells the Blackstone *Commentaries* story with the word that Lincoln took the bulky volume wherever he went. He tells how Lincoln borrowed law books from John T. Stuart of Springfield, reading at times while walking. The author tells of Lincoln's meager beginnings in Springfield, sharing a room with Josua F. Speed. Description of law partnerships follows, and riding the circuit of the Eighth Judicial Circuit of Illinois. In addition to precise physical description, the author details his courtroom demeanor. Townsend describes his cross-examination of witnesses, his courteousness, his relaxed relationship with witnesses, and his success as a trial lawyer. Townsend credits his power of analysis, logic, and grasp of subject with his winning the majority of his cases before the state supreme court, and several before the Supreme Court of the United States. Townsend mentions Lincoln's honesty, and his good humor. He considered that Lincoln was foremost of the Illinois bar at the close of his legal career.

--- ----. Freeport, N.Y.: Books for Libraries Press, 1972, ©1959.

95
Kuhn, Isaac.
Abraham Lincoln: A Vast Future: Selected Articles Published Over More Than
a Century Reflecting the Foresight and Influence of the Great Illinois Lawyer
and President. Champaign, Ill.: J. Kuhn, 1946.
50 p. illus., port., facsim.

The book is a memento of the Jos. Kuhn and Co. eighty-year anniversary,
the theme of which is based on Lincoln's words "The struggle of today is not
altogether for today; it is for a vast future also."

A speech by Congressman William A. Rodenberg before the Illinois
General Assembly honors Lincoln's 110th birthday on February 12, 1919, by
noting that Lincoln taught respect for the law. An address by C. C. Burford
before the Kiwanis Club of Champaign-Urbana on February 8, 1945, concerns
Lincoln's association with pioneer railroads--where the author contends the
building of the railroads aided Lincoln into emerging prominence and eventually
greatness. It was the first "big business" with which Lincoln was associated as
an attorney. With a new form of transportation came new problems to solve
and explore. Lincoln represented these railroads with legal aid and advice,
thereby growing with the railroads.

Burford discusses the McLean County tax case against the Illinois Central
Railroad, the result of which enabled the railroad to expand rapidly without
being crippled by various county taxes. This case led to another famous Lincoln
case when he had to sue the railroad for his $5,000 fee. The Rock Island Bridge
case, or "Effie Afton" case, was of vital importance to the railroads and it was
well represented by Lincoln. "We will hazard the opinion that fewer cases at
any time have been taken better prepared into United States Courts, than this
one."

96
Kyle, Otto R.
Abraham Lincoln in Decatur. 1st ed. New York: Vantage Press, 1957.
176 p. illus.

The author traces the many ties Lincoln had with the city of Decatur.
Lincoln's first home was in Decatur until he moved a year later to New Salem.
But he would return to Decatur as an attorney riding the Eighth Circuit. In the
chapter "Lawyer Lincoln" Kyle describes Decatur in those days, telling about the
attorneys' activities and accommodations. He discusses numerous cases in which
Lincoln was involved, including the one in which he represented Richard J.
Gatling, "of machine gun fame." Lincoln's case load in Decatur was heavy up
until about 1855 when it began to lessen. A slander suit of 1838 found Lincoln
opposing Stephen A. Douglas for the first time. The author based his description
of Lincoln's manner in the courtroom on Judge David Davis' words.

The appendix lists Lincoln's law cases in Decatur with very brief description of each; Lincoln's plea of justification in the case of *David Adkins v. Robert Hines*, and an affidavit for a new trial for Robert Hines by Stephen Douglas. Includes bibliography.

97
Lamon, Ward H. (Hill)
The Life of Abraham Lincoln from His Birth to His Inauguration as President.
Boston: James R. Osgood, 1872.
xiv, 547 p. illus., ports., facsims.

Lawyer Lamon, one of Lincoln's close friends, was determined to write a biography. He had material in his possession, and learned that Herndon was similarly engaged. The object of both men was to create a real history and make the character of Lincoln known. Lamon deplored the many publications pretending to be biographies. There was only one, that by Holland, of which he spoke with respect. Herndon cooperated by placing his collection of materials at Lamon's disposal. Coupled with his own, he was able to prepare an authentic history of Mr. Lincoln. Lamon mentions three enormous volumes of original manuscripts garnered in Herndon's labors, and calls his "a faithful record." Readers were surprised at differences in this portrayal of Lincoln and the laudatory volumes by other biographers.

In Chapter 11 this contemporary of Lincoln describes his settling in Springfield to practice law, his first case, partnerships, and his style. In Chapter 13, he continues with "Mr. Lincoln in His Character as Country Lawyer." He regards Lincoln as a case lawyer, using examples of the Henry McHenry case, the Duff Armstrong case, Illinois Central Railroad Company case and the McCormick Reaper case.

He provides insight into Judge Davis' relationship with Lincoln, by quoting the judge, "He read law-books but little except when the cause at hand made it necessary." Davis indicated that he was self-reliant, rarely conferring with other lawyers, a fair and accommodating practitioner, and in all elements a great lawyer. Judge Davis spoke of his honesty, and his defending wrong cases poorly.

Lamon told how he reasoned at court from analagous causes that had been decided and reported. He noted that in consultation he was cautious, conscientious, and painstaking. Lamon used many quotations, some from Lincoln's letters to Speed.

The authorship of this book has been ascribed by Herndon to Chauncey Black.
Monaghan 926

--- ----. Microfilm. Ann Arbor, Mich.: University Microfilms [n.d.] (American Culture Series, Reel 272.6)
--- ----. Microfiche. Louisville, Ky.: Lost Cause Press, 1977.

--- ----. Microfiche. Chicago: Library Resources, 1970. (Library of American Civilization; LAC 12487).

98
Lamon, Ward H. (Hill)
Recollections of Abraham Lincoln, 1847-1865. Edited by Dorothy Lamon Teillard. Washington, D.C.: Published by the Editor, 1911.
xxxvi, 337 p.

Lamon became acquainted with Lincoln during Autumn 1847, when they were introduced by John T. Stuart. Lamon was Lincoln's local partner, at Danville and later at Bloomington, and they rode the circuit together.

Lamon explains that Lincoln could not learn to charge well for legal services. The lawyers complained, and actually Lincoln and Lamon disagreed on at least one fee in the case of a demented girl. The reader learns of the moot tribunal for Lincoln's lack of proper fees, where he was found "guilty" and fined.

The appendix contains a four-page facsimile of a fifteen-page brief in Lincoln's hand, in which he defends a will.

The editor, Lamon's daughter, utilized material that he had gathered for the foundation of this book.

--- ----. Chicago: A. C. McClurg, 1895. 276 p.
Monaghan 1168
--- ----. Microfilm. New Haven, Conn.: Micrographic Systems of Connecticut, 1986.
--- ----. Washington, D.C.: Dorothy Lamon Teillard, 1911. 337 p.

Lang, H. Jack, ed.
The Wit and Wisdom of Abraham Lincoln as Reflected in His Briefer Letters and Speeches.
See **Lincoln**, Abraham

99
Lincoln, Abraham.
Abraham Lincoln: His Speeches and Writings. Edited with Critical and Analytical Notes by Roy P. **Basler**. Preface by Carl Sandburg. Cleveland: World Pub. Co., 1946.
xxx, 843 p.

The editor has attempted to give a full and accurate text, as Lincoln had written it, of his most important works. Much of the text has been edited from original manuscripts or photostatic copies. In his choice of selections he was guided by literary significance, historical importance, and human interest. He tells of Lincoln's literary growth in the law partnership with Herndon in "Lincoln's Development as a Writer." Several letters pertain to cases.

--- ----. New York: Grosset & Dunlap, 1962, ©1946.
--- ----. New York: Kraus Reprint, 1969, ©1946; 1976, ©1946.
--- ----. Franklin Center, Pa.: Franklin Library, 1979, ©1946.

100
Lincoln, Abraham.
Abraham Lincoln: His Story in His Own Words. Edited and with notes by Ralph Geoffrey **Newman**. Garden City, N.Y.: Doubleday, 1975, ©1970.
117 p.

Using the words of Lincoln, as found in texts, the editor quotes from the literature, and offers some explanation of passages. In this volume, there is a short section entitled, "Springfield Lawyer," in which Lincoln tells of obtaining his law license, moving to Springfield, and beginning to practice law with Stuart.

Other paragraphs provide Lincoln's advice to a young man who wanted to become a lawyer, emphasizing the diligence required. He urged him not to postpone until tomorrow what could be done today, and not to let his correspondence fall behind. He said that the main thing was to get books, read, and study; it did not matter where he was located.

101
Lincoln, Abraham.
Abraham Lincoln: Speeches and Writings. Speeches, Letters, Miscellaneous Writings. Edited by Don E. **Fehrenbacher**. New York: The Library of America, 1989.
2 v.

These two volumes consist of texts from *The Collected Works of Abraham Lincoln*, edited by Roy P. Basler, with texts selected and notes by Don E. Fehrenbacher, Lincoln scholar and Pulitzer Prize winner.

There are several items pertaining to Lincoln, the legal profession and his preparation for it among the letters, memos, fragments, and speeches. There is a letter from Lincoln to Jesse W. Fell, endorsing his autobiography in which information appears concerning his study of law during legislative periods and his relocation to Springfield to practice. In the campaign biography, he mentions going into practice with greater earnestness than ever before upon return from Congress. Other items of interest include a letter explaining that he is away too much for a young man to read law with him advantageously.

There are some writings regarding law cases, and his speech to the jury in the Rock Island Bridge case. Correspondence concerning fees shows that he returned money to a client, saying that he had been overpaid. Lincoln's opinion of judicial precedent is obvious from his speech on the Dred Scott case. The Lincoln-Douglas debates and "House Divided" speech are available among others in this collection. Lincoln's punctuation and spelling have been retained in these writings, which show his clear and direct language.

102
Lincoln, Abraham.
Abraham Lincoln's Stories and Speeches. Including Early Life Stories, Professional Life Stories, White House Incidents, War Reminiscences, etc. Edited by J. B. **McClure**. Chicago: Rhodes & McClure Pub. Co., 1899. 477 p. illus.

The section of this book on Lincoln's "Professional Life Stories" includes those pertaining to his law career. Among others, there is a remarkable lawsuit about a colt, which dealt with the preponderance of evidence. In addition there are: Lincoln's story of a young lawyer; Lincoln defends Col. Baker; the judge and the drunken coachman; Honest Abe and his lady client; how Lincoln kept his business accounts; Lincoln defends the son of an old friend indicted for murder; a revolutionary pensioner defended by Lincoln.
Monaghan 1149

--- ----. Chicago: Rhodes & McClure, 1894. 473 p.

103
Lincoln, Abraham.
An Autobiography of Abraham Lincoln, Consisting of the Personal Portions of his Letters, Speeches and Conversations. Compiled and annotated by Nathaniel Wright **Stephenson**. Indianapolis: Bobbs-Merrill, 1926. 501 p. illus.

The compiler uses a mosaic of Lincoln's literary remains. In it, he includes information that Lincoln provided on law studies, between sessions of the legislature; utilization of Blackstone's *Commentaries*; method of study; and advice to lawyers. During years 1843 to 1847, there were letters to Herndon, in 1848 his notes for law lecture, and in 1853, letters regarding real property. Includes bibliographical references.
Monaghan 2884

--- ----. New York: Blue Ribbon Books, 1926.
--- ----. Microfilm. New Haven Conn.: Yale University Library, 1989.

104
Lincoln, Abraham.
The Collected Works of Abraham Lincoln. The Abraham Lincoln Association.
Springfield, Illinois. Roy P. **Basler**, editor; Marion Dolores Pratt and Lloyd A.
Dunlap, assistant editors. New Brunswick, N.J.: Rutgers University Press, 1953-
55.
9 v. ports, facsims.
Vol. 1, 1824-1848; v. 2, 1848-1858; v. 3, 1858-1860.

This set is comprised of Lincoln's writings or speeches, typescript of his
actual words, and is the result of intensive work of an editorial staff in collecting,
cataloging, and transcribing manuscripts, and annotating each item. These
volumes include nearly twice the number of items printed in earlier "complete
works" of Lincoln, by other scholars. Symbols provide a description of sources
cited.
This primary source material includes some information on Lincoln the
lawyer, although the plan was to gather and publish the legal material in
separate and subsequent volumes at some future date. Nevertheless, where a
document mentions a law case incidental to a letter, it is included. Volumes 2
and 3 are particularly valuable. The index is the key to the following categories:
documents drafted before being licensed to practice; fees and bills; memo of
Lincoln to Stuart re bank account; notes for a law lecture and for argument of
a case; answer to charges of failure to deliver funds; collected on a claim;
certified applications to practice law; advice to law students; letters signed by
Lincoln; student in the office. There is also access to his opinions on several
legal topics through the index, and legal cases mentioned by Lincoln are listed
by case name in the index.

Supplement, 1832-1865. Roy P. Basler, editor. Westport, Conn.: Greenwood
Press, 1974.
xi, 320 p. facsims. (Contributions in American Studies, no. 7)

Second Supplement. Roy P. Basler and Christian O. Basler, editors. New
Brunswick, N. J.: Rutgers University Press, 1990.
In Press.

Basler's Collected Works largely replaces Arthur Brooks Lapsley's *The Writings
of Abraham Lincoln*, 1905; and Nicolay and Hay's *Complete Works of Abraham
Lincoln*, 1905.

A one-volume edition of selected speeches and writings was published in 1946
(See item 99).

--- ----. Special sesquicentennial ed. Washington, D.C.: Lincoln Sesquicentennial
Commission, 1959.
--- ----. New Brunswick, N.J.: Rutgers University Press, 1960.

105
Lincoln, Abraham.
Complete Works of Abraham Lincoln. Edited by John G. **Nicolay** and John
Hay. With a General Introduction by Richard Watson Gilder and Special
Articles by Other Eminent Persons. New and enl. ed. New York: Francis D.
Tandy, 1905.
12 v. illus.

Lincoln's private secretaries collaborated on publication of his letters,
speeches, and writings at the suggestion of Robert T. Lincoln. The first edition
appeared in 1894, 2 v. The 1905 edition was comprised of 12 volumes. These
volumes have been largely superseded by Basler's *Collected Works*.

In the Nicolay and Hay set, there are a number of items pertaining to
Lincoln as a lawyer, such as his advice on the study of law, when admitted to
practice, resumption of practice, his absorption in practice, his license to
practice, and notes for a law lecture. There are notes on "Argumentation in the
Rock Island Bridge Case" as printed from the *Daily Press* of Chicago, September
24, 1857, *Hurd v. Railroad Bridge Co.*
Monaghan 1471.

--- ----. Ultrafiche. Dayton, Ohio: National Cash Register, 1970. (PCMI Library
Collection)
--- ----. Gettysburg ed. New York: Tandy, 1905.
--- ----. Microfiche. Chicago: Library Resources, 1970.
--- ----. Biographical ed. New York: Tandy, 1905. Reprinted from Gettysburg ed.
--- ----. Anniversary ed. New York: Lamb Pub. Co.. 1905.
--- ----. Sponsors ed. Lincoln Memorial University, 1926.
Other variants: Memorial, Commemorative, Presidential, National, and Boy
Rangers of America editions.

106
Lincoln, Abraham.
The Life and Writings of Abraham Lincoln. Edited and with a biographical
essay by Philip Van Doren **Stern**, with an introduction, "Lincoln in His
Writings," by Allan Nevins. New York: Random House, 1940.
863 p. port.

A collection of writings by Abraham Lincoln that includes "all those items
which are of biographical interest or of historical importance." The first quarter

of the book gives an historical account of the life of Lincoln written by Stern. Only a paragraph summarizes the formation of his law partnerships. The remainder of the volume provides reprints of numerous speeches and letters by Lincoln. Only excerpts of some of the longer pieces are printed, the compiler using his editorial privilege in omitting what he considers unimportant. Stern writes a brief introduction to each piece explaining its relevance.

There are several letters from Lincoln to his law partners, not necessarily about the practice, rather about politics, or his melancholy; to John T. Stuart, 1840 and 1841; to William H. Herndon, dated, 1848.

The "headnotes" for Lincoln's brief essay "Notes for a Law Lecture" show that the purpose for which Lincoln penned these notes was unknown.

Nevins, in his introduction notes that these early writings of a "stump speaking lawyer," although intellectually crude, indicate some of his virtues. He tells the familiar story of Lincoln's buying a barrel of rubbish and finding a copy of Blackstone's *Commentaries*.

--- ----. New York: Modern Library, 1940.

107
Lincoln, Abraham.
The Lincoln Treasury. Compiled by Caroline Thomas **Harnsberger**. 1st ed.
Chicago: Wilcox & Follett, 1950.
ix, 372 p. illus., ports.

This volume, designed for the general reader, contains quotations in alphabetical, dictionary arrangement, on topics from A to Z. Explanations precede these short paragraphs, many containing Lincoln's comments pertaining to law, and to lawyers. There are quotations on notes, pleading and oratory, on books and study, and a letter indicating what a studying lawyer should read. The compiler indicates sources, whether they are Lincoln's works or the works of other authors.
Includes chronology, index, and bibliography.

108
Lincoln, Abraham.
The Literary Works of Abraham Lincoln. Selected and arranged, with a foreword, by Carl **Van Doren**. New York: Press of the Readers Club, 1942.
xvi, 302 p.

A selected collection of what Carl Van Doren considers some of Lincoln's most important writings. He includes only works or letters that Lincoln actually wrote himself, omitting any of Lincoln's humorous stories. He begins with Lincoln's address to the people of Sangamon County in 1832 as a candidate for the General Assembly; this includes a paragraph on Lincoln's thoughts regarding existing laws. There are letters to William H. Herndon, his law partner, and to John T. Stuart; a fragment from notes for law lecture. In an autobiographical sketch for J. W. Fell, he mentions briefly his study of law, during a legislative period, and says after his congressional stint, he "practised law more assiduously than ever before." A "Short Autobiography" written at the request of a friend, for campaign purposes, includes information on his study of law and encouragement by John T. Stuart. Several letters to his friend Speed include references to litigation. The book concludes with selected maxims, observations, and comments taken from various Lincoln works.

--- ----. The Heritage Press, 1942. Also 1970.
--- ----. Printed for the members of the Limited Editions Club by the Collegiate Press, 1942.
--- ----. Collector's ed. Columbus, Ohio: Merrill, 1970.
--- ----. Collector's ed. Norwalk, Conn.: Easton Press, 1970.
(Masterpieces of American Literature)
--- ----. Norwalk, Conn.: Easton Press, 1980. (The Library of the Presidents)

109
Lincoln, Abraham.
New letters and Papers of Lincoln. Compiled by Paul M. **Angle**.
Boston: Houghton Mifflin, 1930.
x, 387 p. ports., facsims.

This volume was intended as a supplement to *The Complete Works of Abraham Lincoln*, by Nicolay and Hay; and Gilbert A. Tracy's *Uncollected Letters of Abraham Lincoln*. It includes letters, speeches, legal opinions, and other materials that were not included in the previous collections. Location of this primary material is noted.

New items include: Lincoln's advice on law study; will case of 1855 to break a will in Sangamon Circuit Court, *McDaniel v. Correll*. Notes represent a summary of the status of the case. In 1857, there are notes on *Illinois Central Railroad v. McLean Co.*; in 1858, notes on *Gale v. Morgan Co. Bank*. There are several letters concerning legal matters, during his partnership with Stuart; and with Logan.
Monaghan 3167

--- ----. Microfiche. Chicago: Library Resources, 1970. (Library of American Civilization; LAC 11489)

110
Lincoln, Abraham.
Quotations from Abraham Lincoln. Edited by Ralph Y. McGinnis. Chicago: Nelson-Hall, ©1977.
x, 134 p. illus.

The editor claims that Lincoln is the leader about whom people write most often, with the exception of Jesus of Nazareth. He is also "the most frequently quoted president in United States history." The book is divided into three sections: Quotations representing integrity (ethos), quotations representing intelligence (logos), and quotations representing idealism (pathos).
Several quotations of Lincoln are law related, found in the integrity section. There is a quotation concerning honesty as the first quality every lawyer should possess, several quotations on ethics of lawyers, and his words on hard work and diligence at studying law as well as in practicing it. Other law-related quotations include those on responsibility and logical thinking.
The book includes ten speeches given by Lincoln, and a chronology of events in the life of Lincoln.
Includes selected references.

111
Lincoln, Abraham.
A Treasury of Lincoln Quotations. Compiled and edited by Fred Kerner. [lst ed.] Garden City, N.Y.: Doubleday, [1965]
ix, 320 p.

The compiler has brought together a collection of authentic quotations, using exact words of Lincoln and indicating sources. He utilized Basler's *The Collected Works* to resolve discrepancies in language. Quotations cover subjects, such as lawlessness, laws, with quotations from the speech to the Young Men's Lyceum. He addresses lawyers with quotations from notes for a law lecture and several letters during the period 1855-1858 to Reavis, Grigsby, and Thornton. Additional items are from the years when Lincoln was in law practice.

112
Lincoln, Abraham.
Uncollected Letters of Abraham Lincoln Now First Brought Together by Gilbert A. Tracy. With an Introduction by Ida M. Tarbell. Boston: Houghton Mifflin, 1917.
xxi, 264 p.

"There is a goodly number of legal letters, several of them emphasizing what we already know." Lincoln wrote of law and politics in the same letters to

various lawyers with whom he was associated on the old Eighth Circuit. These provide examples of cleverness and fairness. Several concerned cases.
Monaghan 2346

--- ----. Microfilm. New Haven, Conn.: Yale University Library, 1988.

113
Lincoln, Abraham.
The Wit and Wisdom of Abraham Lincoln as Reflected in His Briefer Letters and Speeches. Edited by H. Jack **Lang**. New York: Greenberg, 1941.
xx, 265 p. port., facsims.

Section 1 includes "Postmaster, Lawyer, Representative of the People, 1832-1860."

There are letters from Lincoln to William H. Herndon and Judge Stephen T. Logan. The latter concerned Jonathan Birch applying for admission to the bar. His notes for a law lecture, described as a lawyer's creed, are included. A letter to J. W. Fell, 1859, provides a two-page sketch of his life in which he mentions that he "removed to Springfield to practice," and from 1849 to 1854 "practiced law more assiduously than ever before."
Bibliography in Acknowledgments.

--- ----. Cleveland: World Pub. Co., 1941.
--- ----. 1965, 1941. (Reprinted for Lincoln Centennial Library)

114
The Lincoln-Herndon Law Offices Volunteer Manual. Compiled by Mark **Johnson**, Marianna Munyer, and Richard Taylor. Springfield: Illinois Historic Preservation Agency. Historic States Division 1986.
v, 173 leaves. illus.

This manual includes information for interpretive teams at the Lincoln-Herndon Law Offices Historical Site, providing designs of the Tinsley Building, post office, law offices, the common room, and jury room. It shows the federal courtroom, 1841-55, judges' chambers, and federal clerks office. Includes a chronology of the Tinsley Building.

115
Lincoln in the State and Federal Courts: A Book of Readings. Compiled by Mark **Johnson**, Colleen Ogg, and Richard Taylor. [Springfield, Ill.]: Illinois Historic Preservation Agency, Historic Sites Division, 1986.

iii, 316 p. illus.

This volume includes reprints of more than a dozen selections, judged most useful by the compilers, related to Lincoln's law practice, and to the judicial system. A number of the articles, from journals and books, are presently out-of-print. This material had been used in designing the Lincoln-Herndon Law Offices State Historic Site interpretation program. The items were largely from the collections of the Illinois State Historical Library.

Benjamin J. Thomas' "Eighth Judicial Circuit" gives background information on the circuit that Lincoln rode in his practice of law; selections from Anton-Hermann Chroust's *The Rise of the Legal Profession in America* give details and general conditions that pertain to a practice in that era. Erwin C. Surrency's "A History of Federal Courts" further enlightens the reader on courts of the period.

116
Lincoln Memorial University.
"Lincoln the Lawyer": Dedication Services for the Bronze Statue "Lincoln the Lawyer," C. S. Paolo, sculptor. Harrogate, Tenn.: The University, 1949.
16 p. illus.

Reprint.
For Annotation, See Journal Articles, **Dedication** of the Bronze Statue "Lincoln the Lawyer," 51 LINCOLN HERALD (June 1949), 2-17.

117
Lincoln National Life Insurance Co.
Lincoln the Lawyer. [Fort Wayne, Ind.: The Company, 1962?]
[6] p.

This pamphlet tells how Lincoln borrowed Stuart's law books, and received his law license at twenty-seven years of age. There is information on his traveling the circuit and enjoying the fellowship. Lincoln became a prominent lawyer for the railroads, and the "Effie Afton" case of 1857 is singled out. When the time came for his departure for the presidency, Lincoln's parting words were that if he lived, he would return and go on practicing law.

118
Lloyd, John A.
Lincoln in Cincinnati. Cincinnati: Queen City Optimists Club, 1988, ©1980.
16 p.

An address delivered to The Queen City Optimists Club, February 9, 1980, describes three visits that Lincoln made to Cincinnati.

As counsel in the lawsuit *McCormick v. Manny*, Lincoln had been employed in 1855 to represent J. H. Manny and Company, reaper manufacturer of Rockford, Illinois, for alleged infringement of patent against Cyrus H. McCormick.

Lloyd describes how Lincoln was sought at his Springfield home and paid a retainer fee, expecting the case to be tried in the United States District Court in Chicago. The trial was moved to Cincinnati where other counsel for Manny were George Harding of Philadelphia and Edwin M. Stanton of Pittsburgh. McCormick was represented by Edward N. Dickerson of New York and Reverdy Johnson of Baltimore. Lincoln was informed rather rudely that he was not actually needed for the proceedings.

The orator explains further how Lincoln spent his time in Cincinnati, and tells of two other visits to the city.

119
Lockridge, Ross F. (Franklin)
A. Lincoln. Yonkers-on-Hudson, N.Y.: World Book Co., 1930.
xiv, 320 p. illus., ports.

The author presents a "short and simple portrayal of the human aspects of the historic Lincoln." He made an effort to seek out contacts, gave careful study to almost every book written on the topic, and visited places on site. He utilized Lincoln's own words and considers him his own best biographer. Lockridge used quotations extensively in building the story of his life.

In the chapter entitled "Lawyer," Lockridge reveals Lincoln's contemplation, considering what he should do: learning the blacksmith trade, or trying to study law, and deciding he could not succeed at that without better education.

The reader learns of Stuart's encouragement in his study of law, lending him books. Lincoln studied alone, and had to abandon his law books whenever the legislature met. In Autumn 1836, he obtained his law license, and in April 1837, moved to Springfield. The author enumerates the three law parnerships. The author mentions his reading habits and time spent in the office of the *Sangamo Journal*. He was most successful upon his return to practice from Congress in 1849, when he practiced with great earnestness. There are stories of circuit riding by horseback or in a hired wagon, later in a "rattling buggy." He enjoyed social life. There are stories to illustrate his arguments to juries. His cases often involved the simple problems of the frontier. He writes of the notes of a lecture to law students, and explains how Lincoln shows his respect for the law in a speech before the Young Men's Lyceum.
Monaghan 3210

120
Lorant, Stefan.
Lincoln: A Picture Story of His Life. New York: Harper, 1952.
256 p. illus. ports., facsims.

The story of Lincoln's life is told with photographs, and pictures of documents, many of which were from the author's extensive collection of Lincoln photographs. Explanatory text accompanies the photos.

A section covers the time when Lincoln was working in Springfield as a lawyer. It shows photos and provides discussion of Lincoln's law partners and their offices. There is a piece on Lincoln "Riding the Circuit." There are photographs of courthouses in which he practiced, and of his law associates. The book includes a phototograph of Lincoln taken immediately after the murder trial of Duff Armstrong, whom Lincoln defended and who was acquitted. There is a facsimile of jury instructions written by Lincoln. His life mask was made when Lincoln tried the *Johnston v. Jones* lakefront case in Chicago in 1860.

Approximately one third of the volume covers Lincoln's prepresidential life. Includes bibliography.

--- ----. Rev. and enl. ed. New York: Harper, 1957. 304 p.
--- ----. Rev. and enl. ed. New York: Norton, 1969. 336 p.
--- ----. Rev. and enl. ed. New York: Bonanza Books, 1975.

121
Lowry, Thomas.
Personal Reminiscences of Abraham Lincoln. London: Privately printed for Beatrice M. Lowry and Her Friends. Minneapolis; [Printed at Chiswick Press, London, by Charles Whittingham for Edmund D. Brooks., 1910.]
31, [1] p. illus., port.

This item begins with the copy of a letter written by Abraham Lincoln in 1850, concerning a case he had for Lowry's father. It dealt with outstanding title to property, owned by neither plaintiff nor defendant. It shows Lincoln's method of coming to a direct point. The letter, described as having been written on old blue "foolscrap" paper, had been folded as an envelope, sealed with red wax and marked "Due 5 cents." Lowry had accompanied his father from Schuyler County to see Mr. Lincoln in his office. Includes information on life on the circuit. Monaghan 1930.

--- ----. [Minneapolis, Minn., 1929] Reprinted from original.

122
Lufkin, Richard Friend.
Mr. Lincoln's Light From Under a Bushel, 1853. Knoxville: S. B. Newman
Printing Co., 1954.
16 p.

Reprinted from 55 LINCOLN HERALD (Winter 1953) 2-14;48.
For annotation see **Lufkin,** Journal Articles.

Reprints from LINCOLN HERALD. See Journal Articles.
Mr. Lincoln's Light From Under a Bushel, 1850. Knoxville, Tenn.:
S. B. Newman Printing Co., 1952.
23 p.
Mr. Lincoln's Light From Under a Bushel, 1851. Knoxville, Tenn.: S. B.
Newman Printing Co., 1952.
26 p.
Mr. Lincoln's Light From Under a Bushel, 1852. Knoxville, Tenn.: S. B.
Newman Printing Co., 1953.
26 p.

123
Luthin, Reinhard H.
The Real Abraham Lincoln: A Complete One Volume History of His Life and
Times.   Englewood Cliffs, N.J.: Prentice-Hall, 1960.
778 p.

Luthin has drawn on historical sources, including the Robert Todd Lincoln
collection for a chapter entitled "Law Office, Court and Circuit." He reminds his
readers of the traditional stories regarding Lincoln's reading of the *Indiana
Revised Statutes*, and presents two versions of his acquiring Blackstone's
Commentaries.

With description of the firm advertisement, he indicates the   start of
Lincoln's practice with Stuart. Lincoln represented the defendant in *Hawthorne
v. Wooldridge*, in which three causes grew out of one business transaction:
contract, trespass, and replevin. Many of his early cases were petty and
uninspiring, although his varied practice included criminal cases also. He
mentions the Truett case in the murder of Early among other cases. He tells of
his first case in the Supreme Court of Illinois, *Scammon v. Cline*, and other
cases.

He reports on the valuable experience Lincoln received as partner of Logan,
and explains that Lincoln did well enough financially to purchase a home. He
singles out the case of the Trailor Brothers.

The author explains that Lincoln maintained his longest term of practice
with Herndon. While business began slowly, it doubled during the second year.

The Denton case is of interest as is the Matson case, in which he expresses the view that Lincoln did not present a listless case.

Chapter 10, "Back to the Law," tells of his return from Congress when the partnership of Lincoln and Herndon flourished again. There is brief description of the law office and furnishings, and the mention of book titles on the shelves. He notes that Lincoln was disorderly in his paperwork and some of the documents of both partners were misplaced from time to time. He points out that Lincoln became counsel in at least eighty-five cases tried in the United States Court between 1855 and 1860. In particular he mentions, *Ambos v. Barret*; *Beaver v. Taylor and Gilbert* and adds that it was a lucrative case. He furnishes some description of the Eighth Judicial Circuit.

In Chapter 11, "Lincoln's Celebrated Law Cases," he gives some detail of the *Illinois Central Railroad v. County of McLean*; *McCormick v. Manny*; "Effie Afton," i.e., *Hurd v. Rock Island Bridge Co.* Criminal cases include that of Duff Armstrong, the Harrison case, and a rape case in which Lincoln was a special prosecutor, *People v. Thomas Delny*. The Sand-Bar case, *Johnston v. Jones and Marsh*, was his last important case.

124
McClelland, Stewart Winning.
A. Lincoln, LL.D. Harrogate, Tenn: Dept. of Lincolniana, Lincoln Memorial University, 1939.
[5] p. illus.
Monaghan 3689

For annotation see **McClelland,** Journal Articles.
41 LINCOLN HERALD (May 1939), 2-6.

McClure, J. B., ed.
Abraham Lincoln's Stories and Speeches: Including Early Life Stories, Professional Life Stories . . .
See **Lincoln,** Abraham.

McGinnis, Ralph Y., ed.
Quotations from Abraham Lincoln.
See **Lincoln,** Abraham.

125
Masters, Edgar Lee.
Lincoln, the Man. New York: Dodd, Mead, 1931.
520 p. illus., ports., facsims.

The author attempts to present the facts and events of the life of Abraham Lincoln as a basis for an analysis of Lincoln's mind and character. "The purpose has been to bring together the testimony in full touching Lincoln's career, so that the reader will be enabled to judge for himself whether that testimony justifies the conclusions which are drawn by way of analytical portraiture." Masters writes in an unfavorable light on Lincoln. He theorizes that Lincoln was made a hero by writers of that time, due to passions and events of the war.

He believes that Lincoln could have read better studies of the Constitution than he did and criticizes him for not reading other great books. He was often in the office telling stories, talking politics, and reading poetry. Masters mentions the lucrative Illinois Central Railroad case, and the "Effie Afton" case. Masters states that Lincoln drafted few legal papers, and had neither order nor method concerning the law. He accuses Lincoln of being unprepared for his cases, and losing cases that any lawyer should have won. When others described Lincoln as one of the best of his day, the author believes that there are no facts to support it. He insists that Lincoln was trying to make money rather than assisting the poor, and that much of this litigation was not important.
Monaghan 3284

126
Mearns, David Chambers.
The Lincoln Papers: The Story of the Collection. With selections to July 4, 1861. Introduction by Carl Sandburg. 1st ed. Garden City, N.Y.: Doubleday, 1948.
2 v. (xvii, 681 p.) illus., ports.

The director of the Reference Department of the Library of Congress tells the story of the largest collection of Abraham Lincoln's writings and papers, which belonged to his son, Robert. With the exception of the Lincoln biographers Nicolay and Hay, access to the collection was not allowed until twenty-one years after the death of Robert Lincoln. In 1947 the Robert Todd Lincoln Collection was opened to the public. Mearns writes a history of the collection itself from the date of Abraham Lincoln's death until the papers were opened on July 26, 1947.

The collection contained 18,000 documents. The remainder of volume one and all of volume two contain selected works from the collection. Mearns indicates that the selections do not constitute the most important, nor the most representative of the entire collection.

In Part II of the first volume, one of the immediate items of interest is Lincoln's autobiography. In it he tells of his beginning to study law, his borrowing the books of Stuart, and studying them earnestly, putting them aside when the legislature was in session. He tells of obtaining his law license, moving to Springfield, and commencing to practice, in partnership with his friend Stuart.

William Dean Howells' notes for the biography he was commissioned to write in 1860 were discovered among the Lincoln papers. Here details of

"Lincoln's Course from 1829 to 1846" appear from Howells' work. Howells had interviewed James Quay Howard, a young law student, who himself had interviewed Lincoln's oldest friends, including those who had known him in New Salem. Some insight is gained from the interviews, such as one describing a case which Lincoln would not take because his client would not have been strictly in the right. From the papers, one is able to visualize his reading Blackstone's *Commentaries* under a tree, turning with the shade.

A letter is included from Judge David Davis suggesting a possible commissionship for Lincoln, and how Lincoln could reenter the law, "get in the Circuit and in the Supreme Court as good a practice as you want." Scattered letters have some interest regarding his law practice, such as one from J. B. Jones, in 1859, asking Lincoln if he would defend his son.

--- ----. New York: Kraus Reprint, 1969. 2 v. in 1 (xvii, 681 p.)

127
Mellon, James, ed.
The Face of Lincoln. Compiled and edited by James Mellon. New York: Viking Press, 1979.
201 p. illus. (A Studio book)

The editor, in a collection of photographic portraits of Lincoln, explains that those persons who wish to know Lincoln must, sooner or later, take a look at him. Therefore this book concentrates on Lincoln's face as it appeared in photographs, from which one can catch a glimpse of him. The oversized book displays large (11" x 14") photographs of Lincoln in varying poses. Text, consisting of pieces written by Lincoln, excerpted from his speeches, or recollected by people who knew him, is intermingled with the photos on various aspects and events of his life.

Although most of the photographs are taken during the last eleven years of his life, they include "The Frontier Lawyer; notes for a law lecture," "His Law Partner William Herndon's Recollections of Lincoln as an Orator," "His Law Partner Remembers him in Two Sketches" (William Herndon), along with several photos of Lincoln during 1850s when he was practicing law. Each excerpt above is a page in length.

Photographic portraits accompanied by texts consisting of "Lincoln's written and spoken words interspersed with eyewitness descriptions of the man."

--- ----. New York: Bonanza, Distributed by Crown, 1982, ©1979.
The editor acknowledges the Meserve collection, from which he has drawn material.
Meserve, Frederick Hill. The Photographs of Abraham Lincoln [by] Frederick Hill Meserve [and] Carl Sandburg. New York: Harcourt, Brace, 1944.

--- ----. New York: Privately printed, 1911. Supplements, 1911-1955.
Monaghan 2001; 2002.
   He utilized twenty of Lloyd Ostendorf's photographs.
   Hamilton, Charles. Lincoln in Photographs: An Album of Every Known
Pose, by Charles Hamilton and Lloyd **Ostendorf**. Norman, Okla.: University of
Oklahoma Press,1963.

--- ----. [Rev.] Dayton, Ohio: Morningside, 1985.

128
Memoirs of Abraham Lincoln in Edgar County, Illinois. [Paris, Ill.]: Edgar
County Historical Society, 1925.
31 p. illus., ports., facsims.

   "Dedicated to the memory of the men who practiced law in Edgar County
when Abraham Lincoln traveled the Circuit of the Eighth Judicial District." This
collection is comprised of articles, poems, and personal recollections of the time
when Lincoln practiced law on the Eighth Judicial Circuit as he made its route
twice each year. Lincoln, who traveled with Judge Davis, often stayed in Paris
and stopped in Bloomfield. The articles were written by county residents who
had personal knowledge and recollections of Lincoln when he stopped in Edgar
County while on the circuit.
   The pamphlet includes the story of how the Eighth circuit came to be
marked, a poem "The Lincoln Circuit," cases in which Lincoln appeared in
Circuit Court of Paris, Ill., 1852-1853, a piece entitled "Lawyers' Fees Small in
1842," and "Lincoln Mementoes and Relics."
Monaghan 2797

129
Miers, Earl Schenck.
Lincoln Day by Day: A Chronology, 1809-1865. Earl Schenck Miers, editor-in-
chief. Washington, D.C.: Lincoln Sesquicentennial Commission, 1960.
3 v.

A revised and enlarged edition of **Pratt**, Harry E., Lincoln, 1809-[1861].

   Volume 2, 1849-1860, of this work gives a day-by-day chronology of
Lincoln's life during the years when he was a practicing attorney. After each day
there is a brief paragraph describing what Lincoln did on a particular day with
a notation regarding source. These volumes are particularly useful in listing
Lincoln's activities pertaining to law cases, as actions are brought, suits filed,
motions made, agreements made, cases dismissed, won, or lost. Details include
amounts awarded, names of parties to cases, and excerpts from correspondence.

130
Milner, Duncan C.
Lincoln on Liquor. New York: Neale Pub. Co., 1920.
155 p. port.

In this book, there is a discussion of "The State Against the Women."
Lincoln volunteered to defend several women who had smashed barrels and
broken bottles of spirits in a grogshop. He changed the name of the case to
"The State Against Mr. Whiskey."
His plea was published in the *Northwestern Christian Advocate*.
Monaghan 2469

--- ----. 2nd ed. With Supplement. Chicago: W. P. Blessing Co., 1926. 185 p.
--- ----. Microfilm New Haven Conn.: Yale University Library, 1988.

131
Moores, Charles Washington.
The Career of a Country Lawyer: Abraham Lincoln. Read before the American
Bar Association at Chattanooga, Tennessee, September 1, 1910. [S.l.: s.n.], 1910.
38 p. facsims.

Reprinted from Proceedings of the American Bar Association. 35 REPORTS
OF THE AMERICAN BAR ASSOCIATION (1910), 440-477.

Includes Appendix: p. 35-38. "Lincoln's Cases in the Illinois Supreme Court."

(The author's typescript is located at Butler University, with numerous
holographic notes and inserts of the full texts of his interviews with friends and
acquaintances of Lincoln. Gisela Hersch lists accompanying manuscript materials
in *Lincolniana: A Collection of Pamphlets, Booklets, Manuscripts, Magazine and
Newspaper Articles Relating to the Life and Times of Abraham Lincoln 1809-1865*.
Indianapolis: Butler University, 1983.)
Monaghan 1938
For annotation see **Moores**, Journal Articles.

132
Morris, Richard Brandon.
Fair trial. Fourteen Who Stood Accused from Anne Hutchinson to Alger Hiss.

1st ed. New York: Knopf, 1952.
xv, 494 p.

"Armstrong's Acquittal by Almanac; Lincoln Starts a Legend," p. 204-224.

This case illustrates the importance of a first-rate trial lawyer. The author shows that two men were on trial for a murder. One, James H. Norris, went to prison. Duff Armstrong, who had Abraham Lincoln for a lawyer, went free. He tells the tale of Lincoln's shrewd interrogation of the witness, and his use of an almanac. For this trial, no stenographic record was preserved. Newspapers gave it no coverage. To get at the facts, this author has had to depend on recollection of the sequence of events from eyewitnesses, judge, the accused, his family, and Herndon.

There is discussion of which almanac was used and whether it had been altered, also on ownership of the slung shot. Then, there is the surprising statement from Duff Armstrong years later that the moonlight did not matter since the fight was in a bar where there were candles.

"The Armstrong case is as interesting for what it suggests about Lincoln's own attitude toward his client as for what it reveals about Lincoln as a jury lawyer."

--- ----. Rev. ed. New York: Harper, 1967. (Harper Torchbooks; TB1335.

133
Morse, Howard Newcomb.
Lawyer Lincoln: Accounts of Six Law Cases in Which Abraham Lincoln Participated as Counsel, edited by Howard Newcomb Morse. Atlanta, Ga.: Peachtree Publications, [n.d.].
40 p.

This booklet was intended to provide an insight into types of court cases typical of Lincoln's private practice.

In "Lincoln Represents a Business Man," suit was brought by a contractor for masonry and plastering, *Garrett v. Stevenson*. Lincoln, defending the owner, lost the case.

"Lincoln Represents a Doctor" describes a medical malpractice case. The author, a counselor-at-law, calls it a foundation case in the law of medical malpractice. Lincoln lost this case for the physician/surgeon whom he represented.

In "The Rail Splitter a Tree Cutter," the Supreme Court held for Vandever, who had Lincoln for counsel. The plaintiff, Whitecraft, had brought action to recover a statutory penalty for the cutting of trees felled by Vandever.

The fourth case, "A Lincoln Partnership Case," involved a suit that was decided by the Supreme Court of Illinois in 1849. Moffett had brought suit against Lewis and Johnson for an equitable division among three partners of assets realized from sale of patent rights owned by the firm.

In "Another Partnership Case," *Major v. Hawkes*, Lincoln was counsel for Hawkes and others who brought action against Major to recover indebtedness to them as co-partners.

In "Lincoln Represents an Agent," concerning a patented invention, Lincoln was counsel for Reuben Miller, *Miller v. Whittaker*. The Supreme Court of Illnois held for Lincoln's client, and reversed the decision of the lower court.

134

National Archives and Records Administration. Great Lakes Division.
Lincoln at the Bar: Selected Case Files from the United States District and Circuit Courts, Southern District of Illinois 1855-1861. Records of District Courts of the United States, Record Group 21. Washington, D.C.: National Archives Trust Fund Board, 1989.
10 p.   (National Archives Microfilm Publications Pamphlet Describing M1530)

The records listed in this pamphlet represent the extant files of cases from the records of the United States district and circuit courts at Springfield with which Abraham Lincoln has been identified as legal counsel, 1855 to 1861. They represent the only federal district and circuit court case files identified with Lincoln that survive in the official records. The 122 cases are listed by microfilm roll number, case number, and case title. The records are in custody of the National Archives-Great Lakes Region.

Information is provided that U.S. Supreme Court Lincoln records are in Record Group 167, National Arhives and Records Administration, Washington, D.C. Supreme Court of Illinois and Illinois state court case records are in the Illinois State Archives, Springfield. Introductory remarks by Shirley J. **Burton**.

135
Neal, Tom (Thomas A.)
Lawyer On the Circuit. Los Angeles: Dawson's Book Shop, 1945.
9 p.

Limited edition of 50 numbered copies for Lincoln Fellowship of Southern California; 100 copies for Dawson's Book Shop.

The year 1834, in which Lincoln was elected to the state legislature, presented him with the opportunity to study law. Credit goes to Stuart who allowed him to borrow law books and afterward took him into the partnership. This item tells of Lincoln on the Eighth Judicial Circuit during a picturesque period. It depicts six hundred words in the hand of Lincoln, "Lincoln for DEFT," *Nerckles v. Wilson*, a case involving cattle dealers in 1856.

136
Nevins, Allan, ed.
Lincoln and the Gettysburg Address: Commemorative Papers. [By] John Dos
Passos [et al.] Urbana: University of Illinois Press, 1964.
133 p.

This book is comprised of six articles written by various authors concerning
the Gettysburg address. Authur Lehman **Goodhart's** article entitled, "Lincoln
and the Law" concerned Lincoln's emphasis on respect and obedience to the
law. Goodhart contends, "Unless we remember that Lincoln was a lawyer we
cannot fully understand the things that he said or did." He describes Lincoln's
legal education, attributing Lincoln's reading of Blackstone's *Commentaries* as
the cornerstone of his legal foundation. Goodhart believes Lincoln purchased his
copy at an auction in Springfield in 1831, and had not found it in the bottom of
a barrel as popularly believed. He believes Lincoln's short, precise, with "not a
single unnecessary word," in the Gettysburg speech is a result of his training as
a lawyer. He compares parts of the speech to traits and skills used by lawyer
Lincoln. Goodhart states that this was the foundation on which Lincoln's
political ideas were based.

137
Newcomb, Rexford.
In the Lincoln Country: Journeys to the Lincoln Shrines of Kentucky, Indiana,
Illinois, and other States. Philadelphia: J. B. Lippincott, 1928.
191 p. illus., port., maps, facsim.

The chapter entitled "The Springfield of Lincoln's Early Residence" includes
information on the Stuart and Lincoln Law Office and the Logan and Lincoln
Office. It refers to "Homan's Row," a contraction of the Hoffman's Row
location. Information is found on the Lincoln-Herndon Office in "The
Springfield of Lincoln's Married Life." Another chapter describes the "Eighth
Judicial District - the Lincoln Circuit." There are maps of the circuit and an
indication of what life was like on court days. The author says that Lincoln was
not the most popular lawyer on the circuit in volume of business, and in trial
work he was no more successful than many others. He had an enviable record
in the higher court. The author tells of the old court houses and county seats.
He includes a description of Herndon's last meeting with Lincoln.
Monaghan 3051

--- ----. Microfilm. New Haven, Conn.: Yale University Library, 1988.

Newman, Ralph G. (Geoffrey), ed.
Abraham Lincoln: His Story in His Own Words.

See **Lincoln**, Abraham.

138
Newman, Ralph G. (Geoffrey), ed.
Lincoln for the Ages. Edited and with an Introduction by Ralph G. Newman.
Foreword by David C. Mearns. Garden City, N.Y.: Doubleday, 1960.
519 p.

This collection, comprised of "creative scholarship of eminent living students," has been an attempt at an objective reappraisal of Abraham Lincoln, "in contemporary thought and action."

Among other essays, it includes "Lincoln the Lawyer," by Willard L. King, and "Lincoln and Herndon," by Albert A. Woldman.

King, p. 90-95, sees Lincoln as a "Lawyer's lawyer," the bulk of his practice coming from other attorneys. He quotes Judge Davis in saying that he had few equals, and was recognized in many communities at least ten years prior to his election. The words he emphasized were "industry" and "diligence." He characterized Lincoln as being thorough in his investigation of facts and the law, although there was not always opportunity for preparation. He was methodical, meticulous, scrupulous, conscientious, and genuine. He was known for his integrity, resourcefulness and facile speech. He believed in compromise, and was generous in judgment.

Woldman, p. 101-106, describes the law practice, from December 1844, when the shingle of Lincoln and Herndon was hung, through the years they were associated in the practice of law. He expressed surprise at Lincoln's confidence in Herndon, choosing him as partner when he had just been admitted to practice December 9, 1844. Lincoln did not want the restraint of an authoritarian figure. He had learned in his association with Logan, one of the ablest attorneys in the state, and finally went into association with a novice, whom he could train according to his own terms. Although they had conflicting personalities, there was no personal controversy. They had respect for each other. Their parting is a well-known scene.

139
Newton, Joseph Fort.
Lincoln and Herndon. Cedar Rapids, Iowa: Torch Press, 1910.
367 p. illus., ports.

This is a study of the personal and political fellowship between Abraham Lincoln and William H. Herndon. The author, a clergyman, through correspondence dated 1854-1859, between friends Theodore Parker, a noted Boston reformer, and William Herndon, introduces new material (at that time in history), shedding light on the Lincoln-Herndon association. The chapters

"The Junior Partner" and "Lincoln and Herndon" contain material on Lincoln's law practice and career in some detail.

The work portrays Herndon with "reference to his service to Lincoln as friend and adviser, and later as biographer." The author's concern "is with the personal and political side of their partnership, their mutual confidence and inspirations, their influence upon each other. . . ." The theme is illustrated by the Parker-Herndon letters. The latter part of the book deals with Herndon after Lincoln's death in regard to his position as Lincoln's defender and biographer.
Monaghan 1942

140
Nichols, Clifton.
Life of Abraham Lincoln, Being a Biography of His Life from his Birth to His Assassination: Also a Record of His Ancestors, and a Collection of Anecdotes Attributed to Lincoln. Springfield, Ohio: Mast, Crowell & Kirkpatrick, 1896. 320 p. illus., ports. (Farm and Fireside Library; no. 132)

A chapter, "Lincoln as a Lawyer," has information on riding the circuit. The courthouses are described, as well as the United States Court in Springfield. A chapter entitled "Lincoln's Most Famous Law Cases" includes *McCormick v. Manny and Duff Armstrong*. There is information on the slave girl case, as well as an unusual one of a colt's proving its ownership by finding its mother. The author relates an incident pertaining to the location of the Stuart and Lincoln law office above the courtroom.
Monaghan 1202

141
Nicolay, Helen.
Personal Traits of Abraham Lincoln. New York: Century, 1912.
387 p.

The author, daughter of John Nicolay, wrote this book from material that her father had collected and marked "personal traits," which was to have been used but omitted from *Abraham Lincoln: A History*, by John Nicolay and John Hay.

The book is a study of Abraham Lincoln's character through his nature, personal traits, and attitudes. She explores Lincoln's anecdotes and similes, his attitude toward money, and his moral fiber among other traits.

A chapter entitled "Eighth Judicial Circuit" describes the circuit itself and its vast expanse of territory over which the circuit judge and lawyers traveled twice a year. She describes Lincoln's lighthearted spirits, traveling with a jovial group, and his entertainment of fellow travelers, only occasionally being silent and moody.

The Eighth Circuit was the setting for numerous anecdotes. She paints the picture of his being undisturbed by the inadequate accommodations of the day, describing only one incident when Lincoln was angered. She describes legal and political aspects of court week in the county seats. Lincoln was popular due to his wit, and his ability to listen. In the court, he was able to get to the core, and gave points to his opposition until an essential question dealing with the issue arose. His speech was clear, simple, and deliberate, and he told an occasional anecdote when applicable. She notes his expert handling of witnesses. He was seen one of fair play, taking only cases that appeared just.
Monaghan 2049

--- ----. New York, Century, 1919.
--- ----. New York: D. Appleton Co., 1939.

142
Nicolay, John G. (George)
Abraham Lincoln: A History, by John G. Nicolay and John Hay.   New York: Century Co., 1890.
10 v.

These volumes were published twenty-five years after the death of Lincoln by these two contemporaries. The authors' purpose was to write the life of Lincoln to "show his relations to the times in which he moved," the issues, and the associates. They have tried to ascertain the truth and present "absolutely honest history." Friendly critics responded to their first efforts in *The Century Magazine*.

Nicolay and Hay have not relied on memory in their ten-volume work but have based their findings on memoranda, diaries, documents, and reports. Several chapters deal with Lincoln's law practice. In "Early Law Practice," topics include: early legal customs; Lincoln's popularity in law and politics; correspondence with Stuart. The chapter entitled "The Campaign of 1844" includes: partnership with Stephen T. Logan; Lincoln becomes a lawyer. The chapter "The Circuit Lawyer" includes: growth and change of legal habits; Lincoln on the circuit; his power and value as a lawyer; opinions of Lincoln by David Davis and Judge Drummond; incidents in the courts; and Lincoln's wit and eloquence.
Monaghan 1071

--- ----. 1890. Microfilm. Emporia, Kan.: William Allen White Library, 1972.
--- ----. 1890. Microopaque. New York: Readex Microprint, 1975.
--- ----. New York: Century Co., 1917.
--- ----. Ultrafiche. Dayton, Ohio: National Cash Register, 1970. (PCMI Library Collection 000855-000856)
--- ----. New York: Century Co., 1918, ©1914, Copyright renewal.

--- ----. Manuscript ed. [S.l.]: American Historical Foundation, 1914.
--- ----. Abridged ed. Chicago: University of Chicago Press, 1966. 394 p. (Classic American Historians)

143
Nicolay, John G. (George)
A Short Life of Abraham Lincoln. Condensed from Nicolay & Hay's Abraham Lincoln: A History. New York: Century, 1902.
xvi, 578 p. port.

A condensed version of Nicolay and Hay's *Abraham Lincoln: A History* covers the life of Abraham Lincoln from beginning to end. At least three quarters of the book deals with the Civil War era. The final chapter relates Lincoln's life to his environment in affecting his character and attitude, how early failures were eventually turned into successes, and how his achievement awarded him a place in history. Among other details, it singles out his beginning the study of law, practice of law, rules for a lawyer, law and politics. Note is made of the distinctively new period of Lincoln's career dating from the time of his entrance into a law partnership with John T. Stuart. Nicolay chose not to trace in detail his progress in his new and chosen vocation. Lincoln climbed the path from a five-dollar fee before a justice of the peace to a five-thousand dollar fee before the Supreme Court. Mention is made of the law partnership with Logan, and Lincoln's notes intended for a lecture to law students.
Monaghan 1376

--- ----. Microfilm. New Haven, Conn.: Yale University Library, 1988.
--- ----. Special ed. New York: Century, 1903, ©1902.
--- ----. New York: Century, ©1930.

144
Oakleaf, Joseph Benjamin.
Abraham Lincoln as a Criminal Lawyer: An Address by Judge Benjamin Oakleaf at the Banquet of Illinois State's Attorneys' Association Held at the Close of Their Annual Session, December 7, 1912, at Hotel Sherman, Chicago. Rock Island, Ill: Augustana Book Concern, 1923.
15 p. illus., port.

Caption title: Lincoln as a Criminal Lawyer.

The author contends that Lincoln "abhorred criminal practice." He states, "If Lincoln appeared in a criminal case at all it was invariably in defending some poor unfortunate who was unable to hire an attorney. . . ." He believes that if Lincoln had taken up criminal practice, he would have been a success, since he

had mastered the art of cross examination. Lincoln had a knack of framing his question so that no matter how a witness answered it would be favorable to Lincoln's side. He had a faculty for presenting the points that the jury could best understand, using simple logic. The author, by analogy to presidential actions, concludes that Lincoln would have been a success had he specialized in criminal law as either a prosecuting or defending attorney.
Monaghan 2657

145
Oates, Stephen B.
The Illinois Lawyer: Why Should the Spirit of Mortal be Proud? Gettysburg, Pa.: National Historical Society, 1976. 15 p.
For annotation, See **Oates**, Journal Articles.

146
Oates, Stephen B.
With Malice Toward None: The Life of Abraham Lincoln. 1st ed. New York: Harper & Row, 1977.
xvii, 492 p. illus.

This contemporary biography by a history professor deals with all significant aspects of Lincoln's life, devoting several pages to the legal phase. Oates describes Lincoln's rise to the top of the legal profession, and his reputation as a first-rate lawyer. He depicts a typical working day, so that the reader can visualize him on the way to his office dressed as well as the average western lawyer of his day. He portrays him as a "lawyer's lawyer" arguing appeals cases for other attorneys. He gives an account of a man of substantial wealth, using his money to measure his worth. The suggested annual salary of $5000, is more than most other biographers have estimated.

Oates sets the stage for life in Lincoln's law office, and describes court time, his care in selecting a jury, compiling his own annotated list of prospective jurors for a trial. He had his own view in judging the characteristics of the jury by appearance. He took a variety of cases; the author mentions *Bailey v. Cromwell*, and the Matson slave case in particular. Lincoln was the only lawyer who rode the entire Eighth Judicial Circuit, with the exception of state's attorney. He tells of his friends on the circuit, Jesse W. Fell, of the Bloomington *Pantagraph*, Leonard Swett, a criminal lawyer, and Henry C. Whitney, involved with Lincoln in circuit court litigation, as well as Judge Davis, and Ward Hill Lamon.

He notes Lincoln's involvement in the McCormick reaper patent case, and his reputation as a railroad lawyer, although he had not always represented the railroad interests. Lincoln's advice on honesty appears in the final paragraph dealing with the lawyer. There are scattered references to other cases, such as "Effie Afton" and Duff Armstrong. The author presents an objective study of the

lawyer, referring to traditional sources, and presenting his biography in a modern volume.
Includes bibliographical references.

--- ----. New York: New American Library, 1978, ©1977. 542 p.
--- ----. Collector's ed. Norwalk, Conn: Easton, 1988. 492 p.

147
Oberholtzer, Ellis Paxson.
Abraham Lincoln. Philadelphia: George W. Jacobs, 1904.
389 p. port. (American Crisis Biographies)

In the chapter entitled "Benedick and Lawyer" the point was made that Lincoln's knowledge of the law was imperfect. He read under his own direction, and became the partner of Stuart, who was often absent for political reasons. Then he joined Logan as a partner in 1841. This was fortunate for his own advancement, Logan being regarded as one of the most able attorneys in the "West," who pursued law for its own sake, not as the means to political advancement. The author tells of Lincoln's establishing his own office in a business relationship with Herndon as partner.

He describes life on the circuit for the itinerant lawyers in the fourteen counties of the Eighth Judicial Circuit. Finally, he relates a few incidents of Lincoln's life, reminding the reader that he was original and unfettered.
Includes bibliography.
Monaghan 1443

--- ----. Microfilm. New Haven, Conn.: Yale University Library, 1988.

148
Oldroyd, Osborn H.
The Lincoln Memorial: Album-immortelles. Original Life Pictures, With Autographs From the Hands and Hearts of Eminent Americans and Europeans. Contemporaries of the Great Martyr to Liberty - Abraham Lincoln. Collected and edited by Osborn H. Oldroyd. With an Introduction by Matthew Simpson and a Sketch of the Patriot's life by Hon. Isaac N. Arnold. Chicago: Gem Pub. House, 1883.
571 p. illus., port., facsims.

Arnold Isaac N., p. 29-69, "Abraham Lincoln," includes a subsection "A Lawyer," p. 35-38.
Arnold, a contemporary of Lincoln, points to differences between the log courthouses of the frontier and the halls of Westminster. He believed that Lincoln was a great lawyer, seeking to convince by application of principle, rather than relying on citation of authority. He was strong with a jury, and he

did not know of a more successful advocate before the jury than Abraham Lincoln. He impressed people in his favor, and was an accurate reader of character. He had a candid manner and a direct method, being anxious for truth and justice. He excelled in the statement of a case, and had ability in examining witnesses, bringing out important facts. He could make a jury laugh or weep. He compelled truth, and never misstated evidence. He preferred right cases, and had to have faith in his case. He was involved in leading cases in federal and state courts, with a large clientele.
Monaghan 987

--- ----. New York: G. W. Carleton, 1882.
--- ----. Microfilm: New Haven, Conn.: Micrographic Systems of Connecticut, 1986.
--- ----. Boston: D. L. Guernsey, 1882.
--- ----. Jersey City, N.J.: N. Gesner, 1882.
--- ----. New York: Norman D. Sampson, 1883.
--- ----. Springfield, Ill.: Lincoln Pub. Co., 1890, 1882.

149
Packard, R. D. (Roy Dwight)
A. Lincoln, Successful Lawyer, by R. D. Packard. Cleveland: Carpenter Printing Co., 1948.
14 p. facsim.

Packard credits Lincoln's love of public speaking and his power of analysis as the deep seated reasons for his pursuit of a law career. Encouraged by John Todd Stuart to study law, Lincoln was admitted to practice, and became Stuart's partner. His second partnership with Stephen T. Logan taught him court technique and how to study a case. Lincoln's third and last partnership was with William Herndon. Lincoln did much of his law work on the Eighth Judicial Circuit of Illinois. The author describes Lincoln's life on the circuit and his actions in the courtroom. "He was regarded by lawyers and judges as an almost infallible judge of human nature."

The author discusses types of cases in which Lincoln was involved, his contemporaries' views of him, and his reputation as a lawyer. He looks at Lincoln's fees and assets, and notes, "Like many another lawyer, Lincoln died intestate." He credits his political and diplomatic success with his legal training.

This pamphlet shows the fascimile of a letter written by Lincoln with advice on how a student should study the law.

150
Pratt, Harry E. (Edward)
Lincoln and Bankruptcy Law. Chicago: The Poor Richard Press, 1943.
9 p. illus.

Reprinted.
For annotation, see **Pratt** Journal Articles.

151
Pratt, Harry E. (Edward)
Lincoln, 1809-1839. Being the Day-by-Day Activities of Abraham Lincoln from February 12, 1809 to December 31, 1839. Springfield, Ill.: Abraham Lincoln Association, 1941.
lxxxvii, 256 p. illus., maps.

Cover title: Lincoln Day by Day, 1809-1839.

The Illinois State Historian prepared a calendar-type publication which explains in daily entries where Lincoln was, and what he was doing at particular times, whenever information was available. This volume shows March 24, 1836, as the day Lincoln's name was entered on the record of Sangamon Circuit Court. In 1837, Stuart and Lincoln cases appear in the entries, following announcement of the practice, with legal filings, deeds, motions, etc. Dates of court with terms are entered.

Introductory text includes information on Lincoln's admission to practice, and the fact that he had responsibility for the firm during Stuart's lengthy absences. Lincoln had written "Commencement of Lincoln's Administration" in the fee book.

A table of Stuart and Lincoln cases appears in "The Young Lawyer in Springfield, 1837-1839," p. lxi. Also, a "Table of Appearances and Continued Cases and Leading Lawyers, Sangamon County, 1837-1839." This table includes chancery, common law, and criminal cases.

152
Pratt, Harry E. (Edward)
Lincoln, 1840-1846. Being the Day-by-Day Activities of Abraham Lincoln from January 1, 1840 to December 31, 1846. Springfield, Ill.: Abraham Lincoln Association, 1939.
xli, 391 p.

Cover title: Lincoln Day by Day, 1840-1846.

The book follows the pattern of a daily calendar for the years 1840-1846, listing Lincoln's activities by date and place. It includes courts, docket listings, case names, actions, notes of preparation for trials, scheduled speeches, and other details. Spaces are left blank for unaccounted activities.

The introduction contains information on his law partnerships, and the Eighth Judicial Circuit, including maps, as well as names of other lawyers practicing on the circuit. Data are included concerning material used in the daily log, as well as some explanations for the missing material.

There is the semblance of a trilogy, when this volume covering 1840-1846 is combined with Benjamin P. Thomas' *Lincoln: 1847-1853* and Paul M. Angle's *Lincoln: 1854-1862*.
Monaghan 3708

153
Pratt, Harry E. (Edward)
Lincoln, 1809-[1861] Being the Day-by-Day Activities of Abraham Lincoln from February 12, 1809 to [March 4, 1861]. Springfield, Ill: Abraham Lincoln Association, 1933-1941.
4 v. maps
For annotation, see **Pratt** above.

Later edition revised and enlarged published under title: Lincoln Day by Day: Chronology, 1809-1865 by U.S. Lincoln Sesquicentennial Commission. See **Miers**, Earl Schenck, editor.

154
Pratt, Harry E. (Edward)
The Personal Finances of Abraham Lincoln. Springfield: Abraham Lincoln Association, 1943.
xiii, 198 p. illus., ports., facsims.

Chapter 2, "Income From the Law," contains information on the matter of fees. Lincoln said that, although fees were important, exorbitant fees should not be claimed, and never a whole fee in advance, lest the attorney lose interest in a case. Wealth was not his ambition, and he admitted that he knew nothing of money. In studying his law practice, it is impossible to determine fees for a year, but it is possible to ascertain amounts of fees for individual entries in the Stuart/Lincoln fee book. (This fee book had been retained by Lincoln, and left in Herndon's office.) Stuart and Lincoln divided their fees equally, and Lincoln and Herndon followed this practice; however, Lincoln received only one-third of fees in the Logan and Lincoln law partnership.

155
Pratt, Silas G.
Lincoln in Story: The Life of the Martyr-President Told in Authenticated Anecdotes. Edited by Silas G. Pratt. New York: D. Appleton, 1901.
xv, 224 p. illus., ports., facsims.

Chapters 8 and 9 deal with the fifth period of Lincoln's life, "The Legislator-The Lawyer" (1837-1855). They include among other topics: his partnerships;

saving two young men from dishonesty; the widow's pension case; skin Wright and close; he gives a mean lawyer some good advice; gives his opponents their case because it was right; his defense of William Armstrong.
Monaghan 1359

--- ----. Microfilm. New Haven, Conn.: Yale University Library, 1988.
--- ----. Microfilm. Emporia, Kans.: William Allen White Library, 1971.

156
Quarles, Benjamin.
Lincoln and the Negro. New York: Oxford University Press, 1962.
275 p. illus.

While this book deals with the topic as a whole, the chapter "Lincoln: The Shaping Years" includes several passages dealing with Lincoln the lawyer and cases involving black persons: Bailey v. Cromwell, the John Shelby incident, the Matson slave case, and his representation of his barber, William de Fleurville in William Floville [*sic*] v. James Allen. Includes bibliography.

157
Randall, J. G. (James Garfield)
Lincoln the President: Springfield to Gettysburg. New York: Dodd, Mead & Co., 1945.
2 v. (American Political Leaders)

Volume one of this set deals with Lincoln from Springfield to Gettysburg. The author, a professor of history, states that the serious study of Lincoln as a lawyer has been covered elsewhere, and provides in a footnote a list of a dozen works that speak to the topic. Nevertheless, he discusses some aspects of Lincoln's life as a lawyer, including his social and professional standing. He notes that it is inadequate to refer to Lincoln as a country lawyer, as he was one of the outstanding lawyers of Illinois. He describes his partnerships, and explains that Lincoln handled important cases, and practiced before the Supreme Court of Illinois. He practiced in the federal courts, being admitted to practice before the Supreme Court of the United States. He suggests that Lincoln could be described as a corporation lawyer of that era. Lincoln's name carried prestige in the courts, and he argued more civil than criminal cases. Randall quotes Paul M. Angle, saying that Lincoln was more successful in the higher courts than on the circuit. Lincoln has become identified with the Eighth Circuit; however, much of his practice was outside that circuit.
Randall reviews some of Lincoln's characteristics. He explains Lincoln's knack of going directly to the essential point of a complicated subject. He pointed out that Lincoln had a high conviction of ethics, and had been known

to withdraw from a case; he was a businessman in charging for his services and collected what was owed to him. He was good natured in acknowledging that sometimes others snubbed him. He mentions several of his well-known cases, such as the Illinois Central Railroad case, McCormick case, *Lewis v. Lewis*, and Duff Armstrong.

This author has gone beyond other biographies, taking only basic material, and discarding that which he considered irrevelant or unhistorical. He did this, particularly with regard to some of the Herndon contributions, aiming toward historical restoration. Includes bibliography.

--- ----. Gloucester, Mass.: P. Smith, 1976, ©1945. 2 v.
--- ----. Lincoln the President. New York: Dodd, Mead, 1945-55.
4 v. (American political leaders) Vol. 4, by J. G. Randall and R. N. Current.
Volumes 1-2, Springfield to Gettysburg.

158
Rankin, Henry B. (Bascom)
Intimate Character Sketches of Abraham Lincoln. With a Foreword by Ida M.
Tarbell. Philadelphia: J. B. Lippincott, 1924.
344 p. ports., facsim.

Rankin was a twenty-year-old youth when he entered the law office of Lincoln & Herndon in Springfield in 1856. For four years he watched, and through this volume was able to provide a picture of the intellectual life of the two partners. He gives an idea of the extent and thoroughness of Lincoln's studies and his mental habits. He describes the location of the law office and furnishings. He quoted Charles W. Moores in saying that almost all pleadings of Stuart and Lincoln and of Lincoln and Herndon are in Lincoln's handwriting. Rankin reports, further, that while he was a student in that office, he never had any hesitancy about going to Lincoln with a question on a point of law, or details of legal documents. Lincoln was never impatient with him. He offers some sidelights of Lincoln on the circuit.
Monaghan 2718

--- ----. Microfilm. New Haven, Conn.: Yale University Library, 1988.

159
Rankin, Henry B. (Bascom)
Personal Recollections of Abraham Lincoln. With an introduction by Joseph Fort Newton. New York: G. P. Putnam's Sons, 1916.
xvi, 412 p. illus. ports., facsims.

The author, Rankin, was one of the few remaining friends who knew Lincoln personally. He includes his own interpretation of the Blackstone *Commentaries* story. Lincoln told the office boys who were reading it for the first time that he caught his first inspiration in the art of defining words and stating principles from it. Sometimes he read it aloud.

Law partner Stuart's courteous manners assisted Lincoln in his first legal work in the courts, but Stuart would never have selected him if his mental abilities had not forecast a promising future.

The author finds it impossible to describe Logan in a few lines so does not attempt to do so. Then Rankin describes Herndon, Lincoln's last and most influential partner, in some detail. Lincoln's readings during his partnership with Stuart and with Logan were largely confined to law. He read only authorities and precedents connected with clients' cases. His reading habits changed after his association with Herndon, who had become a reader of state library books and some that he had purchased himself. Lincoln was influenced to some degree by the "office family" there and by educated friends who were book lovers. Monaghan 2262

--- ----. Microfilm. New Haven, Conn.: Yale University Library, 1988.

160
Ransom, William L.
Abraham Lincoln--Profession as a Lawyer. In **The Lawyer's** Treasury: An Anthology Selected by the Board of Editors from Articles ... Representative of the Best to Appear in the Forty-Year History of the American Bar Association Journal. Edited by Eugene C. **Gerhart**. Indianapolis: Bobbs-Merrill, 1956.
p. 470-480.

--- ----. Indianapolis: Charter Books, 1963.
For Annotation see **Ransom**, Journal Articles.

161
Raymond, Henry J. (Jarvis)
The Life and Public Services of Abraham Lincoln: Together with His State Papers, Including His Speeches, Addresses, Messages, Letters and Proclamations, and the Closing Scenes Connected with His Life and Death. To Which Are Added Anecdotes and Personal Reminiscences of President Lincoln, by Frank B. Carpenter.
New York: Derby and Miller, 1865.
808 p. illus. ports.

Information on the lawyer aspect of Lincoln's life in this first full-length biography is sparse. Yet the reader learns that politics interfered with his legal studies, that he was admitted to the bar in 1836, and in April of 1837 settled permanently in Springfield. Merely a sentence acknowledges Stuart as a law partner. However, the full account of the Duff Armstrong case as it appeared in the *Cleaveland* [sic] Leader is printed, and Raymond quotes the *San Francisco Bulletin* on another phase of Lincoln's legal career, his popularity on the circuit.

Enlarged edition of Raymond's *History of the Administration of President Lincoln*. Also published with title: *Lincoln: His Life and Times*. Monaghan 691. See also 692 and 347.

--- ----. Ultrafiche. Dayton, Ohio: National Cash Register, 1970. (PCMI Library Collection)

162
Rice, Allen Thorndike, ed.
Reminiscences of Abraham Lincoln by Distinguished Men of His Time. Collected and edited by Allen Thorndike Rice. New and rev. ed. New York: Harper, 1909.
x, 428 p. port., facsims.

Rice, editor of the *North American Review*, includes two selections that deal with Lincoln's life as a lawyer.

Weldon, Lawrence, p. [123]-141, a lawyer and contemporary who moved to DeWitt County, Illinois, in 1854, discusses Lincoln's life as a lawyer. He had already known of Lincoln, with his stronghold upon the public and confidence of the people. He was a leader of the bar, known as "Old Mr. Lincoln." Weldon tells of incidents with Judge Douglas, describing circuit practice, and indicates that Lincoln enjoyed the atmosphere. He was happy when Judge Davis was on the bench, and often knew the jury. The author remarked on his use of old-fashioned language.

He mentioned Lincoln's service as attorney for the Illinois Central Railroad. He was frequently engaged in criminal trials, although he was not a criminal law specialist. He did not have great legal knowledge, nor encyclopedic knowledge of cases, but he had ability in application of principles, and the author had great confidence in him.

Swett, Leonard, p. 455-468, tells "Lincoln's Story of His Own Life." In Autumn 1849 he met Lincoln for the first time. Both men had litigation in David Davis' court. He describes attending circuit court in fourteen counties, and indicates court terms. In 1853 while riding with Lincoln, by buggy, from DeWitt County to Champaign, Swett initiated a conversation about curious incidents in

his early days. Lincoln told him of his early history and Swett presents it in these reminiscences as accurately as he can.
Monaghan 1026

--- ----. Microfilm. New Haven, Conn.: Yale University Library, 1988.
--- ----. New York: North American Pub. Co., 1886. 656 p.
--- ----. New York: North American Review, 1888. 656 p.
--- ----. Microfiche. Chicago: Library Resources, 1970.
--- ----. Microfilm. New Haven, Conn: Micrographic Systems of Connecticut, 1986
--- ----. New York: North American Pub. Co., 5th ed.; 6th ed.; 7th ed., 1888; 8th ed., 1889.
--- ----. New York: Haskell House, 1971.

163
Richards, John T. (Thomas)
Abraham Lincoln at the Bar of Illinois: An Address delivered before the Chicago Bar Association, Thursday Evening, February 11, 1909. [Chicago: s.n.], 1909.
14 p.

John T. Richards, a member of the Chicago Bar, discussed the limited requirement for Lincoln to be accepted into the Illinois bar in 1837. He described the courts in those days as much less dignified and formal than they were at the time of his address. He claims Lincoln took any legitimate advantage he could which the record of the cases might furnish. This contradicts some Lincoln biographers in claiming he never took advantage of technicalities. He also cited the supreme court case of *Scammon v. Cline* and circuit court case (Tazewell County) of Maus v. Worthing to verify his claim.

The author discussed the *Bailey v. Cromwell* case in which Lincoln represented the defendant, pleading lack of consideration of the purchase of a negro girl. He talked of the numerous areas of law in which Lincoln practiced, and the great lawyers of his day with whom he crossed swords. Richards believed that Lincoln would have proven himself to be the "greatest constitutional lawyer of the nineteenth century" had he lived.
Monaghan 1855

--- ----. Microfilm, New Haven, Conn.: Yale University Library, 1988.

164
Richards, John T. (Thomas)
Abraham Lincoln, the Lawyer-Statesman. Boston: Houghton Mifflin, 1916.
vi, 260 p. illus., ports., facsims.

The Tinsley Building, Springfield, Illinois, where Lincoln had his law office, from a woodcut in the Illinois State Journal, *June 1, 1850. (Courtesy of The Lincoln Museum, Ft. Wayne, Indiana, a part of the Lincoln National Corporation)*

Law office of Abraham Lincoln, Fifth Street, Springfield, Illinois, from Frank Leslie's Illustrated Newspaper, *December 22, 1860. (Courtesy of The Lincoln Museum, Ft. Wayne, Indiana, a part of the Lincoln National Corporation)*

This book is a well-recognized biography of Lincoln's life as a lawyer, beginning with his training to be a lawyer, his law-practice days, and finally his views on universal suffrage, reconstruction, and his attitude toward the judiciary during his presidency. Fully one half of the text deals with Lincoln in the courtroom and the other half as a lawyer/president using the skills he developed as a lawyer to direct the nation.

An extensive appendix lists cases, with a brief description of each, wherein Lincoln appeared as counsel before the Supreme Court of Illinois and the United States Supreme Court.
Monaghan 2266

--- ----. Microfilm. New Haven, Conn.: Yale University Library, 1988.

165
Rothschild, Alonzo.
"Honest Abe": A Study in Integrity Based on the Early Life of Abraham Lincoln.
Boston: Houghton Mifflin, 1917.
374 p. ports.
Chapter 2 is entitled "Truth in Law," and chapter 3, "Professional Ethics."

This "study" is presented in popular embellished narrative. It describes Lincoln's journey April 15, 1837, into Springfield, and the contents of his saddlebag. His honesty and integrity are exemplified with incidents. There is discussion of the fees in the law offices of his partners, and the fact that he had a financial creed of his own.

He was conscientious, with scupulous attention to the interests of people seeking legal aid. His office was a "court of conciliation." He discouraged litigation, and advised others to do so; there were examples of compromise in settlement and arbitration. He was "perversely honest," devoted to truth, and not in the least mercenary. He had to believe in the right of a case. He was candid in self-appraisal.

There were anecdotes to illustrate his patience and courtesy to opposing witnesses, and an unusual example of reprimanding a witness.
Includes notes and a list of books cited.
Monaghan 2334

--- ----. Microfilm. New Haven, Conn.: Yale University Library, 1988.

166
Sandburg, Carl.
Abraham Lincoln: The Prairie Years. With 105 illustrations from photographs, and many cartoons, sketches, maps, and letters . . . New York: Harcourt, Brace, 1926.
2 v. illus., ports, facsims, maps.

This chronological biography of Abraham Lincoln covers Lincoln's years as a lawyer, including his cases and travels on the Eighth Judicial Circuit.

Accounts of the times are intermingled with Lincoln's personal history. Much of this is devoted to his political life and law practice, including a chapter "Lawyer in Springfield." The author at times uses his creativity in depicting scenes.
Monaghan 2876

--- ----. Abridged ed. New York: Harcourt, Brace, 1929, ©1926. 604 p.
--- ----. New York: Blue Ribbon Books, [1931?] 604 p.
--- ----. New York: Sangamon ed. New York: Scribner, 1939 [1926] 2 v. (6 v. include 4 v. The War Years.)

167
Sandburg, Carl.
Lincoln Collector: The Story of Oliver R. Barrett's Great Private Collection.
New York: Harcourt, Brace, 1950.
344 p. illus.

The volume is about the Lincoln collection of Oliver R. Barrett presenting, with collateral text, description of items from that collection. The extensive and far-reaching Barrett collection included letters from Lincoln to his friend Joshua Speed. One of these involved the Trailor Brothers' murder trial. It also discussed some of Lincoln's early legal documents. Includes illustrations of Lincoln memorabilia.

--- ----. lst ed. New York: Harcourt, Brace, 1949.
--- ----. New York: Bonanza, 1960, ©1949.

168
Scripps, John Locke.
Life of Abraham Lincoln. Edited with introduction and notes by Roy P. Basler and Lloyd A. Dunlap.   New York: Greenwood Press, 1968, ©1961.
192 p. facsims.

Although a chapter is listed as "Merchant--Surveyor--Legislator--Lawyer," little information is included on the lawyer phase. Nevertheless, that which appears is valuable because it is considered the most authoritative of the campaign biographies.
Stuart urged Lincoln to study law and offered him books. When the legislature met, his law books were laid aside. But it resumed after the legislative session. In Autumn 1836, Lincoln was admitted to the bar. He became

a co-partner of Stuart, and moved to Springfield. A footnote shows the date of his law license, and cites his first case as *Hawthorne v. Wooldridge*. Includes footnotes.

The introduction to Scripps is valuable in explaining the relationship of this book to other biographies. Thirteen separate campaign biographies were published in English in 1860, and others in foreign languages. Most of those biographies were published in great quantities and were cheap, such as the biography written by John Lock Scripps. "The Most authoritative and influential of the lot was the 32 page pamphlet written by Scripps and published by the *Chicago Press and Tribune*." A New York edition was published by the *New York Tribune*. There has been some debate over the date of the actual issue of biographies by Scripps, Howard, and Howells. The biography by Howells was published in cloth binding from the same manuscript.
See also **Howells.**
For earlier editions of Scripps, see Monaghan 79, 80, 81.

--- ----. Bloomington: Indiana University Press, 1961.

The original campaign biography attributed to Scripps was published in 32 pages: Life of Abraham Lincoln. Chicago: Chicago Press and Tribune Co., 1860. 32 p.

--- ----. Microfiche, Ann Arbor, Mich.: University Microfilms International, 1981. (Presidential Election Campaign Biographies; PE 154)
--- ----. New York: H. Greeley, 1860. New York Tribune. (Tribune Tracts; no. 6) 32 p.
--- ----. Microfiche. Ann Arbor, Mich: University Microfilms International, 1980. (Presidential Election Campaign Biographies; PE 155)
---. 1860 Campaign Life of Abraham Lincoln Annotated. Foreword and Notes by M. L. Houser. Peoria: Edward J. Jacob, 1931.
72 p.

169
Selby, Paul.
Stories and Speeches of Abraham Lincoln: Including Stories of Lincoln As a Lawyer, Presidential Incidents, . . .   Lincoln's Letters and Great Speeches Chronologically Arranged with Biographical Sketch by Paul Selby.   Chicago: Thompson & Thomas, 1900.
469 p.

Chapter "Stories of Lincoln as a Lawyer" includes among other sketches, advice to a young lawyer, and Lincoln as a lawyer.

In the latter, he indicates that two things are necessary to his successful managing of a case: time and the feeling of justice for the cause represented. He often went far back in legal history for precedent and argued on the presumption that the court knew nothing.

There is information on "Lincoln and Finances." Lincoln defends the son of an old friend indicted for murder and defends a widowed pensioner with success. Among other sketches are "Hold on, Breese," and "Colonel Baker Defended by Lincoln," finally, "The Old Sign, 'Lincoln and Herndon'."
Monaghan 1306

170
Shirley, Ralph.
A Short Life of Abraham Lincoln, by the Hon. Ralph Shirley. Illustrated American ed. New York: Funk & Wagnalls, 1919.
188 p. illus., ports.

This American edition of a book by a British member of Parliament deals with "Legal Practice," and "Lincoln as Member of Congress." Lincoln "retired" from his first partnership with Stuart, who had been elected to Congress. He went into partnership with Stephen T. Logan, who enjoyed the reputation of being the best *nisi prius* lawyer in the state and presented a contrast to Lincoln. Logan was orderly, methodical, and had a grasp of the details of law. He was helpful to Lincoln, who lacked mastery of detail, order, and method. Following severence of the Lincoln and Logan firm, he got Herndon to become his partner.

He writes of travel on the circuit, meetings of the state supreme court at Springfield once a year. He discusses Lincoln's fees, the Illinois Central Railroad and McLean County case, and the Duff Armstrong case. Lincoln was honest, and defended a wrong case poorly. Shirley describes Lincoln and Herndon's primitive business methods, with Lincoln wrapping Herndon's share of a fee and placing it in a drawer, and keeping documents in the lining of his hat. The author believed that his mind worked slowly, but no one was better at holding the interest of the jury. Politics was his first and last love.
Monaghan 2424

171
Sigelschiffer, Saul.
The American Conscience: The Drama of the Lincoln-Douglas Debates. New York: Horizon Press, 1973.
488 p. illus.

While the title of this volume might suggest the Lincoln-Douglas debates *per se*, scattered material concerning Lincoln as a lawyer is included as the author traces "development of the thinking of the two opponents."

He described the junior law partner, Billy Herndon, and the relationship of Lincoln and Herndon. The detailed description of Lincoln by Herndon is quoted, regarding his physical appearance and his melancholy. Mention is made of Stuart and Judge Davis; Logan's description of Lincoln appears, as does that of Leonard Swett, lawyer who practiced on the Eighth Judicial Circuit. There is short discussion of Lincoln's law practice, highlighted by the two slave cases Lincoln handled. In the first case, he represented the slave in *Bailey v. Cromwell*; in the second, Lincoln was retained as counsel by slave owner Matson, but indicated that he would rather have represented the slaves, an opportunity which presented itself only after he was committed to the case. Includes bibliography.

172
Simon, Paul.
Lincoln's Preparation for Greatness: The Illinois Legislative Years. Urbana: University of Illinois Press, 1971, ©1965.
xii, 335 p. illus., map, ports.

The author, a former member of the Illinois House of Representatives and presently (1990) a United States Senator (in 1988 a presidential candidate), writes a biography of Lincoln's years in the Illinois General Assembly. The author, while in the House finding no definitive study on Lincoln's legislative years in print, wrote this work about Lincoln's early public service career. It was during Lincoln's second term in the legislature that he was admitted to the bar. The book deals largely with Lincoln's politics, actions, and stands that he took in the House during his four terms from 1834-1842. There are some references to Lincoln's law practice, which he seemed to have attended to mainly between sessions of the legislature. There is an account of Lincoln's voting against a move to tax lawyers ten dollars in each county in which they practiced. Later, the issue concerned fifteen dollars tax for that purpose. Lincoln made the motion that killed the action. He retired from the legislature in 1842. Lincoln's stint trained him in practical politics, elevated his confidence in his leadership abilities, and gave him a statewide reputation.
Includes bibliographical references.

--- ----. 1st ed. Norman: University of Oklahoma Press, 1965.
--- ----. Urbana: University of Illinois, 1989, ©1965.

173
Smith, Elmer A.
Abraham Lincoln: An Illinois Central Lawyer. A Paper read by Elmer A. Smith, senior general attorney of the Illinois Central Railroad Co., at a meeting of the

Western Conference of Railway Counsel, February 13, 1945. [Chicago?: s.n. 1945?]
23 p.

This address is specifically about Lincoln, the Illinois Central Railroad lawyer. It was his wish to be such a lawyer. During a decade he tried many cases for the Illinois Central in the lower courts of Illinois, which he argued with distinction and success. The exact number of Lincoln's Illinois Central cases is not known, and the issues of every case are unknown; some of the litigation is described merely as "little businesses." Smith then considers eleven cases argued by Lincoln for the Illinois Central in the Illinois Supreme Court. He did more work for the Illinois Central than for other clients, and his largest fee came from the Illinois Central Railroad.

There has been some speculation that James F. Joy, counsel for the railroad, wrote letters recommending Lincoln, although Lincoln's name *per se* does not appear. In 1857 Lincoln stated that he had been on retainer for the Illinois Central for two or three years.

Includes bibliographical references.

174
Starr, John W. (William)
Lincoln & the Railroads: A Biographical Study, by John W. Starr, Jr. New York: Dodd, Mead, 1927.
xiii, 325 p. ports., map, facsims.

This work is about Lincoln and his association with railroads throughout his career. His first major association with the railroads was as a second-term legislator supporting extravagant legislation that promoted excessive and expensive railroad building. These expenses burdened the state of Illinois with a debt that proved very nearly ruinous.

Lincoln often represented railroad companies in his law practice and was on retainer by the Illinois Central Railroad. He defended the Illinois Central Railroad and later sued them for the highest fee he ever received as a lawyer. This case and several others where Lincoln defended and opposed the railroads are discussed including the famous Rock Island Bridge case where "he enunciated a right for common carriers which has become an accepted doctrine."

The book includes a chapter on a lucrative offer by the New York Central Railroad to Lincoln to serve as its general counsel in the spring of 1860. Had he accepted the tempting offer as an aspiring lawyer, the course of history might have been different. Includes an extensive bibliography.
Monaghan 2973

--- ----. Microfilm. New Haven, Conn.: Yale University Library, 1988.
--- ----. New York: Arno Press, 1981, ©1927.

Stephenson, Nathaniel W. (Wright), comp.
An Autobiography of abraham Lincoln.
see **Lincoln,** Abraham.

175
Stephenson, Nathaniel W. (Wright)
Lincoln: An Account of His Personal Life, Especially of Its Springs of Action
as Revealed and Deepened by the Ordeal of War. Indianapolis: Bobbs-Merrill,
1922.
474 p. illus., ports.

This is a one-volume biography of Lincoln, by an academic historian. A
chapter entitled "The Second Start" includes some information on the lawyer
phase of Lincoln's life. For a while, Lincoln concentrated on the study of law.
Eventually he rode the circuit with judges and lawyers, going from town to town.
The author describes the circuit and Lincoln's enjoyment of it. There is mention
of his humble style of travel, on an old horse, or with buggy. Stephenson quotes
Herndon in description of life on the circuit. He tells of Lincoln's carelessness
in his work habits, storing letters, memoranda, and other legal papers in his hat.
Generally, he did not care for the mechanical side of his practice and left the
preparation of papers to his junior partner.
    The author tells of Lincoln's ethical sense; his moral and professional views
were inflexible, and he required moral justification of a case. Juries found his
yarns and parables as illustrations irresistible.
Includes bibliography.

--- ----. Microfilm. New Haven, Conn.: Yale University Library, 1988.
--- ----. Indianapolis: Bobbs-Merrill, 1924. 528 p.

Stern, Philip Van Doren, ed.
The Life and Writings of Abraham Lincoln.
See **Lincoln,** Abraham.

176
Stevens, Walter B.
A Reporter's Lincoln. Saint Louis: Missouri Historical Society, 1916.
80 p.

The format of this publication, including the cover, is "notebook" style,
intended to represent a reporter's note book. Stevens assembled recollections
in his "newspaper comings and goings," or newspaper articles and interviews.

Stevens presents "Duff Armstrong and the Almanac," "The Eighth Circuit," and "A Land Case," as he discusses "Lawyer, Philosopher, and Statesman." Monaghan 2275

177
Stoddard, William O.
Abraham Lincoln: The True Story of a Great Life, Showing the Inner Growth, Special Training, and Peculiar Fitness of the Man for His Work. New York: Fords, Howard & Hulbert, 1884.
508 p. illus., facsim.

Chapter 17 deals with the "Young Lawyer," and his being admitted to the bar. The following chapter has material on "An Honest Lawyer," and "Partnerships," as well as the Duff Armstrong case.
Monaghan 1006; 1008.

--- ----. Microfilm. New Haven, Conn.: Micrographic Systems of Connecticut, 1985.
--- ----. Rev. ed. New York: Fords, Howard & Hulbert, 1896.
--- ----. Microfilm. New Haven, Conn.: Micrographic Systems of Connecticut, 1986.

178
Stringer, Lawrence B. (Beaumont)
Abraham Lincoln. Lincoln, Ill., 1943.
28 p.

This item is comprised of a reproduction of chapter XIV, pages 212-231 of Judge Stringer's *History of Logan County*, Illinois. It was designed and printed by Stringer's personal friends for Lincoln College.
Although known as a surveyor and legislator, Lincoln was better known as a lawyer. He was admitted to the bar in 1836, and traveled the Eighth Judicial Circuit, with Judges Treat and Davis. At first he had to borrow a horse for the ride, later he owned a horse and buggy. His journeys to Lincoln, Illinois, were by railroad. In Logan County he shone as a *nisi prius* lawyer. There are stories of his stopping at the tavern, fraternizing with the people, and some anecdotes of Judge Samuel C. Parks of the Logan County bar.
In 1840 Lincoln tried a lawsuit under an oak tree on a farm, heard before the local justice of the peace. The suit was brought by Dement concerning riparian rights. Records of Logan County prior to 1857 have been destroyed; there is no history of Lincoln's legal work. He was one of the attorneys in the first case appealed to the state Supreme Court from Logan County, *Lucien B. Adams v. County of Logan* over removal of the county seat.

He also appeared as attorney in the following cases appealed from Logan County: 1855, *Myers v. Turner*; 1855, *Hildreth v. Turner*; 1857, *Railroad Company v. Dalby*; 1859, *Young v. Ward*; 1860, *Gill v. Hoblit*.

179
Strozier, Charles B.
Lincoln's Quest for Union: Public and Private Meanings.   New York: Basic Books, 1982.
xxiii, 271 p. ports.

The author tells the Lincoln biographical story from a psychohistorical viewpoint, applying concepts of psychoanalytic theory to the documentary evidence. He concludes that Lincoln's personality and character were shaped in his younger days.

A chapter entitled "Law and Order" gives some insight into Lincoln's "legal" life, indicating that at first Lincoln lacked confidence. In his new career, Lincoln's lack of formal training in the law is acknowledged, and the often-repeated story of Lincoln's studying Blackstone's *Commentaries* is told again; with the listing of Chitty's *Pleadings*, Greenleaf's *Evidence*, and Story's *Equity* recommended by Lincoln in counseling an aspiring lawyer. Strozier quotes Judge Davis in describing Lincoln as a practical man, and goes on to say that Lincoln was a litigation man. There is a general statement regarding the types of cases Lincoln tried, with real property, mortgages, simple contracts, and issues of procedure accounting for more than half of his cases, followed by personal property as the next larger category. As he became more mature in his profession, federal trial courts accounted for a substantial percentage of his practice.

There are quotations from Herndon, depicting Lincoln's shrewdness and ability with juries. His casual methods of keeping his office and bookkeeping were noted, but with the qualification that it was not unusual for that period in time. There is description of the primitive conditions on the circuit, and mention of Lincoln's enjoyment of rapport with ordinary citizens. Finally Strozier discusses the findings of John P. Frank in his *Lincoln the Lawyer*.
Includes bibliographical references.

--- ----. Illini Books ed. Urbana: University of Illinois Press, 1987, ©1982.

180
Strunsky, Rose.
Abraham Lincoln. New York: Macmillan, 1914.
xxxv, 331 p. ports.

A chapter entitled "On the Circuit" provides in popular tone a "strange and vital period" in Lincolns' life. The author tells of the division of his time between Springfield and the circuit, and does not overlook shortcomings, such as the haphazard conditions of his office. She reminds readers that he was faulty in legal technicalities, but that he grasped the principle of a case. There is a word about law students in the law office, and Lincoln's first appearance in court. She quotes Judge Davis in saying that Lincoln was "great at *nisi prius* and before appellate tribunal." There are remarks on cryptic notes Lincoln made regarding the Wright pension case. Strunsky sets the scene of Lincoln on the circuit, including his clothing and appearance, based on vivid descriptions by his former colleagues.
Monaghan 2168

--- ----. Microfilm. New Haven, Conn.: Yale University Library, 1988.

181
Suppiger, Joseph E.
The Intimate Lincoln. Lanham, Md.: University Press of America, 1985.
vii, 259 p.

The author, in this work, is concerned with Lincoln in the context of an "examination of the personal and family life of a man who deserves to be known for what he was as well as for what he did." Suppiger studies what Lincoln "loved and feared, knew and accepted, rejected and embraced." The work gives a good description of what Lincoln's life was like: his surroundings, friends and acquaintences, events of the time, social activities, and his thoughts. These factors are intertwined in a chronological setting. Lincoln's life during his time as a lawyer is described in the chapters "Life in Springfield, 1837-1840," and "Life in Springfield, 1840-1847." "Lawyer and Politician" contains information on the topic as well. Suppiger shows Lincoln as a practicing lawyer, including his dress and behavior in court, and his law office. In addition, he discusses several cases. Includes bibliography.

182
Tarbell, Ida M. (Minerva)
In the Footsteps of the Lincolns. New York: Harper, 1924.
xi, 418 p. illus., ports., facsims.

This book includes a chapter "On the Circuit." In it Tarbell describes Lincoln as an "extraordinarily lovable person," welcomed by people as he arrived on a circuit tour. A map of the circuit is provided. Only a few cases are mentioned. She calls Lincoln an able if unconventional lawyer, and tells of an informal side.

Monaghan 2671

--- ----. Microfilm. New Haven, Conn.: Yale University Library, 1989.

183
Tarbell, Ida M. (Minerva)
The Life of Abraham Lincoln: Drawn from Original Sources and Containing Many Speeches, Letters, and Telegrams Hitherto Unpublished, and Illustrated With Many Reproductions from Original Paintings, Photographs, et cetera. New York: Lincoln Historical Society, 1906.
4 v., illus.

This biography of Lincoln, completed at the turn of this century, was begun at the suggestion of *McClure's Magazine* editors in 1894. The purpose was to collect and preserve "the reminiscences of such of his [Lincoln's] contemporaries as were then living," to be presented as a series of magazine articles. The articles (in twelve parts, *McClure's Magazine*, v. 5-8 [November-December 1895; January-August, October-November 1896] were so successful and the material so voluminous that it was developed into this four-volume work.

After discussing Lincoln's beginnings in reading and studying law, the author devotes two chapters in volume 1 to Lincoln's practice of law. One chapter covers his journeys on the circuit, how he prepared cases, examined witnesses, and addressed juries. The second covers some of Lincoln's important cases, such as the Armstrong murder case, the McCormick case, and the Rock Island Bridge case.

The appendix contains almost 200 pages of letters, telegrams, and speeches of Abraham Lincoln, none of which, at that time, appeared in a collection of Lincoln's writings.
Monaghan, 1309-1316.

--- ----. New York: Doubleday & McClure, 1900. 2 v.
--- ----. New York: Doubleday & Page, 1900. 2 v.
--- ----. New York: McClure, Phillips, 1900. 2 v.
--- ----. New York: Lincoln Memorial Association, 1900. 2 v.
--- ----. New York: Lincoln History Society, 1908. 4 v.
--- ----. New ed. with new matter. New York: Macmillan, 1917. 2v.
--- ----. Microfilm. New Haven, Conn: Yale University Library, 1988.
--- ----. Sangamon ed. New York: Macmillan, ©1924. 4 v.
--- ----. New York: Macmillan, 1928. 2 v.

184
Thayer, William M. (Makepeace)
From Pioneer Home to the White House: Life of Abraham Lincoln. With eulogy by Hon. George Bancroft. Enl., rev. and newly illustrated. New York: Hurst, 1882.
469 p. illus. (Log Cabin to White House Series)

Chapter 21, "Successful Lawyer."

Contents include: his practice and poverty; circuit court; saddlebags and buggy; his character; not defend a client in wrong; an interesting case; the old Negress and her son redeemed; Colonel Baker and Lincoln; what Judge Treat relates; deluded into a wrong case; refused to defend his client when convinced he was guilty; another case; a suit against a railroad; refused $250 offered him; what Gillespie thought of him as a lawyer; what Sparks said of him; how he saved Jack Armstrong's son from the gallows; Aunt Hannah and her gratitude; testimony of Judge Davis and Judge Drummond. In addition to the details, the contents present the manners and customs of the times.

The author of this volume wrote *The Pioneer Boy and How He Became President*, for which he used the thirty-two-page campaign life pamphlet attributed to Scripps, and some of the contributed material that had not been used previously. This included names and addresses of early associates.
Monaghan 991

--- ----. Norwich, Conn.: Henry Bill Pub. Co., 1882.
--- ----. Boston: James H. Early, 1882.
--- ----. New York: John B. Alden, 1885.
--- ----. Chicago: Whitman, 1927.
--- ----. Microfilm, New Haven, Conn.: Yale University Library, 1988.

185
Thomas, Benjamin P. (Platt)
Abraham Lincoln: A Biography. 1st ed. New York: Knopf, 1952.
xiv, 548, xii p. illus., port., maps.

This one-volume well-respected biography of Lincoln is by a renowned student of Lincoln's life. It covers the era from the day Lincoln was born on February 12, 1809, outside Hodgenville, Kentucky, until the day he died, shot in the head by an assassin. The author covers the start of Lincoln's law practice in "Frontier Legislator: His Love Affairs." One gleans from the pages that after taking his bar exam, Lincoln followed the custom of treating his examiners to a meal. Subsequently he received his license, then was enrolled by the clerk of the Supreme Court of Illinois. Two days later, he participated in his first Springfield law case, docketed as *Hawthorne v. Wooldridge*.

Thomas devotes chapter 5 to "Lawyer-Politician," in which court of the day is described, as well as the commonplace cases. He tells of law practice with Stuart, later Logan, and finally Herndon, with speculation as to some of the reasons for his change in partners. There is a comparison of Lincoln with Herndon. Several references to Lincoln's law practice are sprinkled throughout succeeding chapters until Lincoln's run for the presidency. After describing Lincoln's practice against the changing times in industrial development and transportation, the author includes the Illinois Central Railroad case and notes that most of his railroad cases established principles of law. The author acknowledges that Lincoln ranked as a distinguished lawyer.

This book provides an overall view of Lincoln's life. It includes an extensive chapter on Lincoln literature directing the reader to other works.
Includes bibliography.

--- ----. New York: Modern Library, 1968, ©1952.
--- ----. New York: Knopf, 1973, ©1951. 1st paperback ed.
--- ----. New York: Book-of-the-Month Club, 1986, ©1952. (The American Past)
591 p.

186
Thomas, Benjamin P. (Platt)
Lincoln, 1847-1853, Being the Day-by-Day Activities of Abraham Lincoln from January 1, 1847, to December 31, 1853. Springfield: Abraham Lincoln Association, 1936.
ix, 388 p. maps.

A Companion volume to Paul M. Angle's Lincoln, 1854-1861.

Lincoln's daily record in chronological diary format, extends back in time to 1847 in this book. In compiling the record of cases in the Supreme Court of Illinois, the original records in the Office of the Clerk of the Court have been used, rather than the *Illinois Reports*, thereby differentiating cases handled by Lincoln or by Herndon.

The introduction outlines circuit riding, docketing of cases, how opinions were handled, and the division of work at the firm of Lincoln and Herndon. It shows Lincoln's growth during this period of his practice.
Monaghan 3541

187
Tilton, Clint Clay.
Lincoln and Lamon: Partners and Friends. Danville, Ill.: Interstate, 1932.
56 p. illus., ports., facsims.

Reprinted from TRANSACTIONS OF THE ILLINOIS STATE HISTORICAL
SOCIETY, no. 38.
Monaghan 3355
For annotation see **Tilton**, Journal Articles.

188
Townsend, George Alfred.
The Real Life of Abraham Lincoln: A Talk With Mr. Herndon, His Late Law
Partner. With Cabinet Portrait, and Mr. Lincoln's Favorite Poem. New York:
Publication Office, Bible House, 1867.
15 p. port.

This description of Lincoln's "real" life, written by poet, lecturer, and
correspondent Townsend was published in the *New York Tribune*, January 25,
1867. He describes ascending the stairs to the office, where he spent two half
days conversing with Lincoln's former law partner Herndon. He says Herndon
gave the author permission to write whatever he chose from their conversation.
He was ready to understand any question, and willing to give direct answers.

Herndon told him that the jury always heard a fair statement of any case
from Lincoln. Later the chief justice of Illinois remarked that he argued both
sides of a case so well that a speech in response was superfluous. As a lawyer,
Lincoln was a close student of cases that interested him and sometimes sat up
all night preparing an argument. Herndon indicated that he was never moody,
rather he enjoyed solitude.

Lincoln's income was not high, but not very different from his Illinois
colleagues. He had been plagued by debt for a fifth of his life; nevertheless,
when he left Springfield for the White House he was worth $30,000. Herndon
described their parting scene. He was always a politician rather than an attorney.
Monaghan 895

--- ----. Microfiche. Ann Arbor, Mich: Microfilming Corp. of America, 1983.
(Pamphlets in American History: Civil War: CW 184)

189
Townsend, William H. (Henry)
Abraham Lincoln, Defendant: Lincoln's Most Interesting Lawsuit.
Boston: Houghton Mifflin, 1923.
vii, 40 p. facsims.

Townsend, a lawyer, considers the case of Abraham Lincoln, "himself a
defendant and the issue involves his own personal integrity," as "Lincoln's most
interesting lawsuit."

Lincoln's father-in-law, Robert S. Todd, who died in 1849, was a partner in a large cotton factory in Fayette County, Kentucky. The surviving partners, Edward Oldham and Thomas Hemingway, filed a petition in 1853 for money allegedly collected by Attorney Lincoln for the firm on a debt owed in Illinois. Lincoln denied ever collecting the debt.

Lincoln, his honor offended, marshaled facts and deposed several witnesses to prove and support his position. The plaintiffs later filed a motion to dismiss, which the court in Fayette County granted. The work contains correspondence between Lincoln and his Kentucky attorney. Photocopies of the original petition appear, as well as Lincoln's answer, various orders, and Lincoln's correspondence relating to the matter. The facsimiles are taken from the records of the Fayette Circuit Court and from Lincoln letters.
Monaghan 2672

--- ----. Microfilm. New Haven Conn.: Yale Univrsity Library, 1988.

190
Townsend, William H. (Henry)
Lincoln and Liquor.   New York: Press of the Pioneers, 1934.
x, 152 p. illus., port., facsim.

In "The Springfield Years," Townsend discusses a number of cases involving alcohol. Lincoln did not let his aversion to liquor keep him from performing his professional duties. In 1846, he represented Munsell of the Bloomington Hotel Bar in a suit against Temple over the validity of a liquor license. In 1852 he was arbitrator in a dispute over the ownership of five gallons of peach brandy. In 1853, he defended Sullivan, Macon Circuit Court for selling liquor without a license. Although the fine was $10.00, he took the case to the Supreme Court of Illinois. In 1854 Lincoln represented nine women in DeWitt Circuit Court; and the same year in Tazewell Circuit Court, *Pearl and Pearl v. Graham et al.* for trespass, entering a dwelling, and destroying liquors. In 1855 Platt and Davidson were fined for destroying barrels of spirits. He handled a case in Sangamon Circuit Court involving the selling of liquor without a license.
Includes bibliography.
Monaghan 3458

191
Townsend, William H. (Henry)
Lincoln the Litigant.   With an introduction by William E. Barton.   Boston: Houghton Mifflin, 1925.
viii, 116 p. illus., port., facsims.

Townsend searched the records of the Illinois courts for all cases in which Abraham Lincoln appeared as a party to the suit. It is suprising that Lincoln, who advised against litigation when possible, was involved in a large number of suits.

He was known for charging modest fees and rendering full services for such fees. Lincoln was not hesitant to bring suit for such fees if left unpaid by the client. He discusses in detail some of Lincoln's cases where he later sued for a fee such as "The Archibald Fisher Murder case" and the last suit involving Lincoln as a plaintiff in "The *Illinois Central Railroad Co. vs. County of McLean.* In the latter, Lincoln, after successfully defending the railroad, presented a bill of $2000 which was rebuffed by the railroad as an amount "as much as Daniel Webster himself would have charged." Lincoln, fifteen months later, sued for and won at jury trial $5,000.

The author discusses Lincoln's first trial as a defendant where he was charged with operating a ferryboat without a license. He speculates that even though the charge against Lincoln was dismissed it sparked his interest in the law. Other cases in which Lincoln was a defendant are included.

The introduction by William E. Barton makes the statement, "Writers on Lincoln as a lawyer will henceforth have to draw upon this book for no inconsiderable portion of their material."
Monaghan 2816

--- ----. Microfilm. New Haven, Conn.: Yale University Library, 1988.

Tracy, Gilbert A.
Uncollected Letters of Abraham Lincoln
See **Lincoln**, Abraham.

192
Tregillis, Helen Cox.
Lincoln and Shelbyville. Shelbyville, Ill.: The Author, 1979.
29 p. illus., port.

Cover title: Lincoln in Shelbyville.

After mentioning Lincoln's entry into Illinois by way of Shelbyville, the author explores the time he spent there later, during his career. As he rode the Eighth Judicial Circuit, his stop was often at Shelbyville. Sections pertaining to his law practice include: Lincoln and his early circuit court days at Shelbyville; Lincoln in Shelbyville Circuit Court (a slander case); courthouses Lincoln knew; Lincoln here in court; Lincoln and the Crocketts; Lincoln and divorce case in Shelbyville; Lincoln and the Todd debts; Lincoln and the railroad. Other short pieces describe his relationship with people of the town, the boarding house and tavern, and social life.

Includes bibliography.

193
United States. Circuit Court. (7th Circuit)
Resolutions presented in the United States Circuit Court in Relation to the
Death of Mr. Lincoln, With the Response of Judge Davis, May 19th, 1865.
Indianapolis: W. Braden, 1865.
8 p.

After general remarks in response to the resolutions, Judge [David] Davis
said that it was appropriate to speak to this audience of Mr. Lincoln as a lawyer.
After acknowledgment of a quarter century of personal friendship, he praised
Lincoln, stating that his career was remarkable, as well as glorious.

He notes that they were admitted to the bar "about the same time," traveled
many years in the Illinois Eighth Judicial Circuit, comprised at that time of
fourteen counties. The people watched for his presence on the circuit. Mr.
Lincoln went with the court to every county, the mode of travel being horseback.
Lincoln loved this simple life and preferred it to practice of law in the city,
where remuneration would have been greater, but opportunity to mingle with
the people would have been less.

Lincoln seized strong points of a case and made his presentation with clarity
and compactness, without indulging in extraneous discussion, claiming the
attention of court and jury, often by his unfailing humor and anecdotes. He
frequently used comparison in a framework of honesty. He was known to defend
a wrong case poorly, and had to be convinced of the right and justice to be most
powerful. He read law books rarely, except when necessary. He rarely consulted
with other lawyers, being unusually self-reliant. He charged little, never taking
from a client more than the service was worth, and he granted favors whenever
possible. He loved his profession and was loved by members of the bar.
Monaghan 698

Van Doren, Carl, ed.
The Literary Works of Abraham Lincoln.
See **Lincoln**, Abraham.

194
Wagenknecht, Edward.
Abraham Lincoln: His Life, Work, and Character. An Anthology of History and
Biography, Fiction, Poetry, Drama, and Belles-lettres. New York: Creative Age
Press, 1947.
xvii, 661 p.

The anthology contains both factual and fictional works concerning Lincoln written by various authors, in an effort to include all types of Lincoln literature. The work is arranged in several sections by areas of Lincoln's life. Reference to him as a lawyer is found in Chapter 1, "Man and Legend," in a short biography, "Lincoln's Life and Public Career," by J. G. Randall, and "His Character," by William E. Barton. Chapter 2, "The Years of Growth," includes an article, "Lawyer Lincoln," by Albert J. Beveridge. Chapter 3, "Fiction and Drama of the Years of Growth," contains "The Counsel Assigned," by Mary Raymond Shipman Andrews, and "Abe Lincoln in Illinois," by Robert E. Sherwood.

195
Wall, Bernhardt.
Following Abraham Lincoln 1809-1865. Etched and printed by Bernhardt Wall, Lime Rock, Conn. Popular ed. New York: The Wise-Parslow Company, 1943. xix, 415 p. illus., port.

These reproductions of etchings were originally printed on hand press by the artist, a well-known etcher. He etched the Lincoln landmarks of America on several hundred copperplates. Placing these etchings in his book, he has text from various sources that he gathered as he did the etchings. The emphasis of the book is primarily on the etchings that illustrate the buildings; text is incidental.

Among etchings pertaining to Lincoln and his family (from before his life to his memorials), are those of Lincoln's Springfield home and various law offices in Springfield. A chapter entitled "Riding the Circuit" depicts courthouses in which Lincoln practiced as well as particular inns and homes that furnished accommodations. He discusses several cases briefly in "Lincoln Gets His First $500.00 Retainer Fee."
Monaghan 3297

--- ----. Lime Rock, Conn.: The Author, 1942. 534 leaves, plates.
--- ----. Lime Rock, Conn.: The Author, 1931-1942. 85 v. By subscription.

196
Wanamaker, R. M. (Reuben M.)
The Voice of Lincoln. New York: Charles Scribner's Sons, 1918. viii, 363 p. port.

Chapters 7, 8, and 9 deal with Lincoln the lawyer. The book was written to answer some of the questions regarding his philosophy of life, gathered from what he said and did, as well as how he lived. Items have been selected from authenticated records that have been compiled by other authors. The words have been examined against the background of significant facts. Many quotations have

been included, such as his comments on case law, and his "Advice to Young Lawyers." There is information on practice, law partners, honesty, legal ethics, and instances depicting ethics of Lincoln in the practice of law. Some of his rules of practice are included. The author quotes from Hill's *Lincoln the Lawyer*, and lists the titles in Mr. Lincoln's law library.
Monaghan 2394

--- ----. Microfilm. New Haven, Conn.: Yale University Library, 1988.

197
Ward, Geoffrey C.
Lincoln and the Law. Springfield, Ill.: Sangamon State University, 1978.
32 p. illus., map, ports.

Of sites associated with Lincoln, this article singles out the law offices. He spent most of his adult life, one quarter of a century, at the practice of law. He was only moderately successful in politics. The law sustained him and his family, helped shape his mind, and sharpened his speaking skills. At New Salem, while he had several different jobs, he retained an interest in the law. There is a legend that he read *The Revised Laws of Indiana* while still a youth. An illustration shows the title page facsimile of Blackstone's *Commentaries*, which he read although he had little schooling. It was not uncommon for American lawyers of the 1830s to omit law school attendance, and instead, to "read law" supervised in a law office. The resolution to succeed was highly important. Ward described his practice on the Eighth Judicial Circuit. Although riding the circuit was an exhausting grind, he enjoyed the friendships, clients, and fellow lawyers. A map outlines the fourteen counties on the circuit. Illustrations include several courthouses, portraits of partners and the client Duff Armstrong. There is a legend that he took only cases he was convinced were right on his clients' side. There is a random sampling of cases over his quarter century of practice illustrating the diversity of his practice.
Includes bibliography.

198
Waste, William H.
Lincoln, the Lawyer. In Lincoln Club, Los Angeles. Addresses Delivered at the Annual Dinners of The Lincoln Club of Los Angeles, 1921-1941. Los Angeles: Privately printed for the Club, 1940.
p. 69-72.

Chief Justice Waste begins by telling how Lincoln was inspired by the volume containing Indiana statutes. He went to school for little more than a year; he was not particularly quick at learning. Since his perceptions were dull, he read and reread. He copied with with quill of a turkey buzzard and ink from juice of briar root. When he had no paper, he wrote on shingles. He had Blackstone's *Commentaries*. "The more I read, the more intensely interested I became." Twenty years later he said to a young man that he should get Blackstone's *Commentaries*, Chitty's *Pleadings*, Greenleaf's *Evidence*, Story's *Equity and Succession*.

Soon after election in 1836 he was admitted to the bar, and began to practice in New Salem. His first fee was three dollars. Six months later, he went to Springfield on a borrowed horse, with no more property than a saddlebag and a few clothes. There he formed a partnership with Stuart. His account book shows that fees were small, not exceeding a total of $1600 a year and seldom more than $10 a case.

The author, seeming to contradict his earlier remarks about Lincoln's perceptions, talks of his quick analytical perception, strong logical power, tenacious memory, liberal estimate and tolerance of the opinion of others. He believed that his work as a lawyer was soon forgotten, overshadowed by accomplishments as a statesman. However, early training and experiences in the legal profession fitted him for the presidency. He knew the common law, understood history and purposes, the scope and limitations of the federal Constitution, and appreciated two sides to every action.

199
Weber, J. R.
Lawyer Lincoln. Davenport, Iowa: Bawden Brothers, 1928.
[24] p.

The author points out in his introduction that writers of journal articles have produced a great deal on Lincoln's home life during all phases, but his legal career had never been accorded proper attention. He utilized archives of the State Historical Society of Illinois, and court records in obtaining his information. Weber gives much background information, finally introducing the legal aspect, with description of Lincoln's friendship with the Armstrongs, followed by the Armstrong murder case. A letter from Lincoln to Mrs. Armstrong appears in typescript, and some details of the case are disclosed.

A description of a bronze tablet in Beardstown, Cass County, includes the inscription, "In memory of Abraham Lincoln, who for a Mother in distress, cleared her son, Duff Armstrong, of the charge of murder, in this hall of justice."
Monaghan 3063

200
Weik, Jesse W. (William)
The Real Lincoln: A Portrait. Boston: Houghton Mifflin, 1922.
xx, 323 p. illus., ports., facsims.

This volume includes several chapters of interest regarding Lincoln's life as a law practitioner. In chapter 11, there are estimates of Lincoln as a lawyer by David Davis and others. There are details regarding the bar, his own admission, his examination of an applicant, and his opinion of examinations. Information is provided regarding his first case, and his last appearance in court. Weik discusses the extent of his practice, his three partnerships, and his fees. Several cases include *Hawthorne v. Wooldridge, Scammon v. Cline, Bailey v. Cromwell,* also *Carman v. Glasscock* involving the navigability of the Sangamon River.

Chapter 12 includes *Green v. Green* divorce case, *Rogers v. Rogers, Miller v. Miller, McKibben v. Hart, Spink v. Chiniquiy, Dungey v. Spencer, Linder v. Fleenor,* and *Dorman v. Lane.*

Chapter 13 describes the scarcity of his written briefs and legal arguments. Details regarding other cases include *Patterson v. Edwards, Smith v. Smith, Hurd v. Rock Island Bridge Company.* Chapter 24 describes his life on the circuit.

Weik utilized manuscript material, court records, and newspapers, as well as information from old friends.
Monaghan 1212

--- ----. Microfilm. New Haven, Conn: Yale University Library, 1989.

201
Whipple, Wayne.
The Story-life of Lincoln. A Biography Composed of Five Hundred True Stories Told by Abraham Lincoln and His Friends. Selected From All Authentic Sources, and Fitted Together in Order, Forming His Complete Life History. Memorial ed. Philadelphia: John C. Winston, 1908.
xii, 708 p. illus., ports., facsims.

The author collected the best from all the great lives of Lincoln, using the true stories for a continuous life story. He records the source at the end of each "sketch."

Chapter 6 includes a subsection entitled "Stuart and Lincoln." Whipple tells the tale of Lincoln's going to the bank and borrowing $30,000 in legal tender, for a transaction involving a land claim, and later returning the money, "Thirty Thousand Dollars Handed to Him Without a Scratch of the Pen." Chapter 8 is entitled "State Capital and Eighth Circuit."

Monaghan 1639

--- ----. Microfilm. Emporia, Kans.: William Allen White Library, 1971.

202
Whitney, Henry C. (Clay)
Life on the Circuit with Lincoln. Introduction and notes by Paul M. Angle.
Caldwell, Idaho: Caxton Printers, 1940.
530 p. illus., ports.

The author is one of the few men who knew Lincoln personally very well
and later wrote about him. Much of the book is about fascinating detail of
Lincoln's life as a circuit lawyer and his prepresidential political life.

Whitney knew and practiced law on the same judicial circuit with Lincoln
from 1854-1861. Angle writes that "one gets the impression, that here is what
one man remembered about another, recorded exactly as it popped into his
mind. . . ." The book is written in rough semibiographical style. Although the
reading is somewhat laborious, due to discourse on subjects broader than merely
Lincoln, it does provide description of Lincoln as a lawyer particularly in the
chapter "Life on the Eighth Circuit" where "our life on the circuit was like a
holiday." Another chapter, "As a Lawyer," is useful as well.

He believes that Lincoln's character as a lawyer was molded by his
character as a man. He was entirely honest, and being on the wrong side did not
enhance his case. He was respectful of truthful witnesses, and gave away all but
important points. He had a philosophical mind, appreciated elementary
principles of law, and applied those; he discarded useless technicalities. He
understood relationships, reasoned by analogy, and his mode of speaking was
plain. He lacked method and organizing ability, and in mere case law he was
deficient. The author mentions other men on the circuit. Judge Breese regarded
him as the finest lawyer he ever knew, and Judge Davis got him to hold court.

--- ----. With Sketches of Generals Grant, Sherman and McClellan, Judge Davis,
Leonard Swett, and Other Contemporaries. Boston: Estes and Lauriat, 1892. 601
p. illus.
Monaghan 1112
--- ----. Microfilm. New Haven, Conn.: Micrographic Systems of Connecticut,
1986.
--- ----. Microfiche. Chicago: Library Resources, 1970. (Library of American
Civilization: LAC 12558)

203
Whitney, Henry C. (Clay)
Lincoln the Citizen. (February 12, 1809, to March 4, 1861.) New York:
Commemorative ed. Edited by Marion Mills **Miller.** New York: Current

Literature Publishing Co., 1907.
xv, 312 p. port. (Life and Works of Abraham Lincoln; v.1)

The author, who had firsthand knowledge, discusses Lincoln's courtroom characteristics. Lincoln was not well grounded in the law. He had an intuitive sense of justice, without any conception of rules. He had little patience with technicality, was not familiar with decisions, and did not approve precedent. His method was to view each case on its merits alone. He used logic and was strong in analysis and reasoning. When cases had no precedent he had few equals. He was frank and cordial with witnesses, and skillful in cross examination. He paid only slight attention to the rules of evidence and recalled elements of evidence as needed. He remained calm at all times, and did the best he could for the case at hand.

It was morally impossible for Lincoln to argue dishonestly. He was shrewd and had common sense. He promoted compromise, was generally a man of peace, and avoided litigation grounded in vengeance or ill will. He was known for charging insignificant fees. There is reference to the case *Illinois Central Railroad Co. v. Mclean County*.

After his death members of the Illinois bench and bar spoke in eulogy. All agreed on his honesty. However, Judge Davis made disparaging remarks on his managing and organizing abilities and his lack of adherence to technical rules. There is brief description of his law partners and the circuit.

A facsimile of the autobiography of Lincoln is included in his own handwriting. In it he states that during the legislative period he studied law and "removed to Springfield to practice it."
Monaghan 1542;1641

--- ----. Centenary edition de luxe. New York: Lincoln Centenary Association, 1907. 9 v. (v.1)

204
Wilson, Rufus Rockwell.
Intimate Memories of Lincoln. Assembled and annotated by Rufus Rockwell Wilson. Elmira, N.Y.: Primavera Press, 1945.
629 p. port.

This book, by journalist and publisher Wilson is a companion volume to *Lincoln Among His Friends*. It includes several selections on the topic of Lincoln as a lawyer:

Davis, David, and others, i.e., Abram Bergen and Frederick G. Saltonstall, "Lawyer Lincoln as His Associates Measured Him." These three men, through long association and close observation, could speak on Lincoln's methods and capacity as a lawyer.

Kidd, Thomas W. S., "The Crier of the Court on Lawyer Lincoln," was an unusual and informative address presented before the Bar Association of Sangamon County, Illinois, April 25, 1903. For annotation, see **Kidd**.

Somers, William H., "Mr. Lincoln Was Always Kind to Young Men." This clerk of the Circuit Court of Champaign County during Lincoln's last years on the old Eighth Judicial Circuit has new and informative things to say, particularly about Lincoln's helpfulness to young members of the bar. See also **Somers**, Journal Articles.

Birch, Jonathan, "A Student Who Was Aided by Lincoln," was first published in an article by Weik in *The Outlook* of New York, February 11, 1911. For annotation, see **Weik**, Journal Articles.

205
Wilson, Rufus Rockwell.
Lincoln Among His Friends: A Sheaf of Intimate Memories. Assembled and Annotated by Rufus Rockwell Wilson. Caldwell Idaho: Caxton Printers, 1942. 506 p. port.

The following selections deal with Lincoln during the lawyer phase of his life:

Conkling, James C., "Some of Lincoln's Associates at the Bar," p. 105-112. Reprint in part of an address, "The Early Bench and Bar of Central Illinois," delivered by Conkling before the Chicago Bar Association, January 12, 1881.

Conkling, lawyer, and member of the Illinois General Assembly, describes the Sangamon District as one of the nine judicial districts of Illinois. Lawyers were compelled to travel twice a year to the court sessions, over impassable roads, where high [prairie] grasses held water. They went for miles without seeing signs of civilization. He described the hotel accommodations, where the lawyers had some leisure hours, enjoying conversation and stories and where Lincoln was known for his anecdotes.

He believed that Lincoln was a slow thinker. He rejected anything for which there was not sound reasoning. He was entirely honest and would not accept a fee for a bad case. He would not argue a case before the jury when he believed he was wrong. However, he was a strong lawyer on the right side of a case. He was known to illustrate his points with stories.

Cunningham, James O., "With Lincoln on the Old Eighth Circuit," p. 113-123.

This is a reprint of portions of an address by James O. Cunningham before Fireland's Pioneer Association at Norwalk, Ohio, July 4, 1927.

Lawyer Cunningham moved to Urbana, Illinois, in "The West," in what is now Champaign County. It was part of the Eighth Judicial Circuit of Illinois presided over by David Davis. He describes the courthouse and county seat. The circuit court of the county was the only court of general common law and chancery jurisdiction. Twice annually the lawyers traveled in what he described as an "ambulatory bar." Lincoln was deemed the best lawyer of the Springfield section in civil matters.

Cunningham described the hotels where lawyers stayed during the court term, such places being a rallying point where there was good cheer and conviviality, and where Lincoln was known for his stories. He often strolled the towns in a reflective mood. He tells of Lincoln's becoming interested in politics and speaking in Chicago, Springfield, Peoria, and Urbana.

Tree, Lambert, "Lincoln Among Lawyers," p. [124]-128.
Reprinted from 81 CENTURY MAGAZINE (February 1911), 591-593.
For annotation see **Tree**, Journal Articles.

Zane, Charles S., "A Young Lawyer's Memoirs of Lincoln," p. [129]-138.
Judge Zane practiced law in Springfield, and was at one time a partner of Herndon. Although he had applied to the Lincoln and Herndon firm, there was no opening, so he located with the James C. Conkling office. It was his good fortune to see something of the daily life of Lincoln from the organization of the Republican party until his election to the presidency. He found Lincoln courteous and interested in him although he was merely a student. Zane heard him argue a patent case at the United States Circuit Court located in Springfield, and commented on his faculty for comprehensive understanding of machinery. He said, too, that Lincoln recognized the difference between speeches in court and on the political platform.

Zane reports what members of the Springfield bar said of Lincoln when they met at the old courthouse on the day of his death.

White, Charles T., "Lincoln the Comforter," p. [139]-144.
The author secured the papers of Capt. Gilbert J. Greene and recorded reminiscences, the first published originally in the Atlanta *Constitution* and the second in the *Christian Herald*.

Greene met Lincoln while on his way home to the northern part of Illinois from Cairo, where he began walking the distance. He had run out of money and asked for shelter at the Strawn home, where he was told he could stay overnight if he would deliver some legal papers to Abraham Lincoln. He agreed to do it, although it meant a thirty-five-mile walk into Springfield. He depicted Lincoln in his office, and told of Lincoln's giving him five dollars, and writing a message on the margin of a newspaper to the local hotel for the management to put him up overnight.

In his second reminiscence, Greene tells of Lincoln's inviting him to ride into the country where he had to draw up a will for an elderly woman on her deathbed. The will was drawn and witnessed and the woman asked Lincoln to read from the Bible. Instead he recited passages before the woman died.

Bergen, Abram, "When Lincoln Defended Duff Armstrong," p. [145]-151.
This interview was given in 1898 to James L. King, state librarian of Kansas at Topeka.

Judge Bergen was in Cass County, Illinois, when Lincoln resided there. He observed his methods as a lawyer. In 1858, Judge Bergen was entering the practice of law in one of the circuits frequented by Lincoln. Bergen met him in the courts of five counties and noted his words and motions at trials. Although he was remembering Lincoln of forty years prior, he gives great detail regarding his physical appearance.

He saw Lincoln at the Morgan County Court defending Dunlap in an action for $10,000 in damages brought by the editor of an abolition paper. With humor Lincoln destroyed the effect of Ben Edwards, opponent, who had used tears and pathos.

Armstrong, Duff, "Duff Armstrong's Own Story," p. [152]-155.

Duff Armstrong became a respected resident of Ashland, Cass County, Illinois. Three years before his death he gave this information about his trial to J. M. Davis, the only known statement he was known to have given for publication. He described the night of the murder, the altercation, and finally the trial, and his joyous hearing of the "not guilty" verdict.

Armstrong said that the almanac was furnished by his cousin, Jake Jones, and that there was no fraud about it. He said that the fight was in front of one of the bars anyhow where there was light enough from candles for anyone to have seen it. He added that it was only a fist fight and he did not have a slungshot. He said that Norris, who had been convicted for the same offence, was no more guilty than he was.

206
Woldman, Albert A.
Lawyer Lincoln. Boston: Houghton Mifflin, 1936.
viii, 347 p. illus., ports., facsims.

One hundred years after Lincoln's admission to the bar, Woldman pens a thorough and comprehensive book covering Lincoln's career as a lawyer, and the constitutional and legal problems he faced as the Civil War president. The author states, "Lincoln is the law profession's noblest contribution to American civilization" and that "Lincoln's training at the bar prepared, molded, and qualified him for his mighty task and enabled him to meet the unprecedented constitutional questions created by the crisis."

The author explores in detail Lincoln's preparation for law, his three law partnerships with Stuart, Logan, and Herndon, and Lincoln's life riding the circuit, including the men with whom he associated and who were his political allies. The author also examines Lincoln as a trial lawyer, prosecutor, bar examiner, advisor, railroad lawyer, and leader of the Illinois bar. He relates the fact that Lincoln was an acting judge, something not all authors have addressed. Woldman looks at Lincoln's character traits, such as honesty and shrewdness. He discusses his fees and investments and illustrates these subjects with discussions of cases. This author brings out some less-well-known cases.

Later, Woldman establishes the connection between Lincoln's training as a lawyer and his view of the Dred Scott decision, his debates with Douglas and the legal and constitutional problems Lincoln faced when president, including

international aspects in his dealings with foreign nations. Includes footnotes and partial list of Lincoln's federal cases in notes.
Monaghan 3547

See also **Hertz**, Emanuel. Lawyer Lincoln, by Albert A. Woldman. [Book Review] 11 *St. John's Law Review* (April 1937), 354. Journal Articles.

207
Wood, Harlington, Jr.
Lincoln's Early Experience with the Constitution.
In Papers from the Second Annual Lincoln Colloquium. Cosponsored by Lincoln Home National Historic Site and the Sangamon County Historical Society.
[Springfield, 1988]
p. 13-18.

Judge Wood glances over Lincoln's early years and declares him a good lawyer. He reviews Lincoln's interest in becoming a lawyer, and notes that he emerged from New Salem as a lawyer and a legislator. Lincoln did not know it then, but he was preparing for constitutional issues of the presidency. Lincoln focused not only on the Constitution but also on the Declaration of Independence. He had a lawyer's caution, common sense, and a sense of justice, fairness, order and decency, love of independence, and belief in equality. He considered the practical aspects in practice before the legal or constitutional dimensions.
After brief description of the circuit, Wood mentions the "Effie Afton" steamboat case, the criminal case of Truett, and the Duff Armstrong "almanac" case. He notes that Lincoln was a great trial lawyer and a leading appellate lawyer, including statistics on the number of cases. After discussing several constitutional issues, he describes Lincoln's last day at the law office in Springfield. He expressed the fact that although Lincoln was elevated to the presidency, he was still a lawyer.

208
Woodford County Historical Society.
Dedication of Court Scene of Lincoln's Time in the Lincoln Memorial Court House, Metamora, Illinois, Tuesday, June 28, 1932, by the Woodford County Historical Society and State Department of Public Works and Buildings.
[Metamora, Ill.: The Society, printed by the Metamora Herald, 1932.]
[40 p.] illus.

This pamphlet includes minutes of the dedication. There was an enactment of the court scene, and a presentation by Judge George T. Page, "Lincoln and His Associates in Woodford County." This item includes an illustration of the

granite composition monument and bronze tablet in front of the Lincoln Memorial Court House in Metamora. The inscription on the statue reads, "Abraham Lincoln traveled this way as he rode the Circuit of the Eighth Judicial District, 1847-1857."
Monaghan 1313

209
Zane, John M. (Maxcy)
Lincoln, the Constitutional Lawyer. Chicago: Printed for the Caxton Club by R. R. Donnelley at Lakeside Press, 1932.
92 p.

An address was delivered February 12, 1932, in Springfield, Illinois, before the Abraham Lincoln Association. The author portrays Lincoln solely as a lawyer to show his legal mentality. He begins by describing Lincoln, as a practicing attorney, calling him "a versatile lawyer, one of extraordinary resource and legal acumen." He illustrates this view of Lincoln by describing several of his cases. Although Lincoln was the "all around" practitioner, he had a certain style to him, a sense of "prose rhythm" as described by the author. He dismisses as absurd stories of Lincoln's not arguing cases unless moral, and deserting cases if they were not.

After describing Lincoln as a practicing lawyer the author studies Lincoln as a constitutional lawyer. He explores Lincoln's views on the Dred Scott decision and later the legal positions Lincoln took as president on constitutional questions that confronted him caused by seccession and war with the southern states. The author marvels at how Lincoln devised a legal formula, "one of mixed law and politics but its basis was purely legal," which was legally correct, to allow the courts to support his views. A lengthy footnote disputes certain facts as presented in Beveridge, and originally in Whitney, pertaining to *Johnston v. Jones and Marsh*, later *Jones v. Johnston*.
Monaghan 3365

---. An Address by John M. Zane, Delivered Before the Abraham Lincoln Assocation at Springfield, Illinois, in the Old State House, on February 12, 1932. Springfield, Ill.: Abraham Lincoln Association, 1932. Abraham Lincoln Association Papers, 1933.
59 p.
Monaghan 3365

Journal Articles

Journal Articles

210
A. Lincoln v. Timothy D. Lincoln. 1424 LINCOLN LORE (October 1956), 4.

Two lawyers had the same surname in a case tried in the United States Circuit Court, Chicago, in 1857. Abraham Lincoln, with attorneys Judd and Knox, represented the defendant, and Timothy D. Lincoln [et al.] represented the plaintiffs in the "Effie Afton" bridge case. The case, regarding the right of a railroad to bridge a navigable stream, ended in a hung jury, and was dismissed. The contention was finally upheld by the Supreme Court of the United States.

211
Abbott, Lawrence F.
Was He an Oafish Country Lawyer? 144 OUTLOOK (November 17, 1926), 363-365.

The author discusses a Lincoln tradition which he believes erroneous, as set forth by Editor Strachey, of the London *Spectator*. Strachey had used the term "oafish country lawyer" in describing Lincoln as he entered the White House. Abbott was willing to acknowledge awkwardness, ungainliness, or plainness, but he refuted the idea that Lincoln was mediocre in intellect and achievement, or that his law practice was insignificant or disreputable.

He selected quotations from Lincoln's contemporaries to illustrate their belief in the legend that Lincoln's conversion from a backwoods country lawyer to a statesman occurred overnight. Then he points to the records that indicate that Lincoln was a leader of the Illinois bar, was knowledgeable, and had appeared in important corporation cases.

212
Abraham Lincoln. 1 ILLINOIS CENTRAL MAGAZINE (February 1913), 19-23; (March 1913), 15-26; (April 1913), 15-28; (May 1913), 15-27; (June 1913), 15-20.

Lincoln was retained as local attorney for Illinois Central by James F. Joy, chief counsel for the railroad. This article includes a photographic reproduction of Lincoln's railroad pass and a facsimile of his handwritten opinion on construction of the charter. There is discussion of several cases in which Lincoln appeared as attorney, such as *Illinois Central Railroad v. Brock Hays*. It describes *Illinois Central Railroad v. County of McLean*, and Lincoln's suit to collect his fee. Lincoln tried his own case, and photocopies of the original papers prepared by Lincoln for the suit are included.

Lincoln continued an almost unbroken connection with the Illinois Central Railroad as one of its attorneys, appearing for the company about a hundred times in the Supreme Court of Illinois. His record was unparalleled by any other Illinois attorney. Although he always felt a lack of education, he demonstrated to the railroad company that he was a master of the law.

213

Abraham Lincoln--Lawyer. 31 AMERICAN BAR ASSOCIATION JOURNAL (February 1945), 99.

This one-page tribute to Lincoln reminded readers of Lincoln's background as an experienced lawyer who used his skills for his circuit, state, and finally his nation. He talked of "common people" or "plain people" without class consciousness.

214

Abraham Lincoln's New Memorial [Report on Lincoln Circuit Marking Association] 8th Circuit. 8 AMERICAN BAR ASSOCIATION JOURNAL (October 1922), 600; 8 VIRGINIA BAR REGISTER (N.S.) (December 1922), 637-638.

This report of the Lincoln Circuit Marking Association summarizes its completed work on marking the route traveled by Abraham Lincoln and other famous lawyers who made the rounds of the Eighth Judicial Circuit of Illinois.

215

Angle, Paul M.
Abraham Lincoln: Circuit Lawyer.   PAPERS OF THE LINCOLN CENTENNIAL ASSOCIATION (1928), 19-41.

The author used surviving court records to describe Lincoln's practice on the circuit. He found that while Lincoln was ordinarily successful on the circuit, his success rate in higher courts was outstanding. This illustrated his ability to think analytically and to form judgments that would withstand attack.

216
Angle, Paul M.
Lincoln and the United States Supreme Court. 47 BULLETIN OF THE ABRAHAM LINCOLN ASSOCIATION (May 1937), [3]-9.

After the Dred Scott decision in 1857, Lincoln replied to Douglas with a reasoned analysis of the judicial decision he believed erroneous. Judicial decisions absolutely determine the case at hand, and they indicate to the public how similar cases will be decided when they arise. Lincoln had hope for a reversal of the Dred Scott decision based on public opinion. Lincoln's attack was not on the court, but upon the decision as a policy-determining precedent. The latter part of article discussed Lincoln's later appointments to the United States Supreme Court.

217
Angle, Paul M.
Lincoln Defended Railroad. 17 ILLINOIS CENTRAL MAGAZINE (February 1929), 40-43.

There is no question that Lincoln was an attorney for the Illinois Central Railroad. A facsimile of a Lincoln letter helps to explain a discrepancy as to whether he was retained by the railroad, or employed on particular cases.

From the records, it is obvious that he represented the Illinois Central more than once, and he rendered opinions when requested to do so in cases, such as *Walker v. Hedrick* regarding preemption rights on land. Although Lincoln's name does not appear, the decision was in accordance with his opinion. There is mention of the famous McLean County case, and of the suit he instigated against the railroad for his $5000 fee. There is information on a case establishing the principle that common carriers have the right to restrict their liability. Angle provides little-known details of the Illinois Central with regard to taxation and includes a Lincoln letter regarding an impending suit.

218
Angle, Paul M.
Lincoln in the United States Courts 1855-1860   No. 8 LINCOLN CENTENNIAL ASSOCIATION BULLETIN (September 1, 1927), [1]-8.

In 1855 the United States Courts in Illinois were divided into two districts, northern in Chicago, the southern in Springfield. All records were transferred to Chicago where they later burned in a fire. However, a large number of Lincoln legal papers are in the files of the United States Circuit Court in Springfield covering the years Lincoln practiced before it, 1855-1860. Lincoln was of counsel in at least eighty-five of the 1000 cases tried during these five years. The author contends these papers "puncture the notion that Lincoln was averse to office work," noting that Lincoln's papers were neat, precise, "hardly drawn by a man whose heart was not in his work."

A number of Lincoln's cases before the United States Circuit Court involved collections, with S. C. Davis & Co. of St. Louis. Angle discusses several of Lincoln's collection cases such as *Ambos v. Barret*, and *Bacon v. the Ohio and Mississippi Railroad Company*.

The author hoped these papers would shed light on Lincoln's ability as a lawyer. But because a large number of his cases were won on default or settled by agreement, the data were inconclusive. The author furnishes statistics, noting that Lincoln won three of seven jury trials, and four of fourteen tried before the court without a jury. Fifteen of the Lincoln and Herndon cases were dismissed, while twenty-eight were won by default; the rest were tried after Lincoln became president.

219
Angle, Paul M.
Where Lincoln Practiced Law. Address before Lincoln Centennial Association in the Circuit Court Room, Springfield, February 12, 1927. LINCOLN CENTENNIAL ASSOCIATION PAPERS (1927), 15-46.

The author describes the Sangamon County Courthouse where Lincoln tried the first of his many cases. The two-story brick courthouse was built in the public square in 1831 and became the center of the business community of Springfield.

This piece describes the law offices of Stuart & Lincoln in a two-story brick building on Hoffman's Row. It provides a glimpse of the offices of Logan & Lincoln, and later, Lincoln & Herndon. It also describes the new State House, the United States District and Circuit Court buildings in Springfield where Lincoln tried numerous cases.

220
Armstrong, John.
The Brother of Duff Armstrong. LINCOLN CENTENNIAL ASSOCIATION ADDRESSES (1912), 58-61.

John Armstrong, brother of Duff, after being introduced by Judge Humphrey, tells of family relationships with Abraham Lincoln. He had been told that Lincoln, who lived at his father's home about two years, was studying law and acting as surveyor. Then he tells of the 1857 camp meeting where Prescott Metzker was in a fistfight, receiving an injury from which he died a few days afterward. Duff Armstrong was arrested and charged with the crime. Without bail, he was committed to jail where he remained for eighteen months. There was a change of venue and the case was tried at Beardstown, Cass County.

His mother had employed a lawyer, but immediately received a letter from Mr. Lincoln tendering his services, and it was Lincoln who defended Duff Armstrong. In the May 1858 trial, witnesses for the state claimed that it was a bright moonlit night when Duff used a sling-shot to strike Metzker. Both contentions were denied by the defense. The sling-shot was found and a Mr. Watkins swore that he had thrown it away. Then Lincoln produced the almanac showing the dark of the moon on that night. A "not guilty" verdict was handed down.

221
Armstrong, Walter P.
Abraham Lincoln--Lawyer; New Basic Lincolniana Available in 1947.   33 AMERICAN BAR ASSOCIATION JOURNAL (June 1947), 558-562.

A large quantity of Lincoln's papers, pleadings, and his correspondence were released by the Library of Congress. The papers were a gift from Lincoln's son Robert, on the condition they not be published until twenty-one years after his death. The author and other Lincoln historians anxiously awaited the unsealing date of July 26, 1947.

222
Arnold, Isaac N.
Reminiscences of the Illinois Bar: 1840. Lincoln and Douglas As Orators and Lawyers. 47 ILLINOIS BAR JOURNAL (February 1959), 572-578.

Address originally presented before the Fourth Annual Illinois State Bar Association meeting, Springfield, January 7, 1881.

The author was a personal friend of Lincoln's. He calls him "the strongest jury-lawyer we ever had in Illinois." A description of Lincoln's courtroom demeanor follows. "He had in the highest possible degree, the art of persuasion and the power of conviction." The article explores several of Lincoln's cases, including *Bailey v. Cromwell*, probably Lincoln's first extensive study of the slavery issue. There is discussion of the Lincoln and Douglas debates.

Issued also as a separate, Chicago: Fergus Printing Co., 1881.

223

Ashe, Samuel A'Court.
Lincoln the Lawyer. 16 TYLER'S QUARTERLY HISTORICAL AND GENEALOGICAL MAGAZINE (July 1934), 15-20.

In a nonflattering discussion of Lincoln, the author accuses Lincoln in the Armstrong murder case of reading from an almanac of the previous year, a fact denied but often questioned. Ashe also accuses Lincoln of "log rolling" and trading in the offices while he was a legislator.

224

Baily, Harold James.
Abraham Lincoln's Language. 45 AMERICAN BAR ASSOCIATION JOURNAL (September 1959), 934; 10 BROOKLYN BARRISTER (February 1959), 120.

This short article on Lincoln's mastery of the English language theorizes that Lincoln could never have reached such great heights if he had not mastered clear, simple, and precise English, which illustrated the intensity of his feeling and the sincerity of his convictions.

225

Baily, Harold James.
A Lift for Lawyers from Lincoln. 9 BROOKLYN BARRISTER (February 1958), 138-140.

The author notes that Lincoln "studied diligently, worked hard and became a competent, successful lawyer." He claims there is much lawyers can learn from studying Lincoln. "Most American lawyers admire Lincoln and seek to emulate him. . . . This appreciation of Lincoln's qualities is good for our profession, for what you admire you tend to imitate, what you imitate you tend to become. . . . " Basically the author is saying the words and examples set by Abe Lincoln are good ones for today's lawyers to follow.

226

Barondess, Benjamin.
The Adventure of the Missing Briefs. 8 MANUSCRIPTS (Fall 1955), 20-24, 64. For annotation see **Barondess,** Monographs.

227
Barton, Robert S.
Lincoln and the "Effie Afton" Case. FOXBORO RECORDER (Supplement)
(February 7, 1951), [1-4].

The writer describes in great detail the involved 1857 case of *Hurd v. The Railroad Bridge Company*, known as the "Rock Island Bridge Case" or the "Effie Afton Case," in which Lincoln took a leading part.

The new packet steamer "Effie Afton" commanded by Captain Hurd traveling from St. Louis to St. Paul on her maiden voyage passed through the draw of the Rock Island Bridge. Upstream, the boat struck bridge piers. Upset stoves caused a fire that burned the boat and cargo, and the draw section of the bridge was destroyed.

During the case, Lincoln did not present an eloquent speech, merely skillfully gathered facts in logical relationship. The jury was unable to reach an agreement. This was an important case involving steamboat and railroad interests. Although Lincoln did not appear in the case again after the original trial, it was said of him that he "exerted a powerful influence upon the development of the transportation system of the continent."

228
Barton, Robert S.
Lincoln and the McCormick Reaper Case. Drawing by Harry B. Chase.
FOXBORO RECORDER (Supplement) (February 13, 1952), [1-5].

This is considered one of the most notable cases in the history of American courts. In Lincoln history, *McCormick v. Manny* is important because up until this case, Lincoln had not taken part in a case of this magnitude, nor had he matched wits with such eminent lawyers. He was paid the largest retainer he had ever received. The patent infringement case was for recovery of damages and injunction to restrain Manny from further manufacture of the reaping machine.

Lincoln had prepared his argument, but did not have the opportunity to use it. There were other attorneys who maneuvered so that he did not participate. He was deeply hurt, and felt the obligation and desire to perform his duty. Therefore, he gave his manuscript to Peter Watson for Attorney Harding, who threw it into the wastebasket. Lincoln asked Watson whether Harding had read it, and whether he could have it back. It came back unopened. He was in court for this case daily as a spectator.

Manny won the suit, and McCormick instructed the lawyers to appeal to the United States Supreme Court. John H. Manny died two weeks after his victory, so his heirs and associates became defendants in the supreme court suit. The decision of the circuit court was upheld.

229

Beardsley, George

Lincoln as a Lawyer: His Career in the Supreme Court of Illinois; His First Case in That Court; How He Measured Up With Trumbull, Logan and Others. 4 THE MIDLAND MONTHLY (October 1895), 327-331.

The Supreme Court of Illinois met only once a year, in December. Lincoln, as did other lawyers, would travel great distances to attend. There were four judges on the state supreme court in 1840. The article lists other attorneys who argued before the court during that year.

Scammon v. Cline was Lincoln's first case in the Supreme Court of Illinois. The suit was for less than $200. Although there is no official record that Lincoln represented the defendant at the county court level, or in the circuit court, it is assumed that he did. He successfully got a change of venue at the justice court, was dismissed at the circuit level, but remanded by the state supreme court. Thus, Lincoln lost his first case before the Supreme Court of Illinois; he also lost his second one (1 Gilman 143); and won a third case (1 Gilman 173). The Illinois Supreme Court Reports show that Lincoln appeared in 158 cases at the Illinois Supreme Court and won 82, very nearly 52%. The author does some comparison with other legal figures of the day. If Lincoln were an attorney today, he would be considered a corporate lawyer particularly as an attorney for the railroads.

230

Beaver, Paul J.

Another Look at the Duff Armstrong-Alamanac [*sic*] Trial 7 LINCOLN NEWSLETTER (Fall 1988), [1]-3.

Beaver refers to an article in the *Lincoln Courier*, "Rest of the Duff Armstrong Story," by John Whiteside, dealing with the 1858 Armstrong trial in which Lincoln used the almanac to win his acquittal. Details of the case reveal that Armstrong and Norris engaged in a fight with Metzger [*sic*], who fell from his horse several times on his way home, and died [several days] later. Norris was convicted. Armstrong's mother, Hannah, who had been a friend of Lincoln at New Salem, enlisted his aid on behalf of her son. The author reviews the familiar story of Lincoln's producing the almanac to show that the moon was not bright overhead. Additional information in this article shows that the "slung shot" supposedly used as the weapon by Duff, was owned by Watkins, whose testimony revealed that he had thrown it away the day after the fight. A postscript to the case is included based on information furnished by a teacher who lived in the Armstrong home years later. Armstrong, as an old man, related that he had, in fact, killed Metzger with a "neck yoke."

Includes an illustration of Duff Armstrong.

231
Beaver, Paul J.
Lincoln's Political Rise in Logan County, Illinois. 3 LINCOLN NEWSLETTER
(February 1982), 1-2.

This speech was presented to the Lincoln Group of New York, December 2,
1981.

In the precedent-setting Dalby case, during the train trip from Elkhart to
Lincoln, Illinois, there was a dispute over the price of a ticket. As a result, the
Dalbys were put off of the train. Dalby entered suit, and Lincoln came into the
case through Attorney Samuel Parks, of Lincoln, Illinois. This particular suit was
against the railroad, rather than the conductor. Later, Attorney Parks, with other
legal friends became a supporter of Lincoln in his political ambitions.

232
Benjamin, R. M.
Lincoln the Lawyer 68 CENTRAL LAW JOURNAL (March 1909), 217-218;
9 BRIEF (1909), 74.

Lincoln used the power of reasoning and logic to argue cases rather than
depending on precedent and analogy. (Fewer cases were reported in those days.)
He was more apt to use authorities when he had a case before the Supreme
Court of Illinois. Benjamin also provides description of Lincoln as a lawyer by
Thomas Drummand, who was a judge of the United States District Court of
Illinois in the early 1850s.

233
Bennett, J. B.
A. Lincoln: Attorney at Law. 41 ROUGH NOTES (November 28, 1907), 78-79.

This brief article details a little-known incident in Springfield. In 1858, an
insurance adjuster, who suspected fraud in a question of loss, put the case to
suit. The author of the article, Bennett, brought files to Sangamon, and sought
out the claimant, who stated that he would not deal with him, as he had a
lawyer, Abraham Lincoln. Bennett was under the impression that Lincoln was
only a local attorney, but learned that he stood at the head of the bar. Lincoln,
busy at his office, suggested that his associate counsel at the courthouse could
handle the matter. Although the associate counsel proposed a satisfactory
settlement, he had to have Lincoln's final assent and review. Bennett believed
Lincoln to be entirely honest.

234
Bergen, A[bram].
Abraham Lincoln as a Lawyer. 12 AMERICAN BAR ASSOCIATION JOURNAL (June 1926), 390-394.

While the author was studying law, and in his first year after admission to practice, he had the opportunity to observe Lincoln in the courts of five counties. He gives a personal recollection of Lincoln and describes Lincoln's physical and mental characteristics: ". . . his most noticeable characteristic was his extraordinary faculty for correct reasoning, logic, and analysis." The author describes Lincoln's courtroom demeanor including his actions in several trials, such as the Armstrong murder trial, and particularly the Dunlap assault case, in the Morgan County Courthouse.

235
Bergen, A[bram].
Lincoln as a Lawyer: Address. 1897 KANSAS STATE BAR ASSOCIATION, 31

For annotation see **Bergen** above.

(See also James L. King, "Lincoln's Skill As A Lawyer," NORTH AMERICAN REVIEW [February 1898], 186-195, for King's recounting of Bergen's description of the Dunlap assault case.)

236
Beveridge, Albert J.
Lincoln the Lawyer. 13 STATE BAR JOURNAL OF THE STATE BAR OF CALIFORNIA (March 1938), 45-49.

This article, which contains excerpts from the author's *Abraham Lincoln*, describes Lincoln's law partnership with Herndon, based on trust, and the law office out of which they worked. When Lincoln was away in Congress, Herndon kept up the practice. Upon returning, Lincoln offered to withdraw, but his junior partner insisted that he remain with the firm. He describes Lincoln's riding the circuit, helping younger lawyers along the way. Lincoln's courtroom manner is detailed--his short, compact sentences spoken clearly and simply, focusing on the one crucial point in the case. He reports that associates declared that Lincoln had "little knowledge of decisions, or textbooks, but relied upon principle and reason."

237
Blackstone, or Blacksmith. 865 LINCOLN LORE (November 5, 1945), [1]

This article discusses Lincoln's choice of vocation. Little attention has been paid to his statement that he considered becoming a blacksmith. Such a vocation was appealing for several reasons. He thought of trying law, but could not succeed at that without a better education. He did not go into law by luck or chance, instead he took the initiative. There is a brief discussion of his getting a copy of Blackstone's *Commentaries*. The article referred to Howells' Lincoln biography, which Lincoln read and corrected. He left intact the statement that he *bought* an old copy of Blackstone one day at auction in Springfield and returned to New Salem.

238
Borit[t], Gabor S.
Another New Lincoln Text? Some Thoughts Concerning an Outrageous Suggestion About Abraham Lincoln "Corporation Lawyer." 77 LINCOLN HERALD (Spring 1975), 27-33.

In the winter of 1973, the author published a newly discovered text by Lincoln that considered taxation. It was a portion of the Biennial Report of the Illinois State auditor, Jesse K. Dubois. An explanatory note suggested that Lincoln might have written the final part of the report as well, analyzing issues of a suit pending between the State and Illinois Central Railroad. Students of Lincoln were disturbed by this suggestion, as it was not based on internal evidence such as language in this section following that portion written by Lincoln.

Boritt says the legal language of the text does not lend itself to content analysis. He states that it is "not impossible" that Lincoln wrote the last part of the Dubois report. A footnote to the Boritt article notes that *The Supplement to the Collected Works of Abraham Lincoln* (Westport, Conn., 1974) includes the disputed section of the Dubois report, with Editor Roy P. Basler's statement that it was "quite probable" that Lincoln was the author. No definitive conclusions can be reached based on evidence. The text of the last section of the Dubois report is included in this article.

239
Bridges, Roger D.
Three Letters From a Lincoln Law Student. 66 JOURNAL OF THE ILLINOIS STATE HISTORICAL SOCIETY (Spring 1973), 79-87.

"Law students in the early nineteenth century customarily prepared for admission to the bar by working and studying in the offices of licensed attorneys." Gibson W. Harris of Albion, Illinois, arrived in Springfield in September of 1845 to work and study with the Lincoln and Herndon law firm for two years.

The author, with some accompanying background text, republishes three letters written by Harris to a friend while working in the law office. The letters do not refer much to Lincoln's law practice other than to his tales and anecdotes told in the law office, of which Harris states, "I sometimes have to hold my sides at times, so convulsed with laughter, as to be almost unable to keep my seat." (For further information from Harris' point of view, see **Harris'** Articles.)

240
Brown, Charles LeRoy.
Abraham Lincoln and the Illinois Central Railroad, 1857-1860. 36 JOURNAL OF THE ILLINOIS STATE HISTORICAL SOCIETY (June 1943), 121-163.

Brown states the problems with unfavorable interpretation of the railroad charter regarding taxation. In 1857 Lincoln had been acting four years as attorney and had represented the corporation in the McLean County case. He won the case in 1856, and brought suit to collect his fees. The relations between the corporation and the attorney were strained. New work for which Lincoln was engaged was of some delicacy. He proceeded on enactment of an extraordinary statute, and won two original actions. In the second, a long, favorable opinion (rendered in 1860) was not published until 1863, with some omissions. Lincoln had induced the supreme court to reduce valuation of the company's property, setting a precedent on valuation. Some writers have treated this as Lincoln's greatest legal achievement; others, including other counsel for the corporation, believed that if certain sections had been held unconstitutional the railroad company would have been relieved of paying a percentage of its gross receipts.

241
Brown, Kent Masterson.
Mr. Lincoln: The Exemplary Lawyer. 80 LINCOLN HERALD (Winter 1978), 158, 191.

In this editorial Attorney Brown considers Lincoln one of the most beloved men who has served at the American Bar. He quotes Judge David Davis, "In all the elements that constitute the great lawyer, he had few equals." He was great at trial courts and before the appellate. He was not known as a case lawyer; he did not rely chiefly on the precedents set by earlier cases. He was a tireless worker and known for his penetrating logic. He served people in high or low station, rich or poor, and represented powerful corporations. He had a love of the practice of law, and gave advice on how to practice it. There was no conflict in what Lincoln expected of himself and as a professional lawyer.

242
Bullard, F. Lauriston.
When John T. Stuart Sought to Send Lincoln to South America.
47 LINCOLN HERALD (October-December 1945), 21, 29.

Bullard quotes from John T. Stuart's letter of March 5, 1841, to Daniel Webster, secretary of state, recommending Abraham Lincoln of Illinois to be chargé d'affaires at Bogota, New Granada. This information had appeared in Claude Moore Fuess' biography of Daniel Webster, and a footnote suggested that Stuart was evidently trying to secure a change of climate for his law partner, who had been in a depressed mood. The letter was written a few weeks before dissolution of Stuart and Lincoln's law partnership.

243
Burleigh, Nina.
Lincoln as a Lawyer: Historian to Profile His Career. 131 CHICAGO DAILY LAW BULLETIN (August 14, 1985), 1.

The author notes that most people recognize Abraham Lincoln as a president, but few people knew him as what he was for most of his life, a good lawyer.

The article describes how the Illinois State Historical Society has embarked on publication of an annotated edition of Lincoln's legal papers, which spanned his twenty-three-year career as a lawyer. The book will contain affidavits and documents relating to thousands of cases in which Lincoln was involved. Because there were no stenographers in that period, there will not be any official accounts of Lincoln's words at trial. Along with the documents will be summaries of his cases and notations of the people involved in them.

Historian William Beard theorizes that little was written about Lincoln as a lawyer in the late 1800s and early 1900s because the legal profession had a bad reputation and authors did not want to tarnish Lincoln's image. He believes focusing on some of Lincoln's cases may "change the mythical image created for the man." For example, Beard notes that Lincoln was counsel on behalf of a slaveowner in a runaway slave case. He also points out the fact that Lincoln often represented railroad interests.

Tracking Lincoln's legal papers will show the evolution of Illinois from a frontier territory to an industrial one. "Lincoln went from arguing cases about stolen hogs in a cabbage patch to arguing whether railroads could cross the Mississippi."

244
Butler, Donald Hege.
Lincoln's Largest Fee. 2 ILLINOIS QUEST (1940), 27-28.

The Illinois Central, by charter, was exempt from all tax, but was to pay a percentage of its earnings. Eventually, the railroad received an assessment for taxation, and filed suit in McLean County to restrain the collection of taxes.

Lincoln offered his legal services, first to the county officials. When they declined, he wrote to the Chicago attorney for the Illinois Central Railroad that he was free to act for the railroad. The issues of this case, which came to trial in 1853, were whether McLean County had the right to tax Illinois Central property, and whether the legislature had the right to grant exemptions. Lincoln, Brayman, and Joy represented the railroad; among the opposition were Stephen T. Logan, and Stuart, Lincoln's former partners.

The litigation lasted for two years, and ended with a victory for the Illinois Central. Several versions of Lincoln's suit to collect his largest fee appear.

245
Caradine, Mary.
Lincoln the Lawyer. THE FRONT RANK 8-9 (February 10, 1935), [168-169]; THE CLASSMATE (February 9, 1935), 5.

The article mentions the influence of Blackstone's *Commentaries*, and Lincoln's 1837 law practice in New Salem. It describes his figure in the courtroom, and depicts a general practitioner who tried a variety of cases for modest fees, but would not be imposed upon. He refused to use tricks, and clearly defined principles, tried cases fairly and honestly, and preferred peace to prosecution. Photographs that are included are from the National Park Service.

The Career of a Country Lawyer. 44 AMERICAN LAW REVIEW (1910), 886; 45 AMERICAN LAW REVIEW (1911), 78.

See **Moores**, Charles Washington.

246
Carpenter, Richard V.
Lincoln's First Supreme Court Case. 4 ILLINOIS HISTORICAL SOCIETY JOURNAL (October 1911), 317-323.

The first case in which Lincoln appeared before the Supreme Court of Illinois was *Scammon v. Cline*, a case that originated out of Boone County. It was a suit brought by Jonathan Scammon on a note made by Cornelius Cline. Judgment was found for Cline, a local man, in which Scammon, a Chicago financier, appealed. The appeal was dismissed because the circuit court in which it was tried was not in existence at the time of the initiation of the lawsuit. Scammon appealed to the state supreme court. He was represented by a prominent Chicago attorney; Cline's attorney, recognizing young Lincoln's rising abilities and prominence, retained him in the suit.

Tradition has it that Lincoln in oral argument announced to the court that all cases he could find were against his contention. The author contends this is probably false, believing that Lincoln announced there was no precedent and argued the fact. The supreme court ruled that the circuit court improperly dismissed the case and remanded where Cline won again. Thus Lincoln lost his first state supreme court case, although eventually, his client won.

247
Carter, Orrin N. (Nelson)
Lincoln and Douglas as Lawyers. 4 MISSISSIPPI VALLEY HISTORICAL ASSOCIATION PROCEEDINGS (1912), 213-240.

For annotation, see **Carter**, Monographs.

248
Chapman, Francis.
Lincoln, the Lawyer. 9 TEMPLE LAW QUARTERLY (April 1935), 277-291.

This article includes a brief history of Lincoln's ancestry and early childhood. Chapman follows Lincoln's life chronologically to the time he begins his career as a lawyer. The rest of the article is about Lincoln as a lawyer, up until the time of his presidency. The article discusses some of the cases Lincoln tried. The author is not sure whether Lincoln was one of the greatest lawyers who ever lived, as some claim; he basically presents historical facts and asks the reader to decide.

249
Charbonneau, Louis H.
Lincoln the Lawyer. 16 THE DETROIT LAWYER (February 1948), 27-32, 36; 4 JOURNAL OF THE MISSOURI BAR (February 1948), 17-18, 24.

The author discusses the fact that Lincoln's decision to become a lawyer was influenced by his logical and analytical mind and a natural aptitude for independent study. His law partnerships are described, and the locations of his offices. He includes information on Lincoln's riding the circuit, and notes the wide variety of actions. He refers to the Illinois Central Railroad case, the McCormick Reaper case, *McCormick v. Manny*, and the Sand-Bar case, *Johnston v. Jones & Marsh*. He speaks about other well publicized cases, such as *People v. Armstrong*; *Hurd v. Rock Island Bridge Company*. He discusses several versions of the Lincoln suit for collection of his $5000 fee from the Illinois Central

Railroad. He discusses Lincoln's fees, and quotes Lincoln in his notes for a law lecture.

Lincoln's Manual for Lawyers, compiled by Louis A. Warren, accompanies the Charbonneau article. (p. 29) An introduction indicates that the compilation is from Lincoln's notes for a lecture on law, and other original writings of Lincoln.

250
Chase, Charles M.
Lincoln Tries a Suit Well. 47 JOURNAL OF THE ILLINOIS STATE HISTORICAL SOCIETY (Spring 1954), 63-66.

"One of the best descriptions of Abraham Lincoln trying a case" was written by the author, who was editor of the *DeKalb County Sentinel*, when he served on the jury in the United States Circuit Court in Chicago. The defendant in the case of *Farni v. Tesson* was represented by Abraham Lincoln. Chase says "Lincoln tries a suit well," using humor, never making a big fight over a small point, and admits much but not enough to damage his case. "Lincoln is not a great lawyer but he is a good one." The author describes Lincoln's chief characteristics, as "candor, good nature and shrewdness."

251
Chittenden, L. E.
Lincoln as a Lawyer. 1 WEST VIRGINIA BAR (June 1894), 106-108.

The author suggests that a study of Lincoln will make one a better lawyer: ". . . and yet there are some lives which the lawyer cannot study attentively without becoming a better man and much better lawyer." Chittenden remarks that Lincoln also studied and prepared for a case, no matter how small. The author illustrates Lincoln's habit of thorough preparation by discussing the Armstrong murder case and the McCormick reaper patent case.

252
Chroust, Anton-Hermann.
Abraham Lincoln Argues a Pro-Slavery Case. 5 AMERICAN JOURNAL OF LEGAL HISTORY (October 1961), 299-308.

In this article Chroust is dealing with the 1847 case involving status of Kentucky slaves brought to work in Illinois under the Illinois fugitive slave laws. Lincoln was hired as a co-counsel to represent a Kentucky slave owner. Lincoln because of his antislavery stance was accused of "throwing the case" or at best presenting a "weak" case. The author refutes that argument by pointing out that

Lincoln displayed good courtroom tactics and argued the only possible point that favored his client. He raises the question of why Lincoln would accept such a case and concludes that the "slave issue had not yet seared itself into his conscience. . . ." Lincoln's argument is compared to an earlier case in which he had argued the opposite.

253
Chroust, Anton-Hermann.
Lincoln's Ability as a Lawyer. 53 ILLINOIS BAR JOURNAL (February 1965), 512-517.

The author praises Lincoln as a cross-examiner and trial lawyer who had few equals. Simplicity was his strong suit. He never "tried to shoot over the heads of his audience." The author states that Lincoln "was not only a most competent but also a most conscientious lawyer," well admired by his peers. He concludes that Lincoln's training as a lawyer prepared him more than anything else for the presidency.

254
Cleveland, Grover.
The Country Lawyer in National Affairs. THE YOUTH'S COMPANION (February 6, 1906), 63-64.

The ex-president of the United States Grover Cleveland discusses the virtues of lawyers' country practice, the eighteen lawyer presidents, and singles out Lincoln as "the greatest of them all." He says that he need not recite the deeds of Lincoln, then proceeds to suggest the reasons for the prominence of the country lawyer in public life. He believes legal study and practice in the country sharpen all these qualities. He recognizes the struggle a country lawyer has to make a living, and the number of practical things he must understand involving social and business interests. These conditions prepare such a lawyer to deal intelligently with the wide variety of questions in public life. The country lawyer has the advantage over the city lawyer where practice is more specialized. The country person develops more reliability from hard work and tenacity, without labor-saving devices. He believes that a country lawyer learns frugal ways, which influence his economic outlook in discharge of public duty.

255
Coleman, Charles H.
Historical Essays. Special Number EASTERN ILLINOIS UNIVERSITY BULLETIN (May 1962)
67 p.

Includes "Matson Slave Case," p. 31-40. Reprinted from *Abraham Lincoln and Coles County*, p. 104-111.

The author calls this case the most dramatic and controversial in Coles County Circuit Court in which Abraham Lincoln appeared. The case concerned the freedom of Jane Bryant, Negro, and her four children. Farmer Matson brought slaves from Kentucky annually to work in Coles County. Since they were not Illinois residents, he claimed they were not entitled to freedom, although Jane Bryant's husband, a foreman, was free because of year-round residency.

This article includes information on the *habeas corpus* proceedings. During the trial Lincoln argued only the technicalities and did not attempt to justify Matson's claim of equity or justice. The author believed that he took the case only as a professional obligation. One of the men who was being sued by Matson for sheltering his slaves had wanted Lincoln to represent him, but Lincoln had the prior commitment.

256
Cooper, Joseph H.
Abraham Lincoln Wasn't a Yuppie. 9 NATIONAL LAW JOURNAL (February 23, 1987), 13, 24.

The author claims that despite Lincoln's many successes he was never very successful at managing money. He did not have the temperament to do well in business, and spent a large part of his life in debt.

Although a well respected lawyer, he charged very modest fees; that distressed lawyers who practiced around him. Lincoln paid no more attention to dress than he did to his money. A lawyer who often saw Lincoln described him; "Attire and physical habits were on a plane with those of an ordinary farmer."

There were several instances when Lincoln would not charge his clients. Lincoln spoke of overly opportunistic lawyers as "catchem and cheatem."

The author discusses some of Lincoln's taxation policies, and concludes that Lincoln "was truly a man of conscience for whom fairness was the overriding consideration." Lincoln definitely "wasn't a Yuppie."

257
Dautch, Charles.
Abraham Lincoln Attorney-At-Law. 41 COMMERCIAL LAW JOURNAL (February 1936), 76-77.

After writing of Lincoln's early life, Dautch states that Abraham Lincoln was a good lawyer, and he wonders how he was able to reach trial and appellate courts as often as he did with additional involvement in politics. The court reports show that he was involved in important litigation in the development of the Middle West. The author discusses briefly several of his well-known cases, particularly *Illinois Central Railroad v. McLean County*, concerning assessment and taxation of railroad property within the county. In this case Lincoln's opposition included his former partners John T. Stuart and Stephen T. Logan. Although he lost the case in circuit court, his view was sustained in two arguments on appeal to the state supreme court. Lincoln later sued to collect his fee.

Other cases discussed in this brief article include: "Effie Afton"; *McCormick v. Manny*; *Bailey v. Cromwell*; the Matson case; the Fraim case; and a $3.00 pig case, which went to the state supreme court. Records of cases heard on appeal show that Lincoln won a substantial majority of his cases.

258
Dean, William J.
Abraham Lincoln: Pro Bono Digest. 199 NEW YORK LAW JOURNAL (February 11, 1988), 1, 36.

After outlining Lincoln's twenty-four years as a practicing lawyer, Dean explains that his clients ranged from humble farmers to powerful railroad corporations. Lincoln's practice included a wide range of legal matters, from actions of debt to criminal proceedings. He did his own legal research, and sometimes misplaced his correspondence. He had the reputation of being a leading member of the bar on the Eighth Judicial District.

Lincoln advised other young attorneys, assisting and encouraging them. He reminded one young colleague that his client's fate depends on "every word you utter."

Concerning fees, he was fair and realistic, and never charged an exorbitant fee. He advised lawyers not to accept the entire amount at the outset. However, he was forceful in collecting what he had earned. The author reviews several pro bono cases, Armstrong, Daimwood, Wright, and Scott.

259
Death of Lincoln: Proceedings of Bar and Supreme Court of Illinois on Death of Lincoln. 1 CHICAGO LEGAL NEWS (July 3, 1869), 349-350.

Resolutions of the bar and response by Mr. Justice Breese were in tribute to Abraham Lincoln by "the men with whom he had lived and labored, who knew him best and loved him most." This tribute remarked on his attributes with glowing praise and admiration.

260

Dedication of the Bronze Statue "Lincoln the Lawyer," 51 LINCOLN HERALD (June 1949), 2-17.

The statue of Lincoln the Lawyer was unveiled at Lincoln Memorial University on February 11, 1949. The article includes an illustration of the six-foot bronze statue, cast by Roman Bronze Works, Inc., of Corona, New York. Mounted on a pink marble base, it faces the Duke Hall of Citizenship, which housed the university's Lincoln collection. The statue depicts a young, beardless Lincoln as a barrister addressing the court. The sculptor seeks to immortalize this period portrayed by a lawyer in action. The introductory remarks by Robert L. Kincaid, president, tell of chartering the institution in 1897 as Lincoln Memorial University, and the resolution to establish a collection of Lincolniana. R. Gerald McMurtry presented an introduction of the sculptor, C. S. Paolo, who had intended to be present but had not arrived. President Kincaid read the advance copy of Paolo's speech.

The principal speaker, Carl W. Schaefer, indicated that they knew the statue would be beardless for that period of his legal career ended with his nomination for the presidency in 1860. The first portrait of Lincoln with a beard was in 1861. There was discussion of Lincoln's writing to a little girl in response to her advice that he grow whiskers.

Lincoln's admission to the bar was March 1, 1837, in the twenty-ninth year of his life. He was nominated for president in his fifty-first year. "We may take these dates as circumscribing his legal career, a period of twenty-three years." Almost half of his life was spent in the practice of law. His legal career ended with the case of *Dawson v. Ennis*, in the United States District Court, June 20, 1860.

Issued also as a separate, Harrogate, Tenn.: Lincoln Memorial University, 1949.

261

Dickson, W. M.

Lincoln at Cincinnati. 69 HARPER'S MAGAZINE (June 1884), 62-66. The Magazine of History, Extra no. 69 [i.e. 70] 1920.

Lincoln had been appointed original counsel in a patent suit involving the reaper. The argument was adjourned to Cincinnati from the United States Circuit Court for Northern Illinois.

Lincoln had prepared and looked forward to arguing against renowned Baltimore lawyer Reverdy Johnson. It had been understood that a Philadelphia lawyer, George Harding, well versed in the mechanics of reapers, would be associated with Lincoln. He was dismayed to find additional attorneys, Edwin M. Stanton of Pittsburgh and also a Cincinnati lawyer, appointed without his notification or consultation. Among the attorneys, the suggestion was made that only two represent the client. Lincoln, humiliated and mortified, acquiesced. He took little interest in the case, although he remained until its conclusion.

While in Cincinnati, he visited the county and city courts, and enjoyed a morning in superior court, where a unique judge presided. He wished aloud that the jovial judge were located in Illinois.

262

Donald, David.

Billy, You're Too Rampant. 3 ABRAHAM LINCOLN QUARTERLY (December 1945), 375-407.

This article tells of the Lincoln and Herndon association. They could count on each other, as exemplified by Lincoln's paying a fine for Herndon to keep him from going to jail.

When asked why he did not get another partner, Lincoln said that he knew Billy Herndon better than anyone, and intended to stick by him. Herndon was a good law partner and did not mind the office drudgery. Billy Herndon said that he did the reading and Abe did the thinking. There was only a minimum of friction between the two. Abraham Lincoln was noisy in reading his newspaper aloud, and Herndon suffered through repetitious stories and anecdotes. Herndon was impressed by the character of his senior partner.

Of Herndon's numerous projects and enthusiasm, Lincoln said, "Billy, you're too rampant and spontaneous." But, when Lincoln left for the office of president, he indicated that Herndon should leave their shingle up; and if he returned they would continue practicing.

263

Donald, David.

The True Story of "Herndon's Lincoln." 1 THE NEW COLOPHON (July 1948), 221-234.

Donald calls the book by this title the most controversial biography ever published. There were contradictory opinions, with some persons calling it "best" biography, others denouncing the work. He points out that Herndon's personality was complex, full of inconsistencies.

Donald explains how Herndon decided to prepare a biography, collecting with care into a "Lincoln Record" letters and statements from persons who had known Lincoln. Herndon's realistic lectures on the topic were unpopular, causing him to abandon the biography temporarily. By 1880, he had recruited Jesse Weik, of Indiana, and they began to draft their biography, which included a chapter on "Lincoln the Lawyer."

After completion, a reputable publisher could not be found to publish the book, finally a third-rate New York/Chicago firm, Belford, Clarke and Co. agreed. After problems with an uncooperative publisher, the three-volume biography came off the press in 1889. Donald enumerates later editions, including that of 1890; Appleton's two-volume edition, 1892; 1921 and 1922 editions, as well as a one-volume edition edited by Angle. He notes that at least twenty-five editions and imprints of the Herndon biography have appeared.

264
Dondero, George A.
Lincoln the Lawyer. 38 MICHIGAN STATE BAR JOURNAL (February 1959), 22-30.

This short article on Lincoln as a lawyer presents his court mannerisms against a background of history. Dondero describes several of Lincoln's cases, and delves into his finances. The author concludes that Lincoln "was one of the most unexplainable men of all time." Includes a chronology of Abraham Lincoln.

265
Drennan, John G.
A. Lincoln: Once Illinois Central Attorney. 10 ILLINOIS CENTRAL MAGAZINE (February 1922), 7-8.

Abraham Lincoln represented the Illinois Central Railroad often and served for many years. He assisted in getting the company's charter, although there was opposition to it. His association with the Illinois Central appeared to be independent of his law partnership. He was consulted frequently, as legal representative of the railroad, appearing before the Supreme Court of Illinois several times. He won an important tax case for which he presented a bill in the amount of $5,000 to the company. Officials knew that he deserved it, but did not want to pay it routinely, believing that the directors would consider it too large a sum. They agreed that Lincoln should sue them for it. This was a friendly suit, although it was rumored otherwise.

266
Duff, John J.
This Was a Lawyer. 52 JOURNAL OF THE ILLINOIS STATE HISTORICAL SOCIETY (Spring 1959), 146-163.

Duff says that "Lincoln legals" are still coming to light many years after his admission to the bar. His twenty-three years of arduous practice were between 1837 and 1860. He speaks of the range and variety of lawsuits on the Eighth Circuit, and Lincoln's adaptability to all forms of litigation. "Appeals from justices' courts to the circuit court, from the circuit court to the state supreme court, appeals to the United States Supreme Court, actions in foreclosure, debt, replevin, trespass, partition, suretyship, actions for specific performance suits over dower rights, slander and divorce actions, suits to compel stockholders to pay their assessments, personal injury actions, suits involving patent infringements, will contests, actions seeking injunctions, actions to impress mechanics liens." His criminal cases involved offenses ranging from gambling to murder. Lincoln had ability as a draftsman of important legal papers.

This article also provides information on Lincoln's sitting in the place of judges at trials. It tells of his strange and unaccountable ways, but stresses that he was a man of integrity, and among the two or three most sought after practitioners by resident attorneys.

267

Duncan, R. Bruce.
Where Lincoln Practiced Law in Edgar County. 72 LINCOLN HERALD (Winter 1970), 145-147.

The president of Duncan Galleries tells of a rare half-plate ambrotype discovered in Paris, Illinois. Originally Lincoln was believed to be in the crowd scene. Later it was identified as a picture taken at a later date at the Edgar County Courthouse where Lincoln had practiced law, but the building was almost exactly as he had known it.

268

Dunn, Jesse J.
Lincoln the Lawyer [Delivered at the Amalgamated Bar Association]. 14 AMERICAN LAWYER (March 1906), 99-103; 4 OKLAHOMA LAW JOURNAL (January 1906), 215-222, (February 1906), 249-260.

In his speech, Dunn chronicles the history of Lincoln as an Illinois lawyer, calling attention to his courtroom demeanor, and personal characteristics. He uses Lincoln as an illustration of what a poor, undereducated person can accomplish. Lincoln's political debates and speeches were a product of his legal training. The author concludes that Lincoln the president, emancipator, orator, and statesman acquired his power, wisdom, and virtue from his training at the bar as Lincoln the lawyer.

269

E. J.
Lincoln as a Lawyer. 17 LAW NOTES (February 1914), 204-205.

The author, identified only by his initials, explores Lincoln as a lawyer and questions whether his law activities tarnish the halo bestowed upon the head of the "Great Emancipator." Lincoln made frequent appearances before the Supreme Court of Illinois, 164 cases in all, 86 of which he won. Lincoln was often associated with other counsel in these cases, perhaps because he was situated in Springfield where the cases were tried. He mentions Lincoln's contemporaries at the Illinois bar such as Stephen T. Logan, Stephen A. Douglas, Lyman Trumbull, David Davis, and E. B. Washburne.

The author discusses several of Lincoln's cases before the bar, including *Bailey v. Cromwell* where Lincoln argued that there was no consideration for a note to purchase a slave if papers were not produced to show title for the slave. The presumption of law was that every person was free, and the sale of a free person was void. The article also discusses the case of *State v. Illinois Central Railroad Co.* where Lincoln represented a powerful railroad's interest.

The author concludes by wondering what heights Lincoln could have achieved as a lawyer if he had forgone a political career.

270
East, Ernest E.
Lincoln and the Peoria French Claims. 42 JOURNAL OF THE ILLINOIS STATE HISTORICAL SOCIETY. (March 1949), 41-56.

Abraham Lincoln was counsel in four or more cases concerning the question of legal title to lots that had been in possession of American settlers. Congress was making restitution to former inhabitants of Peoria. Lincoln unexpectedly entered such a case by substituting for Peoria Attorney Ballance in his absence. The ejectment suit as described in this article was not decided until sixteen years later; the date when Lincoln became involved was believed to have been 1853. A facsimile of Lincoln's letter to the surveyor general is included.

271
East, Ernest E.
The Melissa Goings Murder Case. 46 JOURNAL OF THE ILLINOIS STATE HISTORICAL SOCIETY (Spring 1953), 79-83.

The record of this case, is "not found in the books on Lincoln as a lawyer." Lincoln was a practical lawyer, willing to lean on public sentiment when it disagreed with the strict letter of the law. The defendant in a murder case, Mrs. Goings, was granted time for a conference with her attorney, Abraham Lincoln, before selection of the jury. She disappeared from the courthouse and was never seen again. The woman remained a fugitive from justice, with no pursuit, and it was ordered that the murder case be stricken from the record. There was little doubt that Lincoln had indicated to the prosecuting attorney that no harm would be done if the aged wife of the murder victim were permitted to go free.

272
The Eighth Judicial District--1847. 463 LINCOLN LORE (February 21, 1938), [1].

Lincoln marked a map with red lines, indicating the Eighth Judicial District route over which he traveled in 1847. A verbatim transcript of Lincoln's memorandum dealing with the Eighth Judicial District is included.

273
The Expurgated Text of Herndon's Lincoln. 207 LINCOLN LORE (March 27, 1933), [1].

No book has been more severely criticized that the biography of Lincoln by William Herndon. It has been favorably mentioned by other critics. When a three-volume work was reduced to two in a later edition, the inference was that historical data unfavorable to Lincoln were omitted. However, the two-volume edition actually had 43 more pages of text, the "so-called expurgated edition" was actually enlarged. The few deletions included paragraphs concerning Lincoln's ancestry, some reminiscences of his boyhood, and an instance of burlesque verse attributed to Lincoln. The first edition contained superior illustrations.

274
Falcone, Flynn.
Lincoln's Legal Partnerships. 40 ILLINOIS HISTORY (February 1987), 104-105.

This high-school student's essay, selected for publication, presents a brief synopsis of Lincoln's early education and discusses Lincoln's relationship with his three law partners, John Todd Stuart, Stephen T. Logan, and William Herndon. Under Stuart, Lincoln gained valuable experience; Logan taught him "the value of thoroughness and precision"; and Lincoln's junior partner, Herndon, handled the affairs of the law firm so Lincoln could pursue his political career. Falcone discusses briefly Lincoln's well-known cases of Truett, Fraim, Trailor and Thomas C. Browne. The author concludes, "Much is owed to Lincoln's partners in law who contributed to the molding of one of the greatest men in American history."

275
Ferguson, Duncan.
True Story of the Almanac Used by Abraham Lincoln in the Famous Trial of Duff Armstrong. 15 JOURNAL OF THE ILLINOIS STATE HISTORICAL SOCIETY (October 1922-January 1923), 688-691.

The author is concerned that no one took the trouble to clear Lincoln's name in speculations that he altered an almanac for use in the famous defense of Duff Armstrong at Beardstown for the murder of Metzker at a camp meeting. The almanac produced by Lincoln showed that there was insufficient moonlight for the witness to have seen the fatal blow.

To clear Lincoln's name, the author uses information gathered by James N. Gridley in a letter of reply from Professor of Astronomy Joel Stebbins of the University of Illinois. He provides details on the quarter of the moon, exact meridian, with latitude and longitude, at the precise minute of the murder. He shows that although a moon was in sight, it did not change Lincoln's honesty and victory, for it was not over the meridian according to sworn testimony by the prosecution's witness.

276

Fifer, Joseph W.
Lincoln--His Historic Lost Speech. 35 COMMERCIAL LAW JOURNAL (December 1930), 715-721.

The author, who began his law practice in 1869, knew many of the men who had associated with Lincoln. From them he picked up the story of Lincoln's "lost speech." The speech was given in 1856 at the first Republican convention upon the forming of a new party. The speech concerned the destruction of the Union. Some say it was the greatest speech they ever heard. But it was never written down or recorded.

The author contends that even if it were written, the effect would not be the same as having been there to hear it. He then tells of some of Lincoln's speeches that he personally heard.

277

Fitzgerald, Mavournee.
"With This Case and Abe Lincoln": Illinois' Prairie Politician Was the Best Jury Lawyer of His Day. 3 TEXAS BAR JOURNAL (February 1940), 51-52, 86.

Abraham Lincoln "one of America's greatest trial lawyers--perhaps her greatest . . . in the examination and cross-examination of witnesses, and in the art of getting across to the jury the simple, unadorned facts of his case, he had no peer. Every anecdote, each dramatic court room scene had a direct bearing on the issue in question and was more eloquent than a series of citations in stating his cause." The author illustrates this point with the libel case where Lincoln in defending his client, laughed so hard he infected the court and jury with laughter. Sympathy for the plaintiff was forgotten and the damage award paltry compared to the sum asked.

Fitzgerald contends that Lincoln was successful because he presented facts in a simple and natural way. He concentrated on principal points in a case brushing aside nonessentials, and his great gift of storytelling drove home his arguments. Fitzgerald tells a number of Lincoln anecdotes and discusses several of his cases including the Matson slave case trial.

278
Ford, Paul V.
The Crime That Baffled Lincoln. CHICAGO SUNDAY TRIBUNE GRAPHIC MAGAZINE (11 February 1951), 3, 14-15.

The Trailor case baffled Lincoln. There was the question as to why Henry Trailor confessed to a murder plot, involving himself and his two brothers. Lincoln, who was one of the defense lawyers, described the mood of Springfield in a letter to a friend. Archibald Fisher had disappeared under mysterious circumstances. One brother confessed to the crime, but implicated his two brothers. Then Dr. Gilmore entered, saying Fisher was alive; he planted sufficient doubt so that the Trailors were discharged. Three days later Fisher appeared in Springfield. The law firm was never paid for this case.

279
Ford, William D.
"Abe" Lincoln the Lawyer. 25 NATIONAL REPUBLIC (February 1938), 13-15, 30.

Lincoln created the familiar phrase, "You can fool all of the people some of the time and some of the people all of the time, but you cannot fool all of the people all of the time." The article provides description of lawyers and judges traveling together to the courthouses on the circuit. A bit of horseplay brings chuckles as the young lawyers played a joke on Judge Davis. There are summaries of several cases in which Lincoln was involved during his circuit tours. During Lincoln's career, he appeared in 176 cases in the Supreme Court of Illinois and won 92 of them. Ford describes the outstanding cases of Rock Island Bridge, McCormick Reaper, *Illinois Central Railroad v. McLean County*, and Duff Armstrong. He quotes Lord Shaw [of Dunfermline] in saying that Lincoln was one of five of the most able lawyers in history.

280
Fowle, Frank F.
A Famous Interference Case: Lincoln and the Bridge. 14 NATIONAL ELECTRIC LIGHT ASSOCIATION BULLETIN (October 1927), 613-622.

Against the historical background of the Mississippi Valley, Western rivers, railroads, steamboats and a controversial bridge, the author tells the story of the steamboat "Effie Afton" colliding with the bridge fifteen days after its opening. The section dealing with the "Lawsuit Against the Bridge Company" tells how Chicago attorney Norman B. Judd, said that Abraham Lincoln was the only man who could win the case. Fowle singles out Lincoln's past involvement in rivers, and ferries, and his background in the Illinois Central Railroad litigation, although he does not declare him a specialist in transportation law. He quotes from Frederick Trevor Hill in his comments on handling of the bridge case. Also, Fowle provides an early engineer's reminiscence of the trial. Quotations from Lincoln's legal argument, which were printed verbatim in the Chicago *Daily Press*, appear in the article.

281
Fox, Edward J.
The Influence of the Law in the Life of Abraham Lincoln. PENNSYLVANIA BAR ASSOCIATION (1925), 349-364.

The Honorable Edward J. Fox in an annual address before the association notes that the tendency during the 1925 era was to have a businessman in the Oval Office instead of a lawyer. Yet at a time of great crisis in this country the fact that a lawyer was at the head of government did much to carry the nation through crisis. The author claims, "My study of his life leads me to believe that it was his pre-eminent ability as a lawyer which was the foundation of his success as a statesman. . . ."

Fox then discusses Lincoln's early life and describes events that influenced Lincoln toward the practice of law. He tells of Lincoln's legal training through partnerships with Stuart and Logan. Lincoln was developing his skill and ability as a lawyer by traveling the Eighth Judicial Circuit from 1849-1860 acting much as an "English Barrister" being called upon by various lawyers to try cases for them. Fox noted, "He attained such distinction at the bar that he was speedily taken into all the important litigation in the Illinois courts." Lincoln's ability and skill as a lawyer enabled him to stand with Douglas in their debates, and influenced friends and colleagues to "insist upon his nomination for the Presidency." This legal ability served Lincoln well when he was confronted with constitutional and international issues.

282
Fox, Edward J.
The Influence of the Law in the Life of Abraham Lincoln. 33 CASE AND COMMENT (Pocket edition) (Jan./Feb./Mar. 1927), 2-6.

This article contains extracts from 1925 Pennsylvania Bar Association 349-364. It is a condensed version of the address by Fox to the association, 1925. An illustration of "The Seventy Volumes of the Lincoln-Herndon Law Library" accompanies the *Case and Comment* article.

For annotation see **Fox** above.

283
Frank, John P.
Lincoln as a Lawyer. 24 NEVADA STATE BAR JOURNAL (April 1959), 82-95.

A speech by John P. Frank before the Nevada State Bar described Lincoln's life as a lawyer. He comments on how Lincoln was "no more a neat and orderly lawyer, than he was a neat and orderly man." Yet as a jury lawyer simplicity was Lincoln's strongest point. Frank remarks on Lincoln's extraordinary ability to find the basic issue and stick to it. The author believes Lincoln was at his maximum effectiveness as a jury lawyer.

284
Friend, Henry C.
Abraham Lincoln and a Missing Promissory Note. 54 AMERICAN BAR ASSOCIATION JOURNAL (September 1968), 863-865; 73 COMMERCIAL LAW JOURNAL (November 1968), 349-351.

A promissory note was made to Joshua Speed, the storekeeper who once housed Lincoln. The maker of the note, Judge Thomas C. Browne, was a member of the Supreme Court of Illinois, a man Lincoln had represented in impeachment proceedings. The author tells the story of the note and Lincoln's attempt to enforce it.

285
Friend, Henry C.
Abraham Lincoln and Commercial Law--Returning Claims. 51 CASE AND COMMENT (July-August 1946), 12-15; 51 COMMERCIAL LAW JOURNAL (March 1946), 45-46.

Friend discusses some aspects of Lincoln's active practice in commercial law. He shows how Lincoln handled criticisms of less than prompt reporting to his clients by writing to them with care and diligence, thereby upholding his professional reputation.

286
Friend, Henry C.
Abraham Lincoln and the National Intelligencer: The Lawyer's Dilemma. 64
COMMERCIAL LAW JOURNAL (February 1959), 42.

In 1849 Lincoln was a member of the Whig party. He was asked by a client
to undertake a substantial claim against Gales and Seaton, publishers of the
National Intelligencer, which spoke for the Whig party. Lincoln accepted the task.
There is a discussion of the letter he sent to collect the debt.

287
Friend, Henry C.
Abraham Lincoln as a Receiving Attorney: Kelly vs. Blackledge.   54
COMMERCIAL LAW JOURNAL (February 1949), 27-30.

This article concerns a case Lincoln handled involving an Ohio judgment
of default on a promissory note. The defendant had moved to Illinois and
Lincoln was asked to pursue the judgment.

288
Friend, Henry C.
Abraham Lincoln's Trust Account. 67 COMMERCIAL LAW JOURNAL
(February 1962), 40.

In this brief article, Friend tells of Lincoln's trust account in which he
deposited his clients' comingled funds. In the task of liquidation as a result of
dissolving the Stuart & Lincoln partnership, Lincoln found an unexplained
surplus of money. He made written record of putting the surplus into his pocket.
". . . not knowing exactly to whom it belongs, I have put in my pocket, holding
myself responsible to whomever may hereafter prove to be the owner." The
author speculates about the origin of the surplus funds, and provides typescript
of several of Lincoln's notes regarding his trust accounts.

289
Gernon, Blaine Brooks.
Chicago and Abraham Lincoln. 27 JOURNAL OF THE ILLINOIS STATE
HISTORICAL SOCIETY (October 1934), 243-284.

For annotation see **Gernon**, Monographs.

290
Gilbert, Barry.
Attorney for William Baker Gilbert. 46 JOURNAL OF THE ILLINOIS STATE
HISTORICAL SOCIETY (Autumn 1953), 290-293.

This article is about the author's father, William Baker Gilbert, when he
was a senior at Shurtleff College, Alton, Illinois. He was suspended from the
college after the college president observed him at a French New Year's
celebration in St. Louis. Although his father and grandfather sought
reinstatement of Gilbert, the faculty refused to readmit him.

When he sought help from the law firm of Lincoln and Herndon, Lincoln
outlined plans for two suits against the college: reinstatement and $3000 in
damages. The faculty voted to reinstate the student, only after they were notified
to appear in the United States Circuit Court. The father refused to let his son
reenter and ordered Lincoln to file papers in a trespass suit for damages.

The case was postponed each term and never brought to trial. Young
Gilbert was attending Harvard Law School by the time the case was dropped.

291
Goldsmith, Harry.
Abraham Lincoln, Invention and Patents. 20 JOURNAL OF THE PATENT
OFFICE SOCIETY (January 1938), 5-33.

Abraham Lincoln in a lecture, "Discoveries and Inventions," stated, "The
patent system added the fuel of interest to the fire of genius." Goldsmith claims
that Lincoln not only had a great interest in science, invention, and patents but
that he was deeply affected by the subject. Lincoln was the only patentee
president of the United States. He was granted a patent in 1849 for a device that
buoyed vessels over shoals. The author describes in some detail the invention
and Lincoln's efforts to secure a patent on it. Lincoln never made any profit
from his invention. He was retained as counsel in at least five lawsuits involving
patents. The last case he ever tried involved a patent. It was said that while
Lincoln rode the circuit he often studied geometry and algebra. He also went
to any scientific shows that happened to be in the town where he was staying as
he rode the circuit.

Lincoln's first case involving patent was *Parker v. Hoyt*, in which he
defended a man against charges of infringement on a waterwheel patent. His
most famous case involving a patent was *McCormick v. Manny*, known as the
"reaper case." It involved the Cyrus H. McCormick Co. suing Manny for
infringement of patents on various components of the reaper. As the case had
implications for all independent reaper manufactures, they joined Manny in his
fight, hiring the two most able patent attorneys of their day. Lincoln, of
Springfield, was hired by the defense as a popular local attorney. Lincoln "had
prepared with perhaps greater thoroughness than ever in his life, to argue this

immensely important case." However, he was shunned by the famous patent lawyers who did not allow him to speak or use his arguments. Instead of sulking, Lincoln resolved to refine his study of law to match the college-bred lawyers of the East.

The last case Lincoln tried, *Dawson v. Ennis*, was also a patent case, which Lincoln, representing the plaintiff, lost. The author concludes, "Lincoln may have been unsuccessful as an inventor, equally so as a patent lawyer. But his failures never led him to lose faith in the Patent System or in invention as a benefactor of man kind and the driving force of progress."

292

Goodhart, Arthur Lehman.
Lincoln and the Law. 50 AMERICAN BAR ASSOCIATION JOURNAL (May 1964), 433-441.

Lincoln was the only lawyer-president to enter the office directly from the practice of law. The author contends that Lincoln's training in the law explains his masterful use of language, analytical approach to national problems, and his ability to stretch the Constitution during the Civil War yet preserve the people's liberties.

This article deals with Lincoln's law training, the few law books he studied and mastered, and how he incorporated this training into the problems he faced as president.

293

Gridley, James Norman.
Lincoln's Defense of Duff Armstrong. 3 JOURNAL OF THE ILLINOIS STATE HISTORICAL SOCIETY (April 1910), 24-44.

The author, upon hearing and reading several versions of the "Armstrong Murder Case" including testimony about the position of the moon, and whether Lincoln altered an almanac, decided to investigate himself.

Gridley researched the position of the moon at that point in time. He interviewed the lone surviving juror to the trial, John T. Brady, and Armstrong's brother, and also examined the record of the trial. He states the facts of the case, and presents proceedings of the trial itself.

Lincoln, an old friend of the Armstrong family, agreed to defend Duff Armstrong, the accused. The key to the case was Lincoln's refuting the testimony of the state's witness, who claimed he saw the murder by the light of the moon. Lincoln introduced an almanac showing that the moon was not out at that time.

The piece includes a statement of juror, Brady, given in his own words. This article provides an account of events of the trial from people who were actually there.

294

Grosboll, P. P.
Reminiscences of P. P. Grosboll. Contributed by Colby Beekman. 14 JOURNAL OF THE ILLINOIS STATE HISTORICAL SOCIETY (April 1921), 90-91.

Lincoln was surveying in the vicinity of Petersburg, Illinois. When he went to dinner at a log cabin occupied by the justice of the peace, he found that a court session was about to begin. The case involved an orphan girl, who had been betrayed by the nephew of the justice. The young man had a lawyer from Beardstown while the girl had no representation until Lincoln volunteered. He said that he was not a regular lawyer, but had been reading law. "In this room, Abe tried and won his first case long before he began to practice law, taking as he always did, the right side of the case."

295

Grupp, George W.
The Railroads and Abe Lincoln. 4 RAILROAD PROGRESS (February 1951), 2-8.

Abraham Lincoln's interest in railroads dated back to his early years when he saw the hardships of the pioneers. When in the legislature, he voted for measures that promoted railroad construction.

A year after the Illinois Central Railroad was granted its charter, James F. Joy secured Lincoln's services as the Springfield attorney for the railroad. Acting on behalf of the corporation, he handled cases involving "land rights, stock subscriptions, personal injuries, losses of cattle and taxes." Two of Lincoln's most important railroad cases were *Illinois Central Railroad v. McLean County* and the "Effie Afton" case.

296

Gunderson, Robert Gray.
"Stoutly Argufy": Lincoln's Legal Speaking. Address at Annual Meeting. Lincoln Fellowship of Wisconsin, Madison, February 12, 1962. No. 21 LINCOLN FELLOWSHIP OF WISCONSIN. HISTORICAL BULLETIN (1963), 1-14; 46 WISCONSIN MAGAZINE OF HISTORY (Autumn 1962), 109-117.

Lincoln's legal career began before he was admitted to the bar on March 1, 1837. In the early 1830s he drafted legal documents for neighbors, as well as legislative documents in the Illinois General Assembly.

Gunderson discusses Lincoln's disorderly and careless law-office procedures, and his life on the Eighth Circuit. He talks of Lincoln's oratorical skills at trial and in speechmaking, where he was known for brevity, economy, and clarity. He tells of Lincoln's many cases ranging from "insignificant squabbles to major questions of public policy." He concludes that Lincoln's principal training to be a great president came from the courtrooms of the Eighth Circuit. His companions during that time were largely responsible for his nomination and election.

297

Halbert, Marvin R.

Lincoln Was a Lawyer First, Politician Second. 8 PENNSYLVANIA LAW JOURNAL REPORTER (October 14, 1985), 10-11.

The author, judge and Lincoln admirer, conducts an interview with Leonard S. Wissow, a past president of the Lincoln Association. Wissow notes that although twenty-three presidents were lawyers "only one of them was a lawyer who happened to be a President." Until Richard Nixon became president, Lincoln was the only one to have gone from law office to presidency. He claims studies of Lincoln show he practiced his skill obtained as a lawyer while in the presidency. "If it is asked how a lawyer thinks, the answer would be, like Abraham Lincoln."

Wissow remarks that Lincoln's law practice was varied with emphasis on criminal and railroad cases. Robert Todd Lincoln was the only one of his children, who, when he reached maturity, carried on Lincoln's law talents as a successful Chicago attorney. Wissow believes that some of Lincoln's advice is still valid for today's attorneys, "Discourage litigation," and "Resolve to be honest at all events."

298

Harper, Ellahue Ansile.

Lincoln the Lawyer. 28 DICKINSON LAW REVIEW (January 1924), 95-112.

This article, which is written in a biblical sense, provides a somewhat different perspective of Lincoln as a lawyer. Harper points out Lincoln's association with many great men of the time who happened to be in the Springfield area. This assisted in his legal training. The author stresses Lincoln's honesty and dignity in his profession, and discusses some of Lincoln's cases.

299
Harris, Gibson William.
My Recollections of Abraham Lincoln. 28 FARM AND FIRESIDE. (December 1, 1904), 22-23; (December 15, 1904), 24, 28; (January 1, 1905), 24-25; (January 15, l905), 24-25; (February 1, 1905), 24.

The author was a law student in Lincoln and Herndon's office from 1845 through 1847. This series of articles appeared with a first-hand account of life within the law office. Harris shares details that only a person in such a position would know.

(December 1, 1904)
Although Lincoln took up law as a means of livelihood, his heart was in politics. During Lincoln's partnership with Herndon, he spoke for the firm as senior partner while Herndon, the junior partner, drew up pleas and other papers. Lincoln was very courteous to young lawyers who were his opponents as well as to others.

(December 15, 1904)
When telling stories, Lincoln was always instructive, entertaining, and almost always amusing. Lincoln used body language when telling stories to enhance the story's effect.

(January 1, 1905)
There was a case in which three brothers were not found guilty of murder as accused; the alleged victim was not actually dead. This was the theory Lincoln maintained throughout his defense of them.

Traveling the circuit involved sleeping in wretched hotel accommodations. The food at the taverns was often badly cooked. Frequently the roads became impassable following the spring thaw.

The Lincoln & Herndon office on the second floor of the post office consisted of one large room. They had a very moderate number of books. The furniture was in poor condition. Although Lincoln frequently told humorous stories, he never did so in his office. His reasoning for this is that an attorney's "den" is about the last place for genial humor.

(January 15, 1905)
Lincoln was a master of the English language, utilizing a large vocabulary. Any information given by a client to Lincoln was always kept in the utmost confidence. Lincoln would never represent a person when he was in the wrong. During the initial consultation, Lincoln would ask the client to tell the weak points in the case because the strong points would take care of themselves. Lincoln's statement of facts was often more powerful than the sworn testimony of witnesses.

(February 1, 1905)
When courts were not in session, the senior partner (Lincoln) spent more time out of the office than in it. He usually was on the street corner discussing the topics of the day with others. When Lincoln tested people for the bar, he did so on principles of law and was lax on pleading and rules of evidence.

300
Hay, Logan.
Lincoln's Attitude Toward the Supreme Court and the Dred Scott Decision.
ILLINOIS STATE BAR ASSOCIATION ANNUAL REPORT (1937), 90-100.

This address by the former president of the Abraham Lincoln Association and of the Illinois State Bar Association examined Lincoln's criticism of the Dred Scott decision. Hay explained that Lincoln believed the Supreme Court would mold its opinions in accord with the prevalent popular view. He sought to reverse the decision through agitation. "This democratic element in the development of common law was a part of Lincoln's background in his practice as a lawyer at the Illinois bar." He quotes another member of the bar in stating that honest and constructive criticism of court decisions should be encouraged, and out of such criticism and discussion the prevailing public opinion will ultimately find expression in court decisions. Such an evolutionary process was the justification for Lincoln's attitude upon the Dred Scott decision, development or modification of law through the democratic process being consistent with the American system of jurisprudence.

301
Haycraft, Julius E.
Lincoln, the Lawyer-Statesman (Address). 33 LAW NOTES (April 1929), 3; 32 LAW NOTES (March 1929), 238-239; 12 MINNESOTA LAW REVIEW (Supp. 1927), 100-111.

The author notes that ninety years have passed since Lincoln was admitted to the bar. "The most forceful, if not the only, argument adduced against the American Bar Association standard for admission to the bar is that it would have excluded Abraham Lincoln." The body of law had grown [by 1929] beyond recognition of Lincoln's time. What was adequate preparation then is no longer true. In addition law schools are more numerous. If Lincoln were alive at this time, it is possible that he would have the opportunity to pursue a law career. The author concludes that if the ABA rules exclude "one Lincoln and a thousand shysters, it may be said to have worked well."

302
Heintz, Michael G.
Cincinnati Reminiscences of Lincoln. 9 BULLETIN OF THE HISTORICAL
AND PHILOSOPHICAL SOCIETY OF OHIO (April 1951), 113-120.

The first record of Abraham Lincoln's visit to Cincinnati is from a letter
written by him on December 25, 1849, addressed to Peter Hitchcock, judge of
the supreme court at Columbus. He explained that he had come to Cincinnati
to see why some briefs had not been filed in a lawsuit, regarding damages to a
client's steamboat in collision on the Ohio River. Lincoln's name does not
appear in the published report. The suit was decided in the same term during
which Lincoln's letter was written. All court papers regarding the case were
missing.

Lincoln's longest sojourn in Cincinnati was for the *McCormick v. Manny*
case, when Lincoln prepared and offered his brief, only to be ignored. He
received a check, which he accepted only upon insistence of his client. Following
the trial he spent several days visiting the Cincinnati area. Other visits to this
city were for campaign speeches, and on the way to his inauguration in
Washington.

303
[Herriott, Frank Irving]
Abraham Lincoln and His Clients. 9 ANNALS OF IOWA. Series 3 (April 1910),
389-391.

This editorial speaks of the relationship of Abraham Lincoln to his clients.
He would refuse to accept retainers, whatever the client's station in life, if a case
was based on fraud. He did not hesitate to drop a case if he had been
misinformed regarding its merits.

The facsimile of a brief letter, dated October 27, 1852, in Lincoln's
handwriting, is used to illustrate another phase of his conduct as a lawyer. In a
case for which he was hired to collect on a note from a poor man, he extended
time for the debtor to locate unlikely evidence rather than press for judgment,
which he could have obtained. He was obviously sympathetic toward the
unfortunate man. Herriott suggests that Lincoln neglected and disregarded his
client's interest. The conclusion of the case is unknown.

304
Hertz, Emanuel.
Abraham Lincoln: His Law Partners, Clerks, and Office Boys. 44 THE
MAGAZINE OF HISTORY, WITH NOTES AND QUERIES. Extra Number
173.

For annotation see **Hertz,** Monographs.

305

Hertz, Emanuel.

Abraham Lincoln: The Jurist of the Civil War. 14 NEW YORK UNIVERSITY LAW QUARTERLY REVIEW (May 1937), 473-501.

    This article tells how Lincoln used fables and stories to stress a point, clarifying vividly by using illustrations. The author is disappointed that so many of Lincoln's anecdotes and stories were either never recorded or recorded only to be lost or destroyed. He compares Lincoln to Shakespeare and Aesop.

    It was Lincoln's practice to state the case of his opposition and then his own. The article gives illustrations of Lincoln's use of stories to help the jury see his point of view. One example given was in Lincoln's representing a defendant in a case with the plaintiff suing for assault/battery. Although the plaintiff was the initial aggressor, he claims the defendant used too much force in self-defense. Lincoln gave an analogy of a farm dog's attacking a man carrying a pitchfork. The man accidentally killed the dog while protecting himself.

    The article explains problems Lincoln faced as president confronting a rebellion of his own people, in terms of the powers of the presidency in light of the Constitution. The article examines some of the decisions Lincoln had to make during the Civil War and how he enlarged his executive powers as perhaps no other president before him.

306

Hertz, Emanual.

Lawyer Lincoln, by Albert A. Woldman. [Book review] 11 ST. JOHN'S LAW REVIEW (April 1937), 354-359.

For annotation see **Hertz,** Monographs.

307

Hertz, Emanuel.

Lincoln as a Lawyer. 43 CASE AND COMMENT (October 1937), 5-9; 7 LAW SOCIETY JOURNAL (May 1937), 778-783.

    The author speaks of the long hours Lincoln worked as a lawyer with a multitude of cases and a great variety of clients. Hertz calls him a "creative lawyer" who would have left a deep imprint on American law even if he had never been elected president. He used cases to illustrate how Lincoln used simple yet convincing arguments.

308

Hertz, Emanuel.
Lincoln the Lawyer. 71 UNITED STATES LAW REVIEW (February 1937), [79]-102.

Hertz, a renowned author on the subject of Abraham Lincoln, writes, "Lincoln was not merely a lawyer who became president. He was a great lawyer who continued to be a great lawyer when he served the nation as president. . . ." He notes that the variety of cases Lincoln handled was remarkable, "He was the ideal all-around lawyer." "Lincoln was unquestionably a great advocate, a great master of the law." Judges, jurors, and lawyers praised his abilities, fairness, and honesty. The depth of Lincoln's ability is illustrated by his being able to solve great constitutional and international problems he later faced as president. What he practiced as a lawyer, he applied as president, such as presenting the arguments of the other side before stating his own.

While most authors have discussed Lincoln's law career during his law practice days, this author contends that the most important part of Lincoln's law career began with the assumption of the presidency, noting that the problems of Lincoln's presidency were largely legal problems. As a legal expert he dealt with them. He had to wrestle with constitutional questions concerning secession, slavery, and war powers. The author discusses further in some detail the interaction among Lincoln, Congress, and the United States Supreme Court on various constitutional issues. The article studies Lincoln in relation to important constitutional issues, and looks at Lincoln's handling of international law issues.

309

Hertz, Emanuel.
Lincoln the Lawyer. Reprint of NEW YORK TIMES (7 February 1937), Sect. 8, pp. 6, 13, "When Lincoln the Lawyer Rode the Circuit." 81 CONGRESSIONAL RECORD, Pt. 9, Appendix, 192-194; 8 BIOGRAPHY: A DIGEST MAGAZINE (June 1937), 7-13.

On March 1, 1837, Lincoln was admitted to the Illinois bar. Lincoln's legal career started in the law offices of Major John Stuart. The author claims Lincoln worked long and hard at the law. Usually working as a trial lawyer, Lincoln was known for his "calm, logical, always fair minded way." The author states that Lincoln was a "great creative lawyer who would have left his deep imprint on American law even if he had never been elected to any public office."

Lincoln explained his argument fairly, directly, and simply. "There was no such thing as misunderstanding Lincoln. The bailiff could comprehend him as well as the judge."

Lincoln knew the law and was always prepared for his cases. Hertz lists areas of law in which Lincoln practiced, and gives examples of how Lincoln worked. Lincoln's knowledge of the law served him well in the White House.

Hertz, Emanuel.
When Lincoln the Lawyer Rode the Circuit. See preceding entry, **Hertz**, Lincoln the Lawyer.

310
Hickey, James T.
A New Lincoln Letter on the Alton and Sangamon Railroad Cases. 65 JOURNAL OF THE ILLINOIS STATE HISTORICAL SOCIETY (Spring 1972), 101-102.

Hickey discusses cases in which Lincoln represented the Alton and Sangamon Railroad in 1851 and 1852, involving subscribers who refused to pay for railroad stock after the railroad changed location or right-of-way. A letter is transcribed within the text.

311
Hickey, James T.
A Small Receipt Reveals a Large Story. 75 JOURNAL OF THE ILLINOIS STATE HISTORICAL SOCIETY (Spring 1982), 73-80.

Joshua F. Speed entrusted several financial matters to his friend and attorney, Abraham Lincoln. Their correspondence of the 1840s is presently housed in the Illinois State Historical Library. The library received an unpublished Lincoln document in 1982, a receipt written by Lincoln. The article contains a facsimile of the receipt in Lincoln's hand.

There was foreclosure against William Walters, Lincoln's neighbor, and one of the leading Democrats in Springfield. He was also editor and publisher of the *Illinois State Register*, and public printer for the State of Illinois. To settle accounts of Speed and Van Bergen, Lincoln brought suit in Sangamon County Circuit Court for Bergen against Walters. Walters did not lose his house because Lincoln arranged to purchase the property for Speed, who agreed to hold it until Walters could afford to buy it back. "We foreclosed on Walter's house and lots & sold them and bought them in in [sic] your name."

312
Hicks, Ratcliff.
Abraham Lincoln as an Advocate. 47 CENTURY MAGAZINE (n.s. 25) (February 1894), 638.

The author spent some time with the Hon. David Davis, then a justice of the Supreme Court of the United States in 1881. He asked him the secret to Lincoln's success as a lawyer. Davis told the story of a time when he was circuit court judge in Illinois to illustrate "the honesty and integrity of Abraham Lincoln as a lawyer." Lincoln and another lawyer, Leonard Swett, were defending two boys charged with murder. Lincoln, believing the boys guilty and the state's witnesses as trustworthy, wanted to plead guilty to manslaughter. The second lawyer would have nothing of the sort, wanting to defend the boys to the end. Since Lincoln did not believe his clients, he had Swett argue the case. He did; it went to the jury, and the men were acquitted. The following day, Lincoln offered his fee of $500 to Swett, saying that he had not earned it himself.

313
Hill, Frederick Trevor.
Lincoln the Lawyer. 71 THE CENTURY MAGAZINE (December 1905),286-298;(January 1906), 469-484;(March 1906), [586-600]; (April 1906), 745-761; (May 1906), 930-953; 72 THE CENTURY MAGAZINE (May 1906), 139-154.

The author, a member of the New York Bar, explained that no one had attempted to sum up Lincoln's legal career. The treatment that historians had accorded his profession seemed inadequate. He writes of Lincoln's career as a lawyer based on examinations of court records and personal investigations in the old Eighth Illinois Circuit. In exploring Lincoln's early years, there was no indication from his family background or one-year education that he would enter the profession of law. The author rebuts the story that Lincoln became interested in law from reading a copy of the *Revised Statutes of Indiana*, "as dull a tome as ever lay between sheepskin covers." It was more likely that Lincoln received his excitement for the law from attending court sessions in Boonville, Indiana, when he was a teenager. In those days the court not only provided the "entertainment" in the area, but it also meant a market for goods. Local Indiana courtrooms, which were double log-cabins were described. It was in New Salem, Illinois, where Lincoln moved with his family, that he became the avid reader and began practicing debating. It was also at this time that Lincoln became known for his integrity and honor; he was nicknamed "Honest Abe."

Lincoln displayed "a trait which few lawyers possess," the ability to present facts clearly, concisely, and effectively without taking undue advantage of them. The author discusses Lincoln's first public argument and early attitude toward the law as Lincoln stated his views while running for the Illinois legislature.

Subjects covered include: Lincoln the law student; admission to the bar; managing clerk; early successes in the courts; notable partnership; Judge Logan and Lincoln; Lincoln the head of a law firm; Lincoln the lawyer in Congress; life on the Illinois circuit; Judge Davis and Lincoln; leader of the bar; jury lawyer; cross examiner; Lincoln in the criminal courts; his legal ethics; Lincoln's great cases; his legal experience and reputation.

See also **Hill**, Monographs.

314
Hill, Frederick Trevor.
Lincoln's Legacy of Inspiration [to Americans.] NEW YORK TIMES 4 February 1909, Sect. 8: p. 3, 5-6.
For annotation, See **Hill**, Monograph Section.

315
Hill, John Wesley.
Abraham Lincoln: Address. 78 pt. 2 CONGRESSIONAL RECORD (January 26, 1934), 1384-1387.

This address, which Hill gave before the Ohio Bar Association at Cedar Point, July 8, 1933, was later printed in the *Congressional Record*. For annotation, see **Hill**, John Wesley, "Lincoln the Lawyer," Monographs.

316
Hill, John Wesley
Lincoln the Lawyer. 6 OHIO STATE BAR ASSOCIATION REPORT (July 24, 1933), 241-246.

For annotation see **Hill**, Monographs.

317
Hilliard, David C.
Footnotes and Dicta. 62 CHICAGO BAR RECORD (November/December 1980), 116-117.

The article provides excerpts from two short speeches given by Lincoln that reveal his attitude toward the law, the first from his address before the Young Men's Lyceum of Springfield, Illinois, January 27, 1838; the second from his law lecture, 1850. Hilliard mentions the Lincolniana collection in the courtroom and chambers of the federal building in Chicago. The author refers to three present-day Lincoln scholars, who are lawyers, one of whom suggests Duff's *A. Lincoln: Prairie Lawyer* in retracing Lincoln's travels on the old Eighth Judicial Circuit.

318
Hopkins, Richard J.
Abraham Lincoln Lawyer (Address). BAR ASSOCIATION OF THE STATE OF KANSAS REPORT (1928), 130-138.

The article begins poetically by praising Lincoln for his honesty and intelligence. As a youth, Lincoln went to a trial and was impressed by Breckenridge, an attorney. He went home to practice speeches in mock trials, involving imaginary parties. An example of Lincoln's humor is provided.

The article gives a detailed description of the medium-sized law office of Lincoln and Herndon. Hopkins notes Lincoln's representation of fairness. In addressing juries, Lincoln took great pains to make sure the jury understood his point. His sentences were short, compact, and distinct. He was frank and openly admitted it when there was a law that went against his case. Hopkins quotes John T. Richards: "The records of the Supreme Court of Illinois, however, reveal the astonishing fact that he never appeared in that court on behalf of any person charged with a felony. . . . he never knowingly defended a person charged with crime unless he believed the accused to be innocent." He was always thoroughly prepared before each case. Lincoln won ninety-six of the 175 cases in the state supreme court.

319
Horner, W. N.
Abraham Lincoln's Law Cases. 52 n.s. NATIONAL MAGAZINE (June 1924), 551-555.

This article by a member of the Chicago Bar describes Lincoln's cases in the Supreme Court of Illinois and the United States Supreme Court. He practiced law for twenty-three years. Although he was in several partnerships, he appeared alone in many cases. The reporters attest to this. He averaged only about $1500 per year because he did not charge very much for his services. Although many of his cases were small ones, they set precedent that we follow today. Lincoln was never involved in a strictly criminal proceeding in the supreme court. The article notes names of justices as authors of opinions, and includes a list of justices with dates of appointment.

320
Horner, W. N.
As a Lawyer Lincoln First Won Fame. 58 n.s. NATIONAL MAGAZINE (February 1930), 217-221.

The article speaks briefly to the cases with which Lincoln was involved in the Supreme Court of Illinois and the United States Supreme Court. Many cases in which Lincoln was victorious are the foundation of today's laws.

At that time attorneys did not have to pass an examination to be admitted to the bar; they were merely required to obtain a certificate of moral character. He became enrolled as an attorney-at-law in 1836, and continued in practice for twenty-three years. The only years during which he did not practice were from

1847 to 1849, when he was in Congress. The *Illinois Reports* reflect his absence from the practice of law during this interim.

Lincoln collected only modest fees as an attorney, seldom over $50.00, earning approximately $2500 per year. Lincoln and his associates had small private law libraries and four volumes of precedents for guidance. His personal library was reported to contain no more than twenty volumes. His briefs contained constant references to English Reports, also to those of Massachusetts and New York. It is believed that he utilized the library of the Supreme Court of Illinois. The scraps of paper connected with any Lincoln case have disappeared from the files in the Office of the Clerk.

321
Hunt, H. Draper.
Educating the President: Abraham Lincoln and Learning, 1809-1854. Learner and Mentor, 1854-1865. 88 LINCOLN HERALD (Fall 1986), 106-113, 114-115.

Lincoln used the word "defective" to describe his education in a biographical questionnaire, and said in his 1860 biography that he picked up what education he had. He was enthralled by *The Revised Statutes of Indiana*, and attended Squire Bowling Green's justice of the peace court in New Salem. He bought Blackstone's *Commentaries* and borrowed Stuart's books. Stuart, and later Logan were mentioned as partners. In 1844 Lincoln took Herndon as partner, with the two men splitting their fees, including the $5000 fee of the Illinois Central Railroad. Their law firm dealt with every cause of action in a variety of cases. The author depicts life on the circuit of the Eighth Judicial Circuit. Lincoln was known for his clarity of expression and effectiveness in fighting for a client in whose cause he believed. He offered practical information to aspiring young lawyers.

Hunt explained in a section, "Learner and Mentor, 1854-1865," that Lincoln grew as a lawyer, particularly during the decade as he argued his most famous cases, such as the Duff Armstrong case of 1858, *McCormick v. Manny*, "Effie Afton," and Illinois Central Railroad cases.

322
Identifying Lincoln's Law Offices. 1220 LINCOLN LORE (August 25, 1952), [1].

An attempt is made to orient the casual student, placing Lincoln in his actual surroundings. Offices are identified in Springfield at 109 North Fifth Street, 108-110 North Fifth Street, 102 South Sixth Street, and 103 South Fifth Street. Stuart and Lincoln had been collaborating on law cases for at least a month by April 15, 1837, when an announcement appeared in the *Sangamo Journal*, "J. T. Stuart and A. Lincoln." Later partners were Logan and Lincoln, followed by Lincoln and Herndon.

323
Illinois. Supreme Court.
Proceedings Upon the Death of Abraham Lincoln Had in the Supreme Court of Illinois. 37 ILLINOIS REPORTS, 7-11

These proceedings provided the opportunity for the formal announcement of the death of Abraham Lincoln to the court. There are resolutions of the bar adopted to express the grief and bereavement along with expressions of appreciation by those who knew and worked with him.

324
Incidents in Lincoln's Life as a Lawyer. 23 GREEN BAG (February 1911), 104-105.

This short article includes anecdotes about Lincoln as a lawyer. It tells of his buying an old barrel from a traveler. At the bottom was a copy of Blackstone's *Commentaries*, sparking Lincoln's interest in law. Other incidents include his famous "almanac" murder trial, and laughing a case out of court.

325
The Insanity Defense in Lincoln's Illinois. 1727 LINCOLN LORE (January 1982), [1]-4.

There is discussion of the insanity defense, which was well established when Lincoln practiced law. In particular there is discussion of the Isaac Wyant case, pleading not guilty by reason of insanity. Wyant was acquitted and became an inmate. Lincoln acted for the prosecution on the theory that Wyant was pretending to be insane. However, after learning more about the man, he believed that such a person might actually be insane and that he had been too severe. In another insanity case, Robert Sloo sought Lincoln as attorney, but Lincoln recommended another lawyer and the man was acquitted by reason of insanity. There may have been other instances of Lincoln's involvement with insanity cases, but lack of a definitive edition of Lincoln's legal papers made it impossible to draw a conclusion. The article notes statements from the state supreme court for the period to see the reasonable nature of the use of insanity defense in Lincoln's Illinois.

326
Isaacs, Alexander J.
The Pig and the President: An Insignificant Contribution to Lincolniana. 16 CHICAGO BAR RECORD (November 1934), 9-10.

The article tells of four cases tried by Lincoln, one of which was particularly amusing. In the case of *Byrne v. Stout* the dispute was over ownership rights to a pig. While the plaintiff and defendant were arguing furiously during the trial, the pig died.

327
Jackson, H. LeRoy.
Concerning the Financial Affairs of Abraham Lincoln Esquire.   34 CONNECTICUT BAR JOURNAL (September 1960), 240-248.

The article concerns fees Lincoln charged in his law practice. Jackson talks of Robert Irwin who handled Lincoln's financial affairs in the 1850s. He discusses Lincoln's presidential salary as well as his net worth at certain other times in his life.

328
Jaffa, Harry V.
Remembering Lincoln: Have Americans Lost Their Historical Perspective On His View of Human Rights?   96 LOS ANGELES DAILY JOURNAL (February 11, 1983), 4.

On the 174th anniversary of Abraham Lincoln's birth, the author reflects on his views toward Negroes' being excluded from rights under the Constitution. The author recalls how Lincoln disagreed with Chief Justice Roger B. Taney's opinion in the Dred Scott decision. Lincoln, in a June 26, 1857, speech refuted both Taney and Stephen A. Douglas, by stating "I think the authors of that notable instrument [Declaration] intended to include all men."
The author concludes, "the principles of the Declaration of Independence-- from which Lincoln said he had derived all his political opinions--are principles of today and tomorrow, no less than of yesterday."

329
Jones, Henry Craig.
Abraham Lincoln's Attitude Toward Education.   12 IOWA LAW REVIEW (June 1927), 336-354.

This article describes what little formal education Lincoln had, and points out Lincoln's never-ending efforts at intellectual self-improvement, noting that Lincoln read all the books he could. He often practiced his grammar and debating skills, which later served him well. Lincoln believed in better education, and in examinations to qualify teachers. As president, he approved the Land Grant College Act.

330
Jones, Warren L.
Lincoln, the Lawyer. 40 FLORIDA BAR JOURNAL (February 1966), 75-79.

Jones comments on the large number of books on every phase of Lincoln's life. His career was not overlooked. He reviews the story of Lincoln's acquiring Blackstone's *Commentaries*, which he perused; in 1836, being admitted to the Illinois Bar; in 1837, becoming the partner of Stuart; 1841, with Logan; and finally with Herndon, a partnership which lasted seventeen years.

While several biographers had a low rating for Lincoln as a member of the bar, an injustice has been done. Although self-trained, he became a leader of the Springfield bar and his reputation extended beyond his own circuit. In fact, there was no equal to him as an advocate. He was skillful in pleading and draftsmanship, and knowledgeable concerning legal fundamentals, exemplified in writings and speeches. He served as attorney in all types of cases, such as ejectment, partition, foreclosure, municipal bonds, and divorce. His practice included criminal cases also. Cases mentioned included the Trailor case, Duff Armstrong, the McCormick Reaper, Rock Island Bridge, and Matson slave case, among others.

331
Judge Abraham Lincoln. 1054 LINCOLN LORE (JUNE 20, 1949), 1.

This article describes Lincoln's presiding as judge in court at the request of Judge David Davis, who sometimes delegated his judicial function to others. Although this practice was approved by all parties to a case, it was not sanctioned by statute. Two cases that Lincoln tried were reversed by the supreme court because of this irregular assignment. Lincoln's name was listed in the Springfield *Register* in 1850 as one who aspired to a judgeship, although it is doubtful that he seriously sought such a position.

332
Kazmark, Leah A.
The Circuit That Lincoln Rode. 16 ILLINOIS CENTRAL MAGAZINE (February 1928), 8-10.

This article is introduced with a popular story-type setting of Lincoln's birth. Then Kazmark proceeds to describe the marking of the Eighth Judicial Circuit route over which Lincoln rode. The last remaining circuit-riding associate of Lincoln, Judge Cunningham, suggested in 1914 that the historic circuit be marked. Consequently, the Lincoln Circuit Marking Association was formed, consisting of the Illinois Daughters of the American Revolution and the Illinois Bar Association.

The road was marked with bronze bust markers, showing the head of Lincoln, mounted on white stone, particularly at county lines where the circuit passed into another county, and at each of the fourteen county seats. These bronze markers were the work of Lorado Taft.

333
Kellerstrass, Amy Louise (Sutton)
Lincoln and Son Borrow Books. 69 LINCOLN HERALD (Spring 1967), 10-21. With illustrations, and revised; Sutton, 48 ILLINOIS LIBRARIES (June 1966), 443-449.

This article was revised by Wayne C. Temple from the original in *Illinois Libraries*.

An old manuscript record of the Illinois State Library, "Register of Books Loaned to Members of the Legislature, Officers and Members of the Illinois State Library," shows the very first entry in Lincoln's handwriting. He had signed, "S. T. Logan," since Logan was a member of the legislature and authorized to use the collection. The book that he checked out on December 16, 1842, was the *Rev[ised] Laws [of] N[ew] Y[ork]*, Vol. 1st, and it was returned the same day. A footnote to the article suggested that he might have consulted it for the case *Averill v. Field*, argued before the supreme court by Lincoln for plaintiff on that date.

334
King, James L.
Lincoln's Skill as a Lawyer. 166 NORTH AMERICAN REVIEW (February 1898), 186-195.

The author writes about recollections of Judge Abram Bergen who began to practice law in 1858 in Cass County, Illinois, one of the circuits frequently visited by Lincoln. He states that Lincoln's most prominent characteristic "was his rare faculty for detecting and disclosing the controlling point in a legal battle. But not less than this was his clear, full, orderly, and accurate statement of a case. . . ." He also claims "Lincoln's tact was remarkable." The author tells of the Dunlap case where Lincoln's laugh reduced a damage claim against his client from $10,000 to a few hundred. He also tells the story of the "Armstrong Murder Case" known as the "almanac case" in which Bergen was a spectator for the trial.

(For Paul Selby's dispute of information in the King article, see Selby, Paul, "The Dunlap Assault Case on Paul Selby in 1853 in Which Abraham Lincoln Appeared as Associate Counsel," 30 CHICAGO LEGAL NEWS [1898], 298.)

335
King, Willard L.
The Case That Made Lincoln. 83 LINCOLN HERALD (Winter 1981), 786-790.

King describes the case of Henry B. Truett who was indicted for murder in the shooting of Dr. J. M. Early, doctor and Methodist preacher. The young Truett had been appointed by President Van Buren as register of the U.S. Land Office at Galena. There were political overtones and a resolution was passed that the appointment of Truett was not in accordance with wishes of the Democratic party, with removal recommended. Stephen Logan and his partner Baker were retained to defend Truett, and Logan retained the firm of Stuart and Lincoln as associates. Lincoln had been admitted to the bar one year before this case. Although the other lawyers were eminent, Lincoln was chosen to make the crucial closing argument. It was generally agreed that Lincoln was one of the best jury lawyers in the state. "He talked to the jury, man to man, in their language as in a conversational tone . . . giving thrust to his sincerity." Since there is no transcript of Lincoln's summation to the jury, there can be only speculation. However, the jury verdict was "not guilty."
    The *Lloyd v. Lloyd* divorce case was used as an example of Lincoln's insistence that he be convinced of right and justice of a matter. The Lincoln Memorial University had acquired a rare document of Abraham Lincoln, written about 1839 when he served as a divorce lawyer practicing in Sangamon County, Illinois. The item dealing with a desertion case is of folio size, comprised of two sides of one sheet.

336
King, Willard L.
Riding the Circuit with Lincoln. 6 AMERICAN HERITAGE (February 1955), 48-49, 104-109.

Subtitle: A new picture of prairie lawyers coping with bad roads and worse living on the Illinois frontier, drawn from David Davis letters.
    In a study of Lincoln's friend and traveling companion of the Eighth Judicial Circuit, Judge Davis, the author writes about what it was like to ride the circuit with Lincoln. The circuit was comprised of fourteen counties when Davis and Lincoln made the three-month circuit, twice a year during the late 1840s and early 1850s.
    The roads were poor, the food and inns often bad. Yet Davis said, "Lincoln was happy, as happy as he could be, when on this circuit and happy no other

place." King gives descriptions of each town on the circuit where they stopped and provides interesting stories about events pertaining to Lincoln and Davis, through letters that Davis had written to his wife. Davis later became United States Supreme Court justice.

337
King, Willard L.
Some Highlights of the Life of David Davis, Lincoln's Most Ardent Supporter. 65 ILLINOIS BAR JOURNAL (January 1977), 300-306.

Although this article deals with David Davis, it includes considerable information on Lincoln. David Davis was a judge who traveled the Eighth Judicial Circuit, made up of fourteen counties, with Lincoln. While others found accommodations of the day less than adequate, Lincoln was never bothered by facilities of the inns while on these trips. He was concentrating on his cases. Lincoln was a master in examining witnesses. He used only one theory in his cases, and would concede nearly everything not pertinent to that theory. Davis comments that Lincoln was very fair and honest, and that Logan, Lincoln's partner, was a great lawyer.

338
Kissell, Deborra L.
Life on the Eighth Judicial Circuit; Historic Courthouses Reflect Hardships, Pleasures of Lincoln's Lawyer Days. 2 HISTORIC ILLINOIS (October 1979), [1]-3.

Kissell describes Lincoln's life in a simple era, including a modest office, in a three-story Greek-revival business building. Every spring and fall, Lincoln left his office with Herndon and joined the "pilgrimage" of lawyers on the Eighth Circuit comprised of fourteen large central Illinois counties covering eleven thousand square miles. They rode by horseback, at four miles per hour over muddy roads and wagon trails, stopping at the circuit's county courthouses to try cases. This piece includes a map of the Eighth Judicial Circuit, and description of less than luxurious overnight accommodations.

339
Knox-Shaw, Thomas K.
Lincoln as a Lawyer, by Lord Shaw of Dunfermline. 77 FORUM (February 1927), 220-229.

The article deals first with Lincoln's early life. The Blackstone *Commentaries* story surfaces again, with description of its being inside a fifty-cent barrel of miscellaneous items. The author concludes that Lincoln became interested in the law through that volume. There are examples of Lincoln's clever speeches, and his use of certain facts to his advantage. The Armstrong murder case provides details of Lincoln's surprise use of the almanac in trapping the prosecution's witness. The article shows how the lawyer's grueling training prepared the politician, his qualities of integrity, courage, practicality, and vision of equality ripened by legal experience. Yet the author believed that the idea of Lincoln's having been a lawyer, going up in the legal profession step by step, was not familiar to the public.

340
Kramer, William.
Major Stuart--Abraham Lincoln's Law Partner. LOS ANGELES DAILY JOURNAL, 25 May 1987, p. 4.

This brief piece describes Lincoln's law partner, Stuart, and suggests that in his early years he was neither well read nor industrious. Nevertheless, he had an extensive practice. He was willing to have Lincoln assume responsibility for the business due to Stuart's interest in politics. Kramer tells how Lincoln assumed the responsibility, litigation being simple, with few precedents, and flexible legal forms. Kramer notes that one of his contemporaries testified that the self-reliant Lincoln did not ask other lawyers for advice.

341
Lambeth, Harry J.
Lawyers Who Became President. 64 AMERICAN BAR ASSOCIATION JOURNAL (February 1978), 222-226.
P. 225, "Lincoln: The Complete Lawyer-President."

Of the twenty-three lawyer-presidents, Lincoln is probably the most prominent. He may have been the best-known poverty-stricken lawyer. Early in his career, he was a true backwoodsman with folksy manner. There is reference to the newspaper notice of the opening of practice with Stuart, April 15, 1837, and later a printed professional card.

Herndon was reported as having said that Lincoln had a keen sense of justice and was a case lawyer. Although no more than ordinarily successful in the lower courts, he was better in appellate cases, where time was on his side. He had learned the value of preparation from his partner Logan. Several of his well-known cases are named.

342
Landis, Frederick.
Lincoln the Lawyer. 19 LAWYER AND BANKER (July-August 1926), 246-257; 70 SOLICITORS' JOURNAL AND WEEKLY REPORTER (July 24, 1926), 825.

In an address before the Lawyers Club of Detroit, the author called Lincoln the greatest natural lawyer who had ever lived. He gives a brief history of Lincoln's growing up, and his hard life as a child. Then he describes life on the Eighth Judicial Circuit and some of the great lawyers who traveled with Lincoln. Landis depicts his courtroom mannerisms. "It has been said of Lincoln that he was the only English speaking lawyer whose statement was more direct and more powerful than the statements of Daniel Webster." He tells of Lincoln's famous Armstrong murder case, and says that Lincoln was an inspirational speaker. The author concludes that "it was Lincoln's training as a lawyer that made him a great free president".

343
Larrabee, Bill.
Charlie, Fick & Abe, Usher and Anthony and Long Jim. 22 ILLINOIS MAGAZINE (January-February 1983), 26-31.

In Moultree County, which was once a part of the historic Eighth Judicial Circuit, there was repartee between James W. Craig, of Mattoon and veteran Sheriff Joseph Thomason. Craig, a leading Illinois lawyer and jurist, was probing for evidence, questioning Thomason about "that first Court" in the county. There was Charlie as judge, and at the bar, Abe [Lincoln] and his contemporaries: Fick, (Orlando B. Ficklin), Usher (Usher Linder, orator of Illinois), and Anthony Thornton (of Shelbyville) who became a wealthy lawyer, a state supreme court justice, a newspaper editor and publisher, and first president of the Illinois State Bar Association. Long Jim Davis had not been mentioned by major historians, Sandburg, Randall, Thomas, Duff, or Coleman. Local histories list him as J. M. Davis, or James Davis, a trial lawyer, not as well educated as his peers, but a successful criminal lawyer, with two terms in the state legislature. Abe was one of a "platoon of ragtag young lawyers who rode horseback on a Circuit of fifteen Central Illinois Counties," and the one who became president. Anthony had said that circuit riding was often pleasant, with congenial young lawyers, racy incidents, and amusing cases.

344
The Law Student--Abraham Lincoln. 59 THE IRISH LAW TIMES AND SOLICITORS' JOURNAL (March 21, 1925), 71.

A brief paragraph describes an article, "Abraham Lincoln," appearing in an American journal, *The Law Student*. The editor states that one of the objects of the journal is "to build professional ambition." Therefore, the career of Abraham Lincoln as a lawyer is dealt with fully. He notes that his apprenticeship with books and practice of law should not be forgotten in his greatness as statesman and leader. The Irish article quotes Isaac Arnold in describing Lincoln in court.

For the original article, see "Lawyers Who Would Not Give Up" 2 THE LAW STUDENT (February 15, 1925), 2.

345

Lawyer Lincoln's Fees. 288 LINCOLN LORE (October 15, 1934), [1].

Lincoln was satisfied to work for small fees. There are quotes from his notes on a law lecture, expressing his opinion regarding fees. He was anxious that fees be generous to other lawyers whom he hired; he saw danger in an underpaid judiciary. Often he did not collect any fee if he failed in a case, therefore offered some degree of gratuitous service.

346

Lawyers Who Would Not Give Up. Abraham Lincoln (1809-1865) 2 THE LAW STUDENT (February 15, 1925), 2.

A list of Lincoln's failures is followed in each instance by an indication of how he dealt with them. The list includes his loss of jobs, failure to get nominated, failure to be elected, and others. In each case he continued striving toward his goals. The editor states that Lincoln's life should be an inspiration to every law student. Behind his leadership and statesmanship were the years with books and everyday practice of law. He believes one of the finest tributes of the study of law was that it produced Abraham Lincoln.

347

Lincoln, Abraham.
Advice from Lincoln. 9 PENNSYLVANIA LAW JOURNAL-REPORTER (February 10, 1986), 1, 15.

Lincoln's notes from a law lecture appear under the headline, "Advice from Lincoln," stating that he is not an accomplished lawyer, and stressing diligence as essential. He urges acting immediately on correspondence, and completing business as far as possible while it is at hand. In bringing suit, he suggests writing the declaration at once, and recommends examining the books for a point of law, noting authorities.

Lincoln makes recommendations regarding defenses and pleas, in examination of title, and drafting orders in advance. He encourages practicing extemporaneous speaking, urges discouragement of litigation, and insists upon honesty.

348
Lincoln, Abraham.
The Autobiography of Abraham Lincoln. 12 ILLINOIS HISTORY (February 1959), 115.

This autobiography is the one that Jesse Fell had Lincoln write for the campaign. He touched upon his law study and practice very briefly. "During this legislative period, I had studied law, and removed to Springfield to practice it." After his stint in Congress, 1849-1854, "both inclusive, [I] practiced law more assiduously than ever before."
(Note: A three-page facsimile of the handwritten autobiography was reproduced by Edward T. Kelly Co., Chicago, with permission of heirs and descendants of Jesse W. Fell.)

349
Lincoln, Abraham.
Letter Written by Abraham Lincoln in 1841. 70 ALBANY LAW JOURNAL (May 1908), 149-150.

This letter from Lincoln to his friend Speed gives in his own words a "personal and complete account of a sensational murder trial in Springfield, in which Lincoln was one of the defendants' counsel in 1841."
There is vivid description of a search for the missing body of Archibald Fisher, supposed to have been murdered, and information regarding the Trailor brothers, the alleged murderers. The statement of the doctor is recorded, believed to be a fabrication by some, that the missing man was alive.
This letter was in the possession of John F. Geeting, editor of the *American Criminal Reports*.

350
Lincoln Among the Lawyers. Edited by Norman L. Dodge. 3 THE MONTH AT GOODSPEED'S BOOK SHOP (March 1932), 195-200.

This small leaflet lists lawyers who knew Lincoln: Herndon, Lamon, and Whitney. Each man wrote of him in his own way, presenting a "living" chapter in Lincoln's life. One had been his partner, and two had ridden the circuit with him. They knew him in his different moods. While later writers have revised the details, it is upon their records that the biographical conception is based. He does not suggest forgetting the intimate knowledge of authors Nicolay and Hay, nor historians Beveridge, Sandburg, and Barton.

351
Lincoln and Seward, Patent Lawyers. 1592 LINCOLN LORE (October 1970), 4.

There is mention of the reaper patent granted to Cyrus McCormick of Rockbridge County, Virginia, and the well-known law case. In a later case Lincoln was employed on the side of the defendant, received a retainer, and prepared a brief, but was not allowed to participate when the case was tried in Cincinnati. There is discussion of the less well known *McCormick v. Seymour and Morgan* case tried in 1854 for infringement of the patent on the original reaping machine in the Circuit Court of the United States for the Northern District of New York, where counsel for plaintiff was William H. Seward.

352
Lincoln and the Bridge Case. 3 THE PALIMPSEST (May 1922), 142-154.

The Steamer "Effie Afton" wrecked against the pier of the Railroad Bridge near Rock Island, 13th day, Tuesday, September 22nd, 1857. A copy of Lincoln's argument in the case, *Hurd v. Railroad Bridge Co.*, before the United States Circuit Court is included. Lincoln was one of the attorneys for the Bridge Company. The copy of his argument in the case was in possession of A. N. Harbert of Iowa City, who loaned it to the State Historical Society of Wisconsin, where it was verified with the original newspaper report in the *Chicago Daily Press*, of September 24, 1857. Lincoln addressed the jury, not with an attitude of assailing anybody, but rather with concern in conflict of testimony. Although he grew earnest, he was not ill-natured in stating that the plaintiffs had to establish the fact that the bridge was a material obstruction and that they managed their boat with reasonable care and skill.

353
Lincoln and the Constitution: An Overview. 1777 LINCOLN LORE (March 1987), 2-4; continued in 1778 (April 1987), 1-2.

This article discusses the unfortunate title of Zane's *Lincoln: The Constitutional Lawyer.* As a lawyer, Lincoln was occasionally involved in constitutional cases. As president, he had tremendous constitutional problems, and had to focus on other constitutional issues that he surely had not considered when he was a lawyer. Yet he did not habitually think first of constitutional aspects; he was practical. There are references to his Lyceum speech and the phrase "reverence for laws."

354
Lincoln and the "Reaper Case," by Emerson Hinchliff in Historical Notes, 33 JOURNAL OF THE ILLINOIS STATE HISTORICAL SOCIETY (March 1940), 361-365.

Hinchliff uncovered numerous "mistakes" in the standard biographies of Lincoln and points them out for the record. In particular he singles out Sandburg's *Abraham Lincoln: The Prairie Years*, Beveridge's *Abraham Lincoln*, and Woldman's *Lawyer Lincoln*. The article by W. M. Dickson, "Lincoln in Cincinnati," concerning the *McCormick v. Manny* case, is criticized as well.

Lincoln as a Lawyer. [By E. J.] 17 LAW NOTES (February 1914), 204-205.

See: **E. J.,** "Lincoln as a Lawyer."

Lincoln as a Lawyer in Illinois. 50 AMERICAN LAW REVIEW (September 1916), 781-788.

For annotation see **Richards,** John T.

355
Lincoln as an Itinerant Lawyer. 5 LAW STUDENT'S HELPER (April 1897), 139-140.

This brief article includes examples of quotations by people who knew Lincoln as he practiced law, stressing his great use of memory and power of persuasion. They told how he rarely used notes, and how he often condensed facts and issues of law into a story.

356
Lincoln Holds Court. 17 ABRAHAM LINCOLN ASSOCIATION BULLETIN (December 1, 1929), 3.

Evidence had just been discovered that Lincoln occasionally sat on the bench in the place of David Davis in court at Springfield. Whitney, in his *Life on the Circuit with Lincoln,* had already told of this practice in Champaign County. In Sangamon on the old judges' docket for 1856, there was a listing of titles of cases and judges' notes indicating disposition of each case. All notes were in David Davis' hand except for the fall of 1856, when there were frequent notations in Lincoln's hand.

357
Lincoln in Logan County. 2 LINCOLN NEWSLETTER (October 1980),[3].

This piece contains tales and stories of Abraham Lincoln in Logan County, some of which are documented. There are quotations from Frederick Trevor Hill's *Lincoln the Lawyer* on James Hoblit, one of the few men living at the time who had faced Lincoln from the witness chair. Hoblit's uncle was in litigation with Paullin over a mule, and James Hoblit, a nephew, had been subpoenaed as witness of mistreatment of the animal. He told how Lincoln questioned him in a friendly manner. He forgot to be hostile, thereby telling more than he had anticipated about the case.

358
Lincoln in Many Law Firms. 8 JOURNAL OF THE ILLINOIS STATE HISTORICAL SOCIETY (October 1915), 498-499.

This article describes material sold from the library of John E. Burton, including seven documents, five in Lincoln's handwriting. "Various firm signatures" indicated a legal association of Ficklin and Lincoln, Logan and Lincoln, Harlan and Lincoln, Lincoln and Lamon, and Goodrich and Lincoln.

359
Lincoln Saved This Man's Life. 133 THE OUTLOOK (February 7, 1923), 263.

This article relates the familiar story of Duff Armstrong as told by Duff's brother at Oakford, Illinois. The wild, reckless Duff in the proximity of a camp meeting was in an altercation. He struck a man with a neck-yoke, and the man died several days later. Mrs. Armstrong had befriended Lincoln early in his life; therefore he defended Duff. The chief witness stated that he saw Duff strike the blow. Lincoln produced an almanac to show that the moonlight was not sufficient for the witness to see on that particular night, and Duff was cleared of the charge. An illustration of Duff Armstrong is included.

360
Lincoln the Lawyer was Lincoln at His Greatest. 14 (no.4) THE ASSOCIATION NEWS, 1.

Published in the interest of General Daniel Davidson Bidwell Memorial Association, Ft. Wayne, Indiana.

Lincoln's happiest years were when he was on the circuit in Illinois trying cases. Once he had mastered a case he rarely needed notes or books to refresh his memory. He never overlooked a chance to laugh a case out of court. The cross-examination of J. Parker Green was an example.

361
Lincoln's Contacts with Law Students. 280 LINCOLN LORE (August 20, 1934), [1].

A number of young men aspired to a place in Lincoln's law office. Vacancies were not always available. Quotations from letters to several young men are included, and this article accounts for contacts with: Isham Reavis, Henry Rankin, William Grigsby, John H. Littlefield, Mr. Widner, Elmer E. Elsworth, J. M. Brockman, and Robert Lincoln.

362
Lincoln's Decision to Study Law. 276 LINCOLN LORE (July 23, 1934), [1].

Lincoln made a major decision in his life when he concluded that he would study law. The article reviews that which brought him to such a decision in 1834, such as his analytical and logical mind, and love for the open forum. There is discussion of persons who might have influenced his decision, noting that even Lincoln might not have been aware of some influences on his life.

363
Lincoln's First Large Legal Fee. 49 LINCOLN HERALD (December 1947), 21-23.

The Illinois Central Railroad Company had retained Lincoln of the Lincoln & Herndon firm at $200 or $250 to assist general counsel of the [rail]road. One of the most important cases, *Illinois Central Railroad v. McLean Co.* dealt with assessing and collecting taxes on railroad properties, and was in litigation for several years. The railroad interests won and Lincoln presented his bill of $2000. (Some persons believe he asked for land parcels.) The Illinois Central personnel said the fee was too high, so Lincoln brought suit for $5000. Eventually he deposited his check of $4800, having already received his retainer. As usual he split his fee with Herndon.

The original check, in restored condition, is located at Lincoln Memorial University.

364
Lincoln's $5000 Fee. 654 LINCOLN LORE (October 20, 1941), [1].

Although Lincoln's $5000 Illinois Central Railroad fee has been well publicized, he actually enjoyed only $2500, since he divided the fee with William Herndon, his partner. Several points concerning the fee have remained controversial, such as motive. The amount itself was unusual; there are several versions about how he presented his bill. The article quotes James F. Joy in saying that Lincoln had wanted land for his fee; since that was not forthcoming, he put in his claim for the $5000. There was discussion of correspondence concerning the fee.

365
Lincoln's Law Library. 619 LINCOLN LORE (February 17, 1941), [1].

It has never been possible to make a complete list of law books to which Lincoln had access. Collector Oliver Barrett believed that Lincoln and Herndon had state reports of every state in their library, or at least had access to them. (Attorneys sometimes agreed about cooperative buying of reference books, exchanging or supplementing the offices of each other.) Lincoln was known to have used the Illinois State Law Library.

This article includes a listing of the complete collection of Lincoln and Herndon law books acquired from a Springfield book dealer. The article mentions those recommended to young students by Lincoln, and fundamental in his own training. It does leave it to your judgment as to how many Lincoln might have used.

Lincoln's Law Offices in the Tinsley Building, 1843-1852. See **McMurtry.**

Lincoln's Manual for Lawyers [compiled by Louis A. Warren].
See **Charbonneau,** Louis H., Lincoln the Lawyer, 16 THE DETROIT LAWYER (February 1948), 27-32, 36.

See also **Manual** for Lawyers.

366
Lincoln's Most Humiliating Law Suit. 1256 LINCOLN LORE (May 4, 1953), [1].

This case was a challenge to Lincoln's integrity and professional ethics. He was the defendant in an action instigated by Levi O. Todd, his wife's brother.

The suit was brought by surviving partners Oldham and Hemingway of Oldham, Todd and Co. They claimed that Lincoln was indebted to them for money collected for them when he acted as their attorney. He vindicated himself in answer to the petition, and the motion was dismissed.

367
Lincoln's Office Equipment. 172 LINCOLN LORE (July 25, 1932), [1].

Items in Lincoln's law office are described such as the bookcase, chairs, desks, inkstands, pens, paperweights, tables, and the sign, or shingle.

368
Lincoln's Oral Argument: Text of Notes for His Only Supreme Court Case. 34 AMERICAN BAR ASSOCIATION JOURNAL (September 1948), 791-794.

Notes for Lincoln's oral argument in *Lewis v. Lewis* (1849) may be viewed in this article. It was the only case of his that went up to the Supreme Court while he was still a member of Congress. The Supreme Court handed down an opinion, by Chief Justice Taney, against Lincoln. The article includes photographs of Lincoln's actual notes. The author refers to Arthur Krock's article in the *New York Times*, 12 February 1948, where the entire text appears.

369
Lincoln's Political Partnerships. 135 LINCOLN LORE (November 19, 1931), [1]

Although this short article is entitled "political partnerships," it is actually a study of the origin and termination of Lincoln's three law partnerships, with John Todd Stuart, Stephen Trigg Logan, and William Henry Herndon. It appeared that Lincoln's first two partnerships were cut short for political reasons.

370
Lindsay, Vachel.
Abraham Lincoln--the Lawyer. 12 KENTUCKY STATE BAR JOURNAL (June 1948), 141-145.

Lincoln had a reputation for honesty. Hence the name "Honest Abe" because of his unique character and natural ability as an advocate with widespread reputation. The author calls him a "true prairie lawyer." He was a "compromiser and conciliator." As a truly honest lawyer he won great respect among his colleagues. Lindsay reviews *Bailey v. Cromwell* and *McCormick v. Manny.*

371
Lindstrom, Ralph G.
Lincoln: Lawyer-Logician. 36 LOS ANGELES BAR BULLETIN (June 1961), 276-280.

Lindstrom, Lincoln scholar and lawyer, gave this address at the dedication of a Lincoln bust in the Los Angeles County Courthouse on Law Day. He gives an account of life on the old Eighth Circuit in Lincoln's day, when lawyers traveled the circuit for three months twice a year. Lincoln and Judge David Davis covered the entire circuit, through all kinds of weather on unimproved trails by horseback or buggy. Lincoln was known to have carried the Illinois Code with him, as well as a geometry book. Local partners joined Lincoln at the county seats, where they interviewed witnesses on the lawn. When court was in session, lawyer Lincoln would appear to give away a case, until he reached a pivotal point.

Lindstrom speaks of the texts Lincoln consulted in writing his First Inaugural Address before leaving Springfield, and he reminds his audience of the constitutional questions Lincoln pioneered. He suggests that as lawyers pass the Lincoln bust they "study the face of this lawyer and civic logician."

372
Lloyd v. Lloyd--Divorce Case. 53 LINCOLN HERALD (Fall 1951), 36.

A rare legal document, ca. 1838, in Lincoln's handwriting was given to Lincoln Memorial University. The typescript reads "To the Honorable the Judge of the Sangamon Circuit Court in Chancery Sitting." The printed contents of this divorce document reveal the request for marriage dissolution, due to abandonment and nonsupport of Eliza A. Lloyd and infant by Peter Lloyd.

373
Logan, Stephen T.
Stephen T. Logan Talks about Lincoln. No. 12 LINCOLN CENTENNIAL ASSOCIATION BULLETIN (September 1928), 1-3, 5.

The original document of an interview, dated July 6, 1875, is in the handwriting of Herndon. Logan tells that his partnership with Lincoln began in 1841. Lincoln's knowledge of the law was small when he took him in. He did not think he studied much; rather, he believed he learned it in the study of cases. He became a pretty good lawyer, though his general knowledge of law was never

formidable. He had been in prior partnership with Stuart, and after joining
Logan became ambitious in the law. He tried to become more knowledgeable
and learn how to prepare his cases. They were in partnership about three years,
when Logan told him he wanted to take in his son, David. They talked it over
amicably and immediately dissolved the partnership.

374
Lorant, Stefan.
A Day in Lincoln's Life: How Honest Abe Saved a Man's Life and Repaid a
Debt of Gratitude. 24 LIFE (February 9, 1948), 111-112, 115-116, 118.

The article reconstructs the story of Duff Armstrong as a defendant in a
murder case. Lincoln repaid the debt of gratitude in defending this son of an old
friend, and was able to secure his acquittal.
    An illustration shows a rare ambrotype photo of Lincoln; here the story of
the photographing unfolds.

375
Lufkin, Richard Friend.
Mr. Lincoln's Light From Under a Bushel, 1850. 52 LINCOLN HERALD
(December 1950), 2-20.

This was the first in a series of articles, each dealing with a different year.
It furnishes a synopsis of Lincoln's life during this one year. Papers in this series
were given as talks to the Lincoln Group of Boston in a Centennial anniversary
series.
    The author, an engineer and cartographer, tracks Mr. Lincoln for the year
1850. He records where Lincoln was, the courts in which he practiced, and types
of law cases he handled. He notes how he spent his time, to whom he wrote,
and high spots of his personal life during 1850. He uses charts, graphs, and maps
to illustrate his accompanying text on the above-mentioned issues. Lufkin
discusses life traveling the Eighth Circuit in depth. Lincoln was an attorney of
record in 109 cases.

376
Lufkin, Richard Friend.
Mr. Lincoln's Light From Under a Bushel, 1851. 53 LINCOLN HERALD
(Winter 1952) [*sic*], 2-25.

The author tracks Mr. Lincoln in the year 1851, using charts, graphs, and
maps to accompany the text. Lincoln spent 176 days in court; he was attorney
of record in 107 cases. Lufkin discusses types of litigation and some individual
cases, as well as noting that Lincoln was the only lawyer to travel the entire

Eighth Circuit with Judge Davis. He lists Lincoln's 1851 correspondence with others. Individual stories include those about two men who were "two thorns in Lincoln's side in 1851," and "financial affairs of Lincoln," among others.

377
Lufkin, Richard Friend.
Mr. Lincoln's Light From Under a Bushel, 1852. 54 LINCOLN HERALD (Winter 1952), 2-26, 60.

This was to be the last year of the old Eighth Circuit and its fourteen county seats in which Lincoln spent of his time trying suits or traveling (at least twenty-seven full days). Lincoln was the attorney of record in 227 cases in 1852. The article discusses some of his interesting cases of that year, including one of the first suits for personal injury damages ever brought against a common carrier in Illinois. Lincoln tried nine cases in the state supreme court that year winning six of them. He also became heavily involved in politics and delivered the eulogy on Henry Clay.

378
Lufkin, Richard Friend.
Mr. Lincoln's Light From Under a Bushel, 1853. 55 LINCOLN HERALD (Winter 1953), 2-14, 48.

The year 1853 was a period of increased public recognition of Lincoln's name. "There was a great expansion in his work as a lawyer." During the year, Lincoln's circuit rides were considerably shortened when six counties were removed from the circuit. The firm of Lincoln and Herndon handled some 300 cases, including several important railroad lawsuits, with representation of the Illinois Central Railroad. Some of Lincoln's larger cases that year are listed; also one in which he is a defendant in a suit. The author again uses maps, charts, and graphs to illustrate the text.

It includes the story of the new town of Lincoln, Illinois, founded in 1853 and named after Lincoln while he was a practicing attorney.

379
Lufkin, Richard Friend.
Mr. Lincoln's Light From Under a Bushel, 1854. 56 LINCOLN HERALD (Winter 1954), 3-24.

A year of hard work was ahead of Lincoln in 1854. The author was impressed by the range of activities of Mr. Lincoln, which were pursued with "apparently tireless energy." Lincoln maintained his law practice, but political activities forced him to cut back some. Lincoln's defense of J. H. Manny Co. on infringement of reaper patents of Cyrus McCormick was begun in 1854. Another of his great cases, defense of the Illinois Central Railroad against taxation of McLean County, took up some of Lincoln's time. Lufkin discusses various other cases of the year. Some information is included about Eighth Circuit travel, although railroads were now beginning to provide more of the transportation. Lincoln made a number of speeches for a friend, Richard Yates, who was running for Congress. In these speeches he began to make a name for himself speaking on the national question of slavery and its extension to the territories.

380
Lufkin, Richard Friend.
Mr. Lincoln's Light From Under a Bushel, 1855. 58 LINCOLN HERALD (Spring-Summer 1956), 17-27.

The author labels 1855 as "Lincoln's year of disappointment." He lost the Senate race for junior senator from Illinois in February 1855. The election saw Lincoln with first-ballot lead, but rough and tumble political maneuvering cost him the election.

The Lincoln-Herndon law practice handled over 250 cases that year. Lincoln's famous J. H. Manny Co. patent infringement suit of the McCormick Reaper Company was a bitter disappointment. Another lawyer for J. H. Manny, Edwin Stanton, was discourteous to Lincoln and disrespectful of his abilities, asking, "Where did that long-armed creature come from and what does he expect to do in this case?" Lincoln's well-prepared trial briefs were not used by the Manny lawyers. Lufkin concludes that 1855 was Lincoln's last comparatively quiet year. "Ambitious Mr. Lincoln was, at the end of 1855, on the threshold of national prominence and greatness."

A bibliography is included in this last in a series of six articles.

381
McClelland, Stewart W.
A. Lincoln, L.L.D. 41 LINCOLN HERALD (May 1939), 2-6.

Lincoln, a self-educated man who never attained a college degree, was granted the "honorary degree of LL.D." in 1860 by the Knox College Board of Trustees. As President Lincoln, he was also granted honorary degrees as doctor of laws from Columbia College in 1861, and the College of New Jersey in 1864. Because of the duties of his office, Lincoln was not able to attend the ceremonies at any of the colleges.

382
McClure, J. Robert, Jr.
On the Practice of Law, A. Lincoln. 76 ABA JOURNAL (October 1990), 98-99.

Excerpts from *Little Masterpieces of Autobiography*. Vol. 1, 1925.
Professional problems of today are not new. McClure interprets Lincoln's message on professionalism in his notes on a law lecture. "Lawyers need the desirable qualities of diligence, perseverence, preparedness, poise, peaceableness, morality, honesty and monetary fairness in one's work."

383
McFarland, Henry B.
Abe Lincoln, Attorney. 109 NEW JERSEY LAW JOURNAL (February 11, 1982), Index p. 115.

The author discusses the famous "Effie Afton" case, *Hurd v. Rock Island Bridge*, where a new river steamer, the "Effie Afton," swept into a bridge pier, and crashed into the first bridge to span the Mississippi River. The boat was a total loss as a result of an overturned stove followed by fire. The case touched off a wave of controversy between river navigation interests and river towns versus railroad and inland communities. As the case was of paramount importance to the railroad, they hired the best counsel available, Abraham Lincoln. The case had little precedent, but Lincoln had previously handled a subrogation claim for the Columbus Insurance Company on an insured canal boat that sank after colliding with a bridge pier on the Illinois River. Lincoln prepared four weeks for the trial that lasted fifteen days and was covered by the national press. The author points out that Lincoln conducted the trial in a "serious and respectful demeanor" with none of the humor found in his earlier cases. The jury was deadlocked, and issues were not resolved until years later.

384
McFarland, Henry B.
Abraham Lincoln and the Illinois Bar. 113 NEW JERSEY LAW JOURNAL (February 9, 1984), Index p. 133.

Lincoln was admitted to the Illinois bar in March of 1837. A man of many occupations, Lincoln was encouraged to study law by John T. Stuart, a running mate of Lincoln's for the Illinois legislature in 1834 and 1836. Lincoln became Stuart's law partner, but Stuart's absence with political activities left the bulk of the work to his partner. Later Lincoln associated with Stephen T. Logan, who taught him painstaking precision and preparedness. His final law partner was William Herndon, who ran the office and did the research, while Lincoln was the trial lawyer, frequently riding the circuit.

Lincoln was often sought by the younger lawyers, not only to try the cases they had prepared, but also for advice. Lincoln was to gain national attention from his famous debates with Stephen A. Douglas in their campaign for the United States Senate. Lincoln's friends from the legal profession helped him gain the nomination for the presidency.

385
McFarland, Henry B.
Abraham Lincoln, Attorney. 107 NEW JERSEY LAW JOURNAL (February 12, 1981), Index p. 113.

Lincoln was quick to use all situations in court to his advantage. He had a thirst for knowledge and would visit courtrooms whenever possible. The author describes Lincoln's brush with the law by operating a ferryboat disregarding the Dill Brothers' monopoly. McFarland believes this incident persuaded Lincoln to study the law. Lawyer John Stuart encouraged Lincoln in his interest in the law, providing books from his law library "one of best in the state capital." Lincoln and Stuart were highly respected attorneys. Lincoln made $1200 to $1500 per year. Compared to a governor's salary of $1200 or a judge's salary of $750, Lincoln was a prosperous attorney. When Stuart was elected to Congress, Lincoln went into a partnership with Logan. After Lincoln and Logan dissolved their partnership, Lincoln began his third partnership with William Herndon, which lasted until Lincoln's death. Lincoln rode the circuit while Herndon ran the office. Lincoln advertised, but set low fees. However, his largest fee was $5000 from a railroad company. Although Lincoln was against slavery, he represented a slave owner trying to regain possession of a slave. The reason Lincoln represented him was because slavery was bound up in the law. Later, when Lincoln argued against slavery, he did not argue morals; rather, he argued the law.

The author refers the reader to two books: *Lawyer Lincoln* by Wolman [*sic*] Woldman; and *A. Lincoln: Prairie Lawyer* by Duff.

386
McFarland, Henry B.
Abraham Lincoln, Lawyer-Statesman. 117 NEW JERSEY LAW JOURNAL (February 13, 1986), Index p. 176-179

Abraham Lincoln was a lawyer, and leader of the Illinois bar, who upon being elected president of the United States used his ability as a skilled attorney to find a settlement to the nation's problems. In this vein the author explores Lincoln's attempt to prevent the outbreak of war, and his diplomatic efforts at keeping foreign nations neutral. This article deals more with Lincoln's use and understanding of international law gained from his years as an Illinois prairie lawyer, than on Lincoln's actual law practice.

387
McFarland, Henry B.
Abraham Lincoln, Preceptor. 115 NEW JERSEY LAW JOURNAL (February 14, 1985), Index p. 170.

The writer insists that one must look at the detailed background of Lincoln's twenty-three years of law practice to complete his picture. His traits were clearly shown in his law office as well as in the courtroom. His training was in the reading of law, and John T. Stuart was his preceptor, a good one since Stuart was college trained and had the best legal library in Springfield. McFarland quotes Judge David Davis in saying that Lincoln was loved by others at the bar. The author has used Lincoln literature to compile a manual for lawyers, "Qualifying for the Bar." He suggests that an aspiring lawyer attach no consequence to the place he is in but strive to get books and read, to be diligent, to become expert in extemporaneous speaking, to work, and to be honest. Books that Lincoln recommended: Blackstone, Chitty, Greenleaf, and Story.

388
McFarland, Henry B.
The Dred Scott Case: Lincoln's Vehicle for National Prominence. 111 NEW JERSEY LAW JOURNAL (February 10, 1983), Index p. 140.

The slave Dred Scott was brought by his owner into Illinois where slavery was forbidden, then returned to Missouri. While in Missouri an abolitionist lawyer petitioned for Dred Scott's freedom. A jury verdict for Scott was overturned by the Missouri Supreme Court. Chief Justice Taney, writing the majority opinion for the United States Supreme Court, held that Dred Scott's status as a free man depended on state law. Taney also said in dicta that "no one of the African race free of slavery could be a citizen of the United States or apply to a Federal Court for justice."

The decision raised a storm of protest in the northern states. One of Taney's supporters, Stephen Douglas, was running for senator from Illinois against Abraham Lincoln. In a series of debates Lincoln denounced the Dred Scott decision. "The debates gave Lincoln national prominence. He was respected for his competence, his honesty and his moderation."

389
McIntyre, Duncan T.
Lincoln and the Matson Slave Case. 1 ILLINOIS LAW REVIEW (December 1906), 386-391.

A Kentucky man, Robert Matson, brought a family of slaves to Illinois. The husband and father was already a free man. After a year, Matson planned to return the wife and children to Kentucky as slaves. The slaves had help in their legal battle, and Matson hired Lincoln, "the best lawyer in the country," to represent him. Lincoln, in his argument, carefully avoided the issue and did not touch upon the question of the right of Matson to return the slaves to Kentucky. His contention was that a *habeas corpus* proceeding was necessary rather than a mere motion. Judgment was that the order for sale of the defendants be set aside, and the defendants discharged from imprisonment.

A footnote to the article indicates that mention of this case had not been located in biographies. (1906)

390
McMurtry, R. Gerald.
Commonwealth v. A. Lincoln. 21 NATIONAL REPUBLIC (March 1934), 5.

Lincoln started his own ferryboat business at the age of eighteen. The story, based on tradition, is that Lincoln was charged in 1827 with a penal offense. Two licensed Kentucky ferryboat operators, named Dill, accused Lincoln of operating his ferry without a license. Lincoln argued his own case. The eighteen-year-old Lincoln was acquitted by Kentucky Justice of the Peace Pate. It is said he became interested in the law at this point, and would row his boat across the Ohio River to listen to Squire Pate's court.

391
McMurtry, R. Gerald.
Lincoln's Law Offices in the Tinsley Building, 1843-1852. 1579 LINCOLN LORE (September 1969), 1-4.

In 1843 the law firm of Logan and Lincoln moved to a large office on the third floor of the Tinsley Building at Sixth and Adams streets in Springfield, Illinois. The building at the time was only three years old and considered a showplace in Springfield. When Lincoln's association with Logan ended, he remained in the office and took in William H. Herndon as a law partner. In 1847 they moved to smaller quarters also on the third floor. Lincoln and Herndon vacated that office in 1852.

Today the building has been restored by the citizens of Springfield and is open to the public. The article includes the history of the Tinsley Building and several photographs.

392
Maddox, John L.
Lincoln: A Lawyer and an Honest Man. 107 HOMILETIC REVIEW (February 1934), 94-98.

Lincoln was regarded with affection by the people for several reasons, including his humble origin, his lack of social graces, and the hardships he had endured. He remained one of the people, not above them, as he moved from rail splitter, grocery clerk, country post master, attorney-at-law, and politician to statesman. He had the ability to think, and was known for his common sense, perseverance, and energy.

In his law practice, he did not charge exorbitant fees, and was fair to plaintiff and defendant. He did his best when representing a righteous cause. He believed in honesty as an inviolable principle, essential for any lawyer, and he put that principle into practice.

393
The Manny Reaper: Some Background Information on the Case of McCormick v. Manny, 1855. 1516 LINCOLN LORE (June 1964), [1]-4.

Lincoln was retained to represent the defense in the patent case *McCormick v. Manny*. The suit was filed 1854 in Circuit Court of the United States for the District of Illinois. In July 1855, Lincoln went to Rockford to study the mechanics of the reaper manufactured by Manny & Co. McCormick was suing Manny on improvement patents rather than the original patents. This article tells of Lincoln's preparing his argument.

Details of the case are omitted, having been related in other accounts, but in summary attention is called to the humiliation of Abraham Lincoln in being ignored during the proceedings. The facsimile of a title page, from *American Law Register*, March 1856, contains the opinion of Justice McLean in the McCormick Reaper case.

394
Mantripp, J. C.
Abraham Lincoln. 12 (n.s.) 65 THE HOLBORN REVIEW (April 1921), 172-188.

The writer provides general information on Lincoln and explains that his law practice was considerable. He was not at his best in any case with which he was not sympathetic, and refused aid to cases of which he disapproved. He enjoyed legal work, and had great respect for the truth. He advised young men not to join the legal profession unless they could retain honesty. During his parting scene with Herndon, he indicated that he planned to return some day.

395
Manual for Lawyers. 327 LINCOLN LORE (July 15, 1935), [1].

The manual was compiled from Lincoln's notes for a law lecture and excerpts from other original Lincoln writings.

See also **Lincoln's** Manual for Lawyers.

396
Mathewson, Mark.
Lincoln the Lawyer. 11 ILLINOIS TIMES (February 6-12, 1986), 1, 4-5, 7-9.

The title "Lincoln the Lawyer" is the cover title of this issue of *Illinois Times*. Mathewson explains that although Lincoln was a lawyer for almost half of his life, few people remember that phase as part of the Lincoln legend, and fewer are familiar with particulars of his practice. Although several biographers have probed Lincoln's law career, the author concluded that the definitive study has yet to be done.

The article discussed some of the findings of the biographers, dismissing several myths, such as his reading the *Indiana Statutes*, and his reading of Blackstone's *Commentaries*. He did read Stuart's law books, and was admitted to the bar, an examination not being required at that time in history. The author championed Lincoln as a politician first and a lawyer second. His entrance to the Illinois bar was far from humble, with political background and connections. With the thrust of partnership, first with Stuart, then with Logan, he eventually gained a reputation as a leader of the Illinois bar. Mathewson, after acknowledging Lincoln's prominence as a lawyer, discussed whether he was a good one. He points to a few of the conflicts within the biographies.

397
Mathewson, Mark.
Uncommon Law. 11 ILLINOIS TIMES (February 6-12, 1986), 8.

The article indicates that a lack of public awareness and interest in Lincoln's legal career is the result of scholarly neglect. The topic has not been entirely ignored; however, several of the titles were more appreciative than scholarly. He pointed out that Beveridge had said Lincoln's legal career deserved but a few paragraphs. The *Collected Works* edited by Basler did not include the legal documents, the author attributing that to the fact that the editor did not think they were very important.

He looks forward to seeing the documentation of Lincoln's professional career, with all raw documents on microfilm--a project progressing in Springfield, Illinois.

398
The Metamora Court House. 3 ILLINIWEK (May-June 1965), 22-23.

A map of the Eighth Judicial Circuit shows where Lincoln traveled at the time of the Goings murder case. Lincoln believed the judge to be prejudiced. Lincoln and Grove were the lawyers for Melissa Goings. Lincoln and the elderly client conferred on the lower floor of the courthouse. When called by the judge, she was not to be found, then or ever again in Illinois. There are different versions of what happened, including the one that Lincoln encouraged her disappearance. She escaped standing trial for murder.

(The Metamora Court House became a Lincoln Memorial Museum, August 1921; one of two remaining courthouses of the old Eighth Judicial Circuit.) Cf. Conn, Robert L.,"Illinois' Most Historic Court House," 26 ILLINOIS BAR JOURNAL (January 1938), 148-149.

399
Miller, Karyn R.
The Stuart-Lincoln Law Firm. 35 ILLINOIS HISTORY (February 1982), 102-103.

A student has drawn on Duff and Frank for information, and presented a description of the law firm. With announcement of the Stuart and Lincoln partnership in the *Sangamo Journal,* Lincoln stepped into an established law practice, an association that provided background for later achievement at the Illinois bar. Among Lincoln's traits, the author recognized Lincoln's concise and clear words, his penmanship, with ability to handle office correspondence and legal papers. Note was made as well of the broad range of cases, from collection claims to murder charges.

400
Montgomery, Harry Earl.
Abraham Lincoln, the Lawyer. 37 AMERICAN LAW REVIEW (May-June 1903), 358-362.

"As a lawyer, Mr. Lincoln stood among the giants of his profession in the State of Illinois." The author uses quotations of others who practiced with Lincoln to describe qualities that made him such a great lawyer, such as: Lincoln would not take a case if he had "to bolster up a false proposition"; his simple and natural presentation of the facts of a case, which seemed to make the jury believe they were trying the case, not Lincoln; on pleading before a jury, he had no equal.

The author continues, describing the era in which Lincoln practiced, going from crude and simple pioneer days in 1837 to the rapid progress of the state in the years following, when the knowledge of the law required one to keep pace, which Lincoln did. He tells of Lincoln's notes for a law lecture and Lincoln's never charging enough for his services. He concludes with comments from Judge David Davis and Judge Thomas Drummond telling why they thought Lincoln was such a great lawyer.

401
Moores, Charles Washington.
Abraham Lincoln, Lawyer. 7 INDIANA HISTORICAL SOCIETY PUBLICATIONS (1922), 483-535.

Reprinted from Proceedings of the American Bar Association, 1910, and enlarged.

For annotation see **Moores** below.

402
Moores, Charles Washington.
Abraham Lincoln, Lawyer. 7 INDIANA HISTORICAL SOCIETY PUBLICATIONS (1922), 483-535.
Reprinted Greenfield, Ind.: William Mitchell Printing Co., 1929.

The author attributed Lincoln's ability to make simple statements in words and phrases that have been remembered through the years to his education as a lawyer. He attributes John T. Stuart, of the Illinois legislature, with encouraging Lincoln to study law. Lincoln became his partner after being admitted to the Illinois bar in 1837. He tells the story of Lincoln's buying a barrel of junk that contained Blackstone's *Commentaries*. Prior to this, his first reading of a law book was of the *Indiana Revised Statutes of 1824*; it also contained the United States and Indiana Constitutions. These works were the beginnings of Lincoln's law foundation.

Moores chronicles the history of Lincoln's law career, describing his law partnerships, office, dress, and mannerisms. He writes of life on the Eighth Judicial Circuit in some depth, including select stories about Lincoln in some of his trials by colleagues who practiced with him.

The Appendix lists Lincoln's state supreme court cases.

403

Moores, Charles Washington.

The Career of a Country Lawyer: Abraham Lincoln. [Read before the American Bar Association, Chattanooga, Tennessee, September 1, 1910.] 35 REPORTS OF THE AMERICAN BAR ASSOCIATION (1910), 440-477; 44 AMERICAN LAW REVIEW (November-December 1910), 886-902; 45 AMERICAN LAW REVIEW (January-February 1911), 78-96.

As background material, the author tells of Lincoln's youth, including his thirst for knowledge. Lincoln would walk fifteen miles to Boonville to attend sessions of court as a mere observer. Lincoln was continually trying to express his thoughts in language that others could easily comprehend. His interest in the *Indiana Revised Statutes* of 1824 is discussed.

Lincoln's honesty and integrity as a lawyer are illustrated in Moores' article. His standing as a lawyer was recognized throughout the Eighth Judicial Circuit. He was known for advocacy only in causes that he believed to be just, and he commanded the respect of his clients, peers, and friends. Lincoln was said to be the strongest jury lawyer in the state. There are references to his peculiarities in the courtroom, as well as his acute memory, simplicity, and sense of humor. The author tells of his law partnerships and details of circuit riding.

Quotations from letters of Lincoln show his recommendations for reading and studying books until every feature is understood, and starting the study of law with Blackstone's *Commentaries*, and after reading it carefully twice, proceeding to Chitty's *Pleadings*, Greenleaf's *Evidence*, and Story's *Equity*, in succession.

Moores considers Isaac N. Arnold's early biography the best, and praises Frederick Trevor Hills' *Lincoln the Lawyer* as an admirable piece of work, where one may find a list of Lincoln's state supreme court cases. Citations to additional cases appear in the footnotes to Moore's article. Examples from the docket are shown also. There is a list of volumes from Lincoln's small library, and the location of those volumes in 1910.

404

Moran, Frank.

Railroad Shares in Lincoln Lore. 37 ILLINOIS CENTRAL MAGAZINE (February 1949), 12-14.

This article by a layperson interested in Lincoln summarizes Lincoln's beginnings in Kentucky, noting that Hodgenville was the first Illinois Central town identified with Lincoln. After he began practice in Springfield, he represented the Illinois Central Railroad in several cases. He tells of Lincoln's drawing on the bank for 150 fees for services to the Illinois Central, lumping cases together and charging $10.00 for each. A map shows Lincoln's association with the Illinois Central Railroad cities.

405
Myers, H. B.
Lincoln at the Bar. 11 THE PHILOMATHEAN MONTHLY (February 1907),
2-5.

Myers speaks, not so much on what Lincoln did, but how and why he did
it. It is certain that he knew but little law as found in books, and never became
skilled in its "technics." Four traits are identified with Lincoln: simplicity,
honesty, confidence in self, and wit. He was also known by his directness of
speech and knowledge of human nature. He could not be persuaded to take a
doubtful case, no matter how much money was involved. With his sense of
justice, the people were assured of the outcome if they had the right on their
side. The author reflects on Lincoln's career from an uncouth lawyer in a
frontier town to a place of importance in the state and nation.

406
Myers, James E.
The Man Who Knew Lincoln Best. CHICAGO TRIBUNE, 6 February 1977, p.
34-35, 37-38.

Billy Herndon, Lincoln's law partner for sixteen years, "knew Lincoln best."
Lincoln appointed him as junior partner in his firm, where Herndon played the
part of a loyal lieutenant. He provided "comfort, counsel, friendship, and
devotion" to Lincoln during his early years, when there were frequent failures.
Herndon had known Lincoln, beginning with days at New Salem, sharing a room
with him in Springfield, extending through the years of law practice, and beyond.
The article indicates that Herndon studied law under Lincoln in the law office
of Logan & Lincoln, before Lincoln selected him as his law partner. He spoke
to Herndon about their being able to trust each other, which might have been
his reason for choosing him as partner. The junior partner also brought his
library to the practice. It was he who shared his knowledge of Lincoln with the
early biographers. Later he wrote a biography of Lincoln showing his human
side; he had trouble getting it published, and it was not popular when it finally
appeared.

407
Nathan, Manfred.
Abraham Lincoln as a Lawyer. 1 SOUTH AFRICAN LAW TIMES
(September 1932), 193-194; (October 1932), 217-218.

Lincoln's interest in the law began in his youth. He was admitted to the bar
on March 24, 1836, and was enrolled as an attorney on September 9, 1836.
Lincoln immediately entered into a partnership with Stuart, and later became
the partner of Stephen Logan. Practice included every sort of case. Lincoln in

his day was known as a leader in law, although somewhat eccentric. The article notes Lincoln's honesty. A lecture is cited in which Lincoln says himself that attorneys must be honest and moral. His methods were generally very direct, and he was clever in using situations and humorous stories in court to his advantage.

408
Nicolay, John G. (George)
Abraham Lincoln: A History, by John G. Nicolay and John Hay. 33 CENTURY (January 1887), 366-369; 33 (February 1887), 536-543.

A section entitled "Law in Springfield" tells of the Lincoln and Stuart office. Lincoln did not gain immediate eminence at the bar. Stuart was busy with political matters and it was only several years later that Lincoln found with Logan the companionship and inspiration he needed to develop into a lawyer.

Milton Hay (later one of the foremost lawyers of Illinois) who became acquainted with Lincoln in the county clerk's office, proposed study in law with him. The author quotes Hay's interesting account of law practice in those days. The young men who made the county clerk's office their place of rendezvous enjoyed Lincoln's stories.

"Six Years of Law Practice" quotes Jesse Fell's autobiography on Lincoln's practicing law more assiduously than ever before upon his return from Congress. Lincoln declined a Chicago offer, and resumed practice on the Eighth Judicial Circuit. He devoted himself to work with more energy than previously and gained new knowledge. The authors quote Judge David Davis in his description of life on the circuit, and they quote Davis and Judge Drummond on description of Lincoln, as well.

Other issues of *Century* are devoted to chapters that were later published in book form under the same title. About half of the book had first appeared in the journal, 1886-1890.
See also **Nicolay**, Monographs.

409
Nolan, Alan T.
Lawyer Lincoln--Myth and Fact. 16 HARVARD LAW SCHOOL BULLETIN (November 1964), 9-11, 22.

In histories of extraordinary men, one has to dig through the myths both pro and con, especially with a controversial figure, to obtain the truth about the man. Nolan refutes myths, such as that of Lincoln's accepting employment only when he "really believed in the justice of his cause," or that he was sympathetic without aggressive tendencies. He also discusses the Matson slave case.

410
Oates, Stephen B.
"Why Should the Spirit of Mortal Be Proud?" Abraham Lincoln's Years As an
Illinois Lawyer. 11 AMERICAN HISTORY ILLUSTRATED (April 1976), 32-
41.

This readable article, with something of a popular frame of reference
indicates that Lincoln was a practicing lawyer, 1837-1860, on the prairies of
Illinois where he had tried thousands of cases by the 1850s. He was described
as one of the leading attorneys, commanding respect of colleagues, and able to
woo judges and juries.

The author describes Lincoln's typical business day, his informal office
demeanor, and his law office, where he is reported to have quoted from the
poem "Mortality," a line of which Oates selects as title of the article.

He advised lawyers to be honest and was fair in setting his own fees. The
large volume of cases that he handled made his law practice profitable.

A wide range of cases was tried, including the well-known "Effie Afton,"
Duff Armstrong, McCormick Reaper at Cincinnati, *Bailey v. Cromwell*, and the
Matson slave case. The author notes that Lincoln defended both sides of fugitive
slave cases.

Issued also as a separate. At head of title: The Illinois Lawyer. Gettysburg,
Pa.: National Historical Society, 1976. 15 p.

411
Ogden, James M.
Lincoln's Early Impressions of the Law in Indiana.   7 NOTRE DAME
LAWYER (March 1932), 325-329.

Lincoln's first recorded interest in the study of law occurred in Indiana,
where he was brought before the justice of the peace in Kentucky for running
a ferry on the Ohio River without a license at the age of seventeen. Lincoln,
then ignorant of the law, would paddle his boat across the Ohio to watch the
justice in court proceedings. The first law book that he read was *The Revised
Laws of Indiana* at the home of a local Indiana constable. He also attended
some sessions of the court in several Indiana towns.

412
The Only Murderer Defended by Lincoln Who Was Hanged for His Crime.
1459 LINCOLN LORE (September 1959), [1]-3.

William (Fielding) Fraim, day laborer on an Illinois River steamboat,
accused of murdering a fellow laborer was defended by Lincoln. The jury found
him guilty and the case was not taken up on appeal. The defendant was

executed by hanging. There is description of the trial and a listing of papers in the files of the circuit court of Hancock County, Illinois. Several facsimiles of the documents are included, one believed to be in Lincoln's hand, removed from the courthouse, and later returned.

413
Packard, R. D.
Cincinnati: Scene of Humiliation and Triumph for Abraham Lincoln. 8 SOHIOAN (February 1936), 2-5.

This article discusses the *McCormick v. Manny* patent infringement case, in which Abraham Lincoln was retained as "local attorney" by P. H. Watson for the J. H. Manny Company. Lincoln had prepared his case carefully as he looked forward to courtroom combat with a recognized attorney. There was change of venue from Chicago to Cincinnati. Hence, there was little need of a "local" Illinois lawyer. Lincoln, however, was not dropped from the case. Packard provides the details, commenting on the behavior of Edwin M. Stanton in insulting Lincoln. As Lincoln tendered an offer to withdraw, the other attorneys accepted it readily. He handed them his carefully prepared argument, which was tossed into the wastebasket. Lincoln remained as a spectator in the courtroom. His spirit was dejected and he spent time walking the streets of Cincinnati. While Lincoln refused his $1000 fee at first, he was persuaded to accept it.

414
Page, Elwin L.
The "Effie Afton" Case. 58 LINCOLN HERALD (Fall 1956), 3-10.

The author contends that *Hurd v. The Rock Island Bridge Co.*, popularly known as the "Effie Afton" case, was the greatest civil case in which Lincoln took an active part. It marked an important turning point in the history of transportation. The "Effie Afton," a profitable steamboat, collided with a railroad drawbridge, the first ever built across the Mississippi River, at Davenport, Iowa. The boat caught fire and was destroyed. The boat owners brought suit against the bridge company. It was basically a clash between river transportation and railroads. Lincoln, with others, was hired for the defense. An in-depth study of the case points out how Lincoln studied the river current and design of the steamboat and bridge. It shows arguments of both sides including Lincoln's argument on the necessity of travel, used by Chief Justice Taney several years earlier in *Charles River Bridge v. Warren Bridge*. Includes list of authorities.

415
Pallette, Edward M.
Abraham Lincoln and Quinn Harrison. 16 BULLETIN OF THE CALIFORNIA STATE SOCIETY SONS OF THE REVOLUTION. (October-December 1937), 4-7.

This trial is cited as an example of Lincoln's influence over juries. Biographers have given accounts of the Quinn Harrison murder trial and also that of Duff Armstrong as being the most prominent criminal cases with which Lincoln identified as attorney. Includes a photograph of Abraham Lincoln's letter in his own handwriting, which had been in the possession of Quinn's sister.

416
Parkinson, Robert Henry.
The Patent Case That Lifted Lincoln Into a Presidential Candidate. 4 ABRAHAM LINCOLN QUARTERLY (September 1946), 105-122.

Parkinson's purpose is to relate information that has come to him from independent and qualified persons who had direct and firsthand knowledge. He preserves this account of the patent case involving certain improvements to the McCormick reaper. The suit, brought in the Northern District of Illinois was important enough to be heard before Justice McLean of the supreme court and Judge Drummond, of the Northern District of Illinois. The case was argued in Cincinnati. Lincoln had been retained as counsel, and led to believe that he was to prepare an argument. He was treated with discourtesy in the summer of 1855. It appeared that he was expected to withdraw from the case. He did so and later sent his roll manuscript containing the prepared argument. After the trial, Lincoln was paid, but returned the check, saying he had made no argument, and was therefore entitled to no more than the original retainer. This check was returned to him.
It was Parkinson's contention that Lincoln used these funds, received fortuitously, to meet the expenses of a campaign he could otherwise not have afforded. Without this "windfall" he might not have become the national leader.

417
Parry, Edward Abbott.
Abraham Lincoln, Advocate. 42 n.s. CORNHILL MAGAZINE (June 1917), 631-42; 294 THE LIVING AGE (July 14, 1917), 89-98.

Lincoln settled in Springfield in 1836 and entered into partnership with J. T. Stuart. Later William Herndon became Lincoln's partner. The article cites *People v. Green* to illustrate pioneer justice. This is a case where the defendant was found guilty of murder. The judge made it clear to the defendant that it was not he who sentenced him to death. Rather, it was the jury and the law. The courts in Lincoln's day were primitive. The courtrooms were makeshift and there were very few law books. As a successful advocate, Lincoln gave his advice on the best way to learn the law.

He neither drank nor used tobacco, but was fond of horseracing and cockfights. He often used illustrations from these pursuits as he argued in front of the jury.

Even if a prospective client had a strong case, Lincoln and Herndon would send him away if they thought that he was in the wrong. Lincoln rarely defended people in criminal matters, and then only if he thought they were innocent. If, during the trial Lincoln found out that his client lied to him, he would not defend him vigorously. The article gives an example of Lincoln's use of situations in court to his own advantage. He never lost sight of the point he was trying to prove to the jury, and often used humor to help win over the jury.

418
Peifer, Mrs. P. F.
The Case of the Stolen Horse. 87 DAUGHTERS OF THE AMERICAN REVOLUTION MAGAZINE (February 1953), 178.

This single page provides a story Mrs. Peifer's grandmother told her. Court was in session in Postville where Lincoln, just admitted to the bar, was to defend a young man for horse stealing. Due to hot weather, they took the court outside. Lincoln advised the young man to tell the judge how it actually happened. He did not steal, but "borrowed" the horse to travel where his sick wife was with their dead baby. The judge listened to Lincoln's appeal.

419
Prairie Lawyer. Edited by Richard M. Phillips. 7 ILLINIWEK (May-June 1969), 18-24.

Lincoln and others cheered when ballot made possible the move of the state capital from Vandalia to Springfield. The next day, March 1, 1837, Lincoln appeared to be admitted to the bar. A replica of his business card is included, "J. T. Stuart and A. Lincoln." A chronology with dates summarizes his career. There is a sketch of the law office, interior, and floor plan of the Tinsley Building. There is a picture as well of the inside of the United States district and circuit courtrooms.

420
The Prairie President. 102 THE PRAIRIE FARMER (May 3, 1930), 10-11.

The case of Duff Armstrong begins with the eruption of a brawl at a camp meeting, 29th August 1857. Norris and Armstrong were indicted for the murder of farmer Metzker, who died three days afterward. Norris had been tried and sentenced, and a change of venue was sought for Duff Armstrong. Lincoln learned of the murder charges against Armstrong, son of his old friend at New Salem. Armstrong's mother accepted Lincoln's offer to defend her son. Lincoln used the element of surprise twice. The state's attorney was surprised that Lincoln was to defend Armstrong, and equally as surprised when the almanac was produced. A "not guilty" verdict resulted.

421
Pratt, Harry E. (Edward)
Abraham Lincoln in Bloomington, Illinois. 29 JOURNAL OF THE ILLINOIS STATE HISTORICAL SOCIETY (April 1936), 42-69.

Lincoln walked the streets of Bloomington in fall and spring, as he followed the circuit courts of the Eighth Judicial District. Three places are marked with tablets: the courthouse, Major's Hall, and Phoenix Hall. The law office of David Davis and that of Swett and Orme were Lincoln's headquarters while in Bloomington. Shortly after the formation of Lincoln's law practice with John T. Stuart in 1837, Stuart sent him to try a case in McLean County. His client, Baddely, an Englishman, was astonished and indignant to see a six-foot-tall, ungainly, and shy young man, clothed in ill-fitting garments. Therefore, he dispensed with Lincoln's services. This article describes court days with Lincoln in the McLean County Circuit Court.

The *Weekly Whig* of Bloomington listed Lincoln as one of the lawyers in attendance in its 1851 notice of the circuit court in session. Pratt's article describes Lincoln's storytelling around the stove to the extent that the judge told him either he would have to adjourn, or the judge would have to adjourn court. Pratt singled out several cases: *Flagg v. Cyrus McCormick*, a patent-infringement case, in which Lincoln had charge of Flagg's interest; and a sensational trial, the murder having been committed in the county clerk's office. There was discussion of Lincoln's suit to collect his $5000 fee from the Illinois Central Railroad; a temperance case; and the Illinois Board of Education, which employed Lincoln to draw up bond guaranteeing the pledge of McLean County subscription to establish Illinois State Normal University. There is further insight into Lincoln's speeches in Bloomington, and his social life there, as well as description of two lots that Lincoln acquired in Bloomington.

Lincoln prepared two autobiographical sketches; one for political purposes to Jesse W. Fell and another sketch of his life for publicity purposes. The last line of the autobiography was unusual and amusing in stating, "No other marks or brands collected," the phrase which sometimes appeared in newspaper notices for stray animals.

Lincoln's ability as a lawyer was judged from the words of his contemporaries in Bloomington. "Lincoln was a great cross examiner." He never asked an unnecessary question, and he knew when and where to stop a witness.

422

Pratt, Harry E. (Edward)

Abraham Lincoln's First Murder Trial. 37 JOURNAL OF THE ILLINOIS STATE HISTORICAL SOCIETY (September 1944), 242-249.

Lincoln's first murder case involved the shooting of Jacob Early by Henry Truett, at the Spottswood Hotel in Springfield (later to be the home of Abraham and Mary Todd Lincoln), over a bitter political quarrel. Lincoln was one among several others engaged to represent Truett. The trial began on October 8, 1838. The author gives a description of the trial itself, and arguments used by both sides. The final plea for the defendant was made by Lincoln, "a short but strong and sensible speech," according to his colleague Stephen T. Logan. The jury found Truett not guilty. Lincoln did subsequent legal work for the parties involved.

423

Pratt, Harry E. (Edward)

The Famous "Chicken Bone" Case. 45 JOURNAL OF THE ILLINOIS STATE HISTORICAL SOCIETY (Summer 1952), 164-167.

Doctors hired Lincoln and his former partner, John T. Stuart, with four Bloomington lawyers to defend them in a malpractice suit. Samuel A. Fleming, whose legs were broken during a fire, brought suit when one leg did not heal correctly after it had been set by the physicians. Defense attorneys, who would have had only a week to prepare for the trial, actually had a year due to continuance of the case. During that time, Lincoln learned bone anatomy and chemistry from one of the doctors, demonstrated with a chicken bone. There were arguments for change of venue, and finally counsel for both sides agreed that the case should be dismissed.

424

Pratt, Harry E. (Edward)

The Genesis of Lincoln the Lawyer. 57 BULLETIN OF THE ABRAHAM LINCOLN ASSOCIATION (September 1939), [3]-10.

In Part One, "The Decision," the author asks the question as to why Abraham Lincoln decided to study law after encouragement from John T. Stuart in 1834, when in 1832 he pondered the study of law and chose shopkeeping.

The author theorizes that the following events exposed Lincoln to the processes of litigation and lawyers in action. In April 1833, in the Sangamon Circuit Court during the case of *Simmons v. Bale*, Lincoln appeared as a witness, followed a week later by an appearance as a witness in *Close v. Ritter*, and he was present as a juryman on three additional cases. Pratt describes the courtroom itself and the lawyers and judges who practiced in it at that time.

Part Two of the article, "Practitioner in Embryo," describes Lincoln's earliest legal document, a bond for a deed dated November 12, 1831. His second document was also a bond for a deed dated January 31, 1833. The author suggests these documents illustrate Lincoln's early interest in the law. The documents were obviously copied from a form book, probably one that Lincoln was purported to have owned at that time. Lincoln also was known to have drawn up petitions and witnessed deeds and mortgages during this time. "That he continued to draw legal documents and to attend the local courts after 1832 indicates the strength of the law's attraction for him."

425
Pratt, Harry E. (Edward)
In Defense of Mr. Justice Browne. 56 BULLETIN OF THE ABRAHAM LINCOLN ASSOCIATION (June 1939), 4-8.

"One of Abraham Lincoln's most interesting cases was the defense of Supreme Court Justice Thomas C. Browne before the Illinois House of Representatives in January, 1843." A group of political opponents of Judge Browne sought his removal from office, by introducing a petition into the House of Representatives praying for Browne's removal "for want of capacity to discharge the duties of his office."

Abraham Lincoln represented Browne in this matter. Much of the trial revolved around the admission of testimony by former Judge Sidney Breese on his opinion of Judge Browne's competency to which Lincoln objected. The objection was overruled but only after long, strenuous arguments on both sides. Judge Browne was eventually acquitted. Breese's testimony proved more helpful than damaging to Browne.

426
Pratt, Harry E. (Edward)
Judge Abraham Lincoln. 48 JOURNAL OF THE ILLINOIS STATE HISTORICAL SOCIETY (Spring 1955), 28-39.

On their way to Taylorville, Lincoln's partner, Herndon, and Attorney Ferguson learned that Judge David Davis, of the Eighth Judicial District could not hold court due to a family illness. Therefore, Davis followed an Illinois circuit court practice of selecting an attorney to preside.

Lincoln is known to have presided for Davis on at least seven occasions. He is also reported to have taken the bench when Judge Davis went out for exercise. (In order to prevent reversal on appeal, the clerk's record would show that the true judge was sitting.) There is evidence in judges' dockets of the Eighth Circuit, with entries in Lincoln's own handwriting, albeit sometimes there is only a single word. These cases were heard in Sangamon, Champaign, Logan, and DeWitt counties.

427
Pratt, Harry E. (Edward)
Lincoln and Bankruptcy Law. 31 ILLINOIS BAR JOURNAL (January 1943), 201-206; 17 JOURNAL OF THE NATIONAL ASSOCIATION OF REFEREES IN BANKRUPTCY (April 1943), 98-100.

Logan and Lincoln handled seventy-seven bankruptcy cases from February 1, 1842, to March 2, 1843, under the bankruptcy law passed by Congress in 1841 and repealed in 1843. The article explains the bankruptcy law itself. Most of the cases were handled by Springfield lawyers, like Lincoln, because that was where the bankruptcy court usually resided. (Records of bankruptcy cases, moved to Chicago, were burned in the 1871 fire; however, record of cases with considerable land involved remain in the office of the clerk of the United States District Court, Springfield.)

428
Pratt, Harry E. (Edward)
Lincoln and Douglas as Counsel on the Same Side. 26 AMERICAN BAR ASSOCIATION JOURNAL (March 1940), 214.

This short article deals with the appearance of Lincoln and Douglas together as attorneys for the defense of an accused murderer, in the case of *People v. Spencer Turner* (May 1840).

429
Pratt, Harry E. (Edward)
Lincoln Defends Tom Patterson. 29 ILLINOIS BAR JOURNAL (October 1940), 56-60.

In the manslaughter trial of *People v. Patterson* Lincoln represented a store owner, Thomas Patterson, in 1858. Patterson was convicted and sentenced to three years. He was pardoned by Governor Wood of Illinois after letters and petitions were sent to him, including one by Abraham Lincoln in August of 1860. A photocopy of Lincoln's letter appears as illustration.

430
Pratt, Harry E. (Edward)
Lincoln's Petitions for Pardon. 30 ILLINOIS BAR JOURNAL (February 1942), 234-240, 261-262.

Pratt discusses Lincoln's pleas to the governor for pardon of some twenty different criminals between 1842 and 1860. A chronological list of the twenty petitions for pardon in which he participated is included. Some of the cases are discussed in detail. There is a facsimile reproduction of one of Lincoln's original petitions.

431
Pratt, Harry E. (Edward)
Lincoln's Supreme Court Cases. 32 ILLINOIS BAR JOURNAL (September 1943), 23-35.

"Abraham Lincoln was one of the foremost lawyers in practice before the Illinois Supreme Court in the 1840s and 1850s." The author claims he appeared in at least 243 cases before the state supreme court. Due to the scattering of files and lapse of time, Pratt concludes it would be almost impossible to do a complete study of Lincoln's work in the Supreme Court of Illinois. Includes an alphabetical list of Lincoln's known cases.

432
Pratt, Harry E. (Edward)
Mr. Lincoln's Introduction to Illinois Law. 42 HOBBIES (February 1938), 18-19.

Pratt discusses Lincoln as a youth and his interest in the law. He tells how people of Kentucky went to court sessions to hear educated lawyers and to observe attorneys when they gave political speeches during recesses. Lincoln took an interest in the constable's *Revised Laws of Indiana*, which he read. Lincoln attended court at several county seats, and became acquainted with Judge Pitcher, the leading attorney. He enjoyed the judge's library, particularly Blackstone's *Commentaries* in which Lincoln wrote his name. He had a chance to read and study the *Revised Code of Laws of Illinois*, with imprint Shawneetown, 1829. He became interested in the Illinois statute describing the Illinois/Indiana boundary, and the "Illinois Black Code," concerning slavery. The author tells of Lincoln's noting a special act regarding a toll bridge. Later, the first bill Lincoln introduced into the General Assembly was authorization for such a bridge. He also showed interest in the elections statute.

433
Pratt, Harry E. (Edward)
Our Growing Knowledge of Lincoln. 39 ILLINOIS BAR JOURNAL (July 1951), 627-629.

Pratt delivered an address to the Legal History Breakfast, calling for a new study of Lincoln as a lawyer, because earlier works are now out of date. He talks about new collections of Lincoln memorabilia that have come to light as recently as 1951. The author makes suggestions on the studies needed.

434
Pratt, Marion D.
Some New Lincoln Finds in the State Archives. 12 ILLINOIS HISTORY (February 1959), 111-114.

The first volume of the "Register of Books Withdrawn from the Illinois State Library" contained Lincoln's signature, although it was in the name of S. T. Logan. The title that he checked out was the *Revised Laws of New York*. Pratt indicated that the book that he had used was believed to be no longer extant at the time of her article. At a later date, he checked out the *Statesman's Manual*.

435
Quinn, James H.
Lincoln, the Lawyer. 21 CASE AND COMMENT (February 1915), 705-709.

This author analyzed the character of Lincoln. Three characteristics sum up Lincoln's twenty-three years of law practice. Lincoln was immovable in his adherence to the right, he sought a moral principle upon which to base his every action, and he promoted human liberty.

The article gives a brief history of young Lincoln as he makes his way into the world of lawyers, and describes the lawyers with whom he associated. "It is exceedingly doubtful if the bar of any other state in the Union equaled that of the frontier state of Illinois in professional ability when Lincoln won his spurs."

436
Ransom, William L.
"Abraham Lincoln--Profession a Lawyer" Address. 22 AMERICAN BAR ASSOCIATION JOURNAL (March 1936), 155-159.

This speech by the president of the American Bar Association referred to Lincoln as a professional lawyer, before the time when being a lawyer was considered a profession. Lincoln was considered "the rugged, active leader of the

Bar of a great state. . . ." He "believed deeply in the Federal Union" and "championed the right of men to be free. . . ."

Ransom concludes that Lincoln was enlightened and farseeing in regard to the Constitution, that the government exists for the people and not vice-versa, and that these views should be heeded in the troubled days ahead (1936).

437
The Replevin Mule Case. 1 LINCOLN NEWS (January 1980), 1.

This humorous case was tried in Logan County. While in the courthouse, Lincoln overheard the court case concerning Henry Palmer's claim of ownership of a mule. Even as Lincoln's friend Attorney Wilford D. Wyatt was defending Palmer, Lincoln laughed aloud. Wyatt, upon losing the case, thought Lincoln's hearty laughter might have been the cause of the verdict. Lincoln wrote to the judge who had heard the case asking for a new trial on grounds of newly discovered evidence. The parties to the case continued to sue over the mule, even after it was dead.

438
Richards, John T. (Thomas)
Abraham Lincoln: His Standing as a Lawyer. 23 CASE AND COMMENT (July 1916), 106-108.

Richards believed that Lincoln's reported interest in studying law after finding a copy of Blackstone's *Commentaries* in the bottom of a barrel was unfounded. He began his study of law after advisement from John T. Stuart, who loaned him the necessary lawbooks during Lincoln's first term in the Illinois legislature. Lincoln "declined to support any measures which he did not believe just." Lincoln became "one of the great lawyers of his generation. . . ."

439
Richards, John T. (Thomas)
[Lincoln as a Lawyer in Illinois]. "The Docket" 50 AMERICAN LAW REVIEW (September 1916), 781-788.

The author draws on Frederick T. Hill's *Lincoln the Lawyer*, which provides an exhaustive account of Lincoln's years of practice in Illinois.

He describes Illinois courtrooms as primitive log buildings, and in some districts the sessions were held in taverns. The proceedings were usually very informal. Judges thought carefully of their own safety before sentencing a defendant. The reader learns of life on the circuit, and in Springfield, of Stuart and Lincoln's law office and the few volumes that comprised the library. It is likely that Lincoln tried more cases between 1849 and 1860 than any other man on the Eighth Judicial Circuit. He was an acknowledged leader of the local bar, whose services were constantly in demand. The article gives examples of how Lincoln would use certain situations in court to his advantage. Lincoln was a good defense attorney in criminal cases only if he strongly believed in his cause. The article gives two examples of Lincoln's refusing to represent a person he believed to be in the wrong. Lincoln was a strong advocate of discouraging litigation and promoting negotiations.

440
S., C. E.
Abraham Lincoln--Attorney and Counsellor at Law.   15 STATE BAR JOURNAL OF THE STATE BAR OF CALIFORNIA (February 1940), 42-44.

Lincoln's "legendary figure of the Great Emancipator and statesman" almost obscures the fact that he was an excellent lawyer. His career in law started when he read a worn edition of Blackstone's *Commentaries* found in the bottom of a barrel of junk he had purchased. It led him to the great heights he achieved as a statesman. The writer describes Lincoln's partnerships and his reputation on the circuit.

441
Saltonstall, F. G.
Recollection of Lincoln in Court.   53 n.s. 31 CENTURY MAGAZINE (February 1897), 636-637.

Before Lincoln's debates with Douglas, "he had won reputation for legal ability and for unsurpassed test in jury trials." Among the most important cases he tried was the Rock Island Bridge case in 1857. The author personally witnessed the trial, which pitted "long and violent opposition of rivermen and steamboat owners to the construction of a railroad bridge across the Mississippi River between Rock Island in Illinois and Davenport in Iowa." The suit was brought by owners of a steamboat that burned after crashing into one of the bridge piers.

The author was impressed by Lincoln's memory of facts and figures and "his comprehension, vigilance, and remembrance of the details of the testimony." Judge McLean "gave his emphatic decision in favor of the Rock Island Railroad Company; it seemed to have received large inspiration from Lincoln's masterful argument."

442
Saunders, Horace.
Abraham Lincoln's Partner, Billy Herndon. LINCOLN GROUP PAPERS, 2nd series. (1945), 145-158.

Horace Saunders pays tribute to Herndon before the Lincoln Group of Chicago. The reader learns how Lincoln and Herndon became partners. As an agitated Lincoln rushed into Herndon's quarters, he said he had determined to sever his partnership with Logan and asked Herndon to go into partnership with him. Herndon was surprised because of his own youth and lack of experience. He had not even received his license to practice. Lincoln uttered the words "Billy, I can trust you if you can trust me." Herndon accepted. He, more than Lincoln, subscribed to papers, bought pamphlets, and had a wide range of correspondence. This piece includes Lincoln's parting words as he left that office for Washington. The author discusses to what extent reliance can be placed on Herndon's truth in his published writings on Lincoln.

443
Scanlon, Ann M.
Dun & Bradstreet's Credit Rating of Abraham Lincoln. 77 LINCOLN HERALD (Summer 1975), 124.

A forerunner of Dun and Bradstreet, Inc., the Mercantile Agency, made credit checks on individuals and agencies. Attorneys were often selected as correspondents because of their practice in debt collection and their access to confidential information. During the 1840s and 1850s Lincoln served as correspondent from Sangamon County. His own credit and standing were scrutinized. In the first entry regarding Lincoln, 1847-1849, he was rated as a "good lawyer." In 1850 it was noted that he was responsible, and in good financial standing, one of the best debt collectors and a first-rate employee of the agency. The law firm of Lincoln and Herndon had also been investigated.

Schaefer, Carl W.
"Lincoln the Lawyer." [Address]

See: "**Dedication** of the Bronze Statue 'Lincoln the Lawyer'" 51 LINCOLN HERALD (June 1949), 2-17.

444
Scoles, Eugene F.
"Abraham Lincoln Being First Duly Sworn . . ." A Fragment from a Lawyer's File. 56 OREGON LAW REVIEW (1977), 649-654.

The author notes that little has been written about Lincoln as a lawyer compared to Lincoln as a president because: 1) "No one thought to save Lincoln manuscripts until he became President," and 2) Lincoln and the Eighth Circuit where he worked kept very few records at that time. The article concerns an original holographic affidavit, used by Lincoln in a contested will case, *McDaniel v. Correll*. The document is located at the University of Oregon Law School; a photocopy appears in the article.

445

Scoville, Samuel.
Abraham Lincoln as a Lawyer. 3 DOCKET [West Pub. Co.] (1927), 3050-1-2, 3058-1-2.

This article explains the informality of trial procedures in the days of Lincoln. It describes client Baddeley, of English origin, who basing judgment of Lincoln on his appearance, refused to be represented by him. Later, the man learned to admire him. Lincoln spent the happiest years of his life walking and riding the one hundred and fifty mile wide circuit, consisting of more than a dozen counties. Lincoln was known for using an anecdote that related to the point he was trying to make.

Lincoln had advice for young lawyers on diligence and extemporaneous speaking, among other things. He believed that it was a mistake to sacrifice honesty for the sake of winning a case. He would take a case only if he had confidence in it, exemplified by his walking out of the courtroom and refusing to continue a trial. He favored negotiation over litigation.

446

Searcy, Earle Benjamin.
A Dead Pig Goes to Court--with Lincoln. 51 LINCOLN HERALD (October 1949), 26-27.

Lincoln held the pig by the hoof, only figuratively, in a $3.00 damage suit in the Supreme Court of Illinois. The appeal concerning a stray pig was the most trivial in his career, and he may have taken the southern Illinois county case out of sympathy. *Byrne v. Stout* was one of the most frivolous suits in the state supreme court, which took the case, and placed it on the agenda for an opinion. A decision was handed down with legal analysis, replete with citations. According to the court rules of that day, lawyers did not have to confine their oral arguments to previously filed briefs and abstracts. They could introduce new evidence, provided they supplied in advance synopses of points and facts they proposed to present.

447
Segal, Charles M.
Lincoln, Benjamin Jonas and the Black Code. 46 JOURNAL OF THE
ILLINOIS STATE HISTORICAL SOCIETY (Autumn 1953), 277-282.

This article is concerned with that portion of William H. Herndon's
biography of Lincoln that deals with a free Negro, John Shelby. He had been
arrested and fined in New Orleans, but was unable to pay the fine. Therefore,
he faced the prospect of being sold into slavery. Herndon and Lincoln
approached the governors of Illinois and of Louisiana in his behalf, but they had
no power to interfere. Lincoln then drew up a subscription list, enlisted the help
of friends to purchase Shelby's liberty, and sent the funds to New Orleans. In
describing the case, Herndon omitted the part Benjamin F. Jonas played in the
case. He was a twenty-three-year-old New Orleans lawyer and son of Abraham
Jonas of Quincy, Illinois. Segal indicates that it was Benjamin F. Jonas who
obtained Shelby's liberty with the funds, whereas Herndon's account notes that
the money was sent to Col. A. P. Field, who applied it as directed. The letters
indicate that Field accepted a fee. The article includes typescript letters from
Annie E. Jonas and B. F. Jonas.

Lincoln became known as a lawyer interested in cases involving rights of
slaves and free Negroes after the campaign of 1854.

448
Segal, Charles M.
Postscript to "Black Code" Article. 46 JOURNAL OF THE ILLINOIS STATE
HISTORICAL SOCIETY (Winter 1953), 428-430.

The original indenture of apprenticeship paper of John Shelby is located at
the Illinois State Historical Library.

449
Selby, Paul.
The Dunlap Assault Case on Paul Selby in 1853, in Which Abraham Lincoln
Appeared as Associate Counsel. 30 CHICAGO LEGAL NEWS (1898), 298.

Paul Selby was a veteran newspaper editor in Illinois. In 1853 he was
assaulted by James Dunlap and Dunlap's friends over a published article
criticizing Trustee Dunlap's administration of a hospital for the insane. Selby
brought suit against Dunlap for damages. Abraham Lincoln appeared as
associate counsel for Dunlap, arguing for mitigation of damages. Selby refutes
the story in the *North American Review* [by James L. King] as told by Judge
Bergen that, after plaintiff's lawyer Benjamin S. Edwards delivered a dramatic
case, Lincoln arose in defense laughing and removing his vest to show one yarn

suspender "the result of which was to destroy the effect of Edwards' tears. . . ." Selby had written statements by others at the trial claiming Lincoln acted in no such manner. The Hon. Henry B. Atherton who was present at the trial, writes, there were "no long and loud laughs; no removing of coat, vest and of cravat down to 'his one woolen suspender'; no weeping by jury or spectators and absolutely no 'Ben Edwards,' whoever he might have been."

450
Selby, Paul.
"Lincoln's Skill As a Lawyer." A Correction. "Part Taken by Lincoln in the Defense of the Man Who Struck Selby," 166 NORTH AMERICAN REVIEW (April 1898), 507-510.

Selby takes issue with the article that appeared in the *North American Review* in 1898, in which the Dunlap assault case as described by Judge Bergen is recorded. Selby explains that he, as editor of the paper, was the person beaten, and he describes events leading up to the assault. He gives first-hand information as he refutes Bergen's description of the courtroom scene in which Lincoln's inappropriate laughter is used to influence the jury. He uses his right, courtesy of the *North American Review*, to set facts straight pertaining to himself, and to vindicate the memory of Lincoln.

451
The Senior Partner. 806 LINCOLN LORE (September 18, 1944), [1].

Lincoln joined John T. Stuart as a law partner at the Hoffman's Row law offices. Although the literature speaks of Lincoln's "old friend" Stuart, he was only fifteen months older than Lincoln. After the Stuart and Lincoln law firm was dissolved, his partnership began with Logan. Finally he was senior partner in the Lincoln and Herndon firm. There is some indication that after Lincoln's permanent departure, that office was not cared for by the junior partner.

452
Sharritt, Charles A.
Abraham Lincoln, Attorney and Counsellor at Law. 15 CALIFORNIA STATE BAR ASSOCIATION AND STATE BAR JOURNAL (February 1940), 42-44.

Sharritt related the familiar story of Lincoln's eager absorption of Blackstone's *Commentaries*. His understanding of human nature, acquired when he was a country lawyer, contributed to his national success. Lincoln had been a law partner in several firms. He was not always victorious. On one circuit trip, he lost every case he tried, representing a total of three months of uninterrupted defeat. Nevertheless, Lincoln was highly respected as a lawyer and sought by many persons to represent them. During nearly a quarter century at the bar, he was regarded as a formidable adversary by his contemporaries. A quotation regarding Lincoln by Justice Caton is included, as well as a statement by jurist Sidney Breese, who stated that Lincoln was one of the fairest lawyers he had ever known.

Shaw, Lord
See **Knox-Shaw**, Thomas K.

453
Shearer, Guy C.
Abraham Lincoln--Spanned the Distance. 40 KENTUCKY BENCH AND BAR (January 1976), 12-14, 32-35.

In fifty-two years Lincoln spanned the distance "from a humble log dwelling on the Kentucky frontier to the White House in Washington, D.C.," and from "poor frontier child to the position of the President of the United States." Shearer believes Lincoln's character was molded by American frontier democracy. He describes Lincoln's humble birth and states, "more books have been written about him than any other non-biblical character."

Lincoln never received formal legal training, yet he became one of the leading lawyers of Illinois. His three law partners were all natives of Kentucky. He talks of books Lincoln read, what education he did have, and tells how Lincoln's words were so simple and direct that it was hard to improve on their meaning, giving wisdom to future generations to come.

454
Shearer, Guy C.
President Abraham Lincoln and Joshua Fry Speed. 13 BULLETIN OF THE LOUISVILLE BAR ASSOCIATION (Fall 1963), 6.

In Springfield, Lincoln joined a debating society similar to the one he had joined in New Salem, where it met in Joshua Speed's room over the store. He also joined the Young Men's Lyceum. Debating played a part in his development. A section on "Lincoln's Law Partners" shows that Stuart, Logan, and Herndon, who were born in Kentucky, influenced his life in different ways. A word is included on Lincoln's local law associates. Springfield attorneys during the Lincoln era are listed, noting the high percentage of Kentuckians.

455
Sherlock, Richard K.
Liberalism, Public Policy, and the Life Not Worth Living: Abraham Lincoln on Beneficient Euthanasia. 26 AMERICAN JOURNAL OF JURISPRUDENCE (1981), 47-65.

The author is concerned with the right of patients to have lifesaving therapy withdrawn or death induced. The question is who decides which lives are not worth saving. The author explores how this concept interacts with liberal regimes which are based on the rule of law. It is almost impossible to define a set of legal criteria for a standard of "life not worth living."
Sherlock compares euthanasia of today with Lincoln's struggle with slavery. Lincoln's message was that slavery was incompatible with civil equality. Lincoln's view of "popular sovereignty," in the context of the slavery issue, was that the majority of the people could not rightfully decide to repeal the fundamental charter of the American regime. The writer contends that euthanasia challenges a liberal regime to make a judgment that some human lives no longer deserve the minimal protections afforded other citizens.

456
Smith, Arthur M.
Abraham Lincoln, Inventor. 20 FEDERAL BAR JOURNAL (Summer 1960), 274-280; 41 JOURNAL OF THE PATENT SOCIETY (July 1959), 447.

Lincoln was the only president to have patented an invention, a patent for "Buoying Vessels Over Shoals." The author distinquishes Lincoln from other mentors in that Lincoln blended "his skills as an inventor with his genius as a statesman." He links men such as Ben Franklin, George Washington, and Thomas Jefferson with Lincoln, who blended an inventor's vision with practical statesmanship. He notes lawyer Lincoln's part in the defense of patent infringement on McCormick's reaper, and follows by discussing some of Lincoln's patent law cases.

457
Smith, Elmer A.
Abraham Lincoln--An Illinois Central Lawyer. 12 I.C.C. PRACTITIONERS JOURNAL (May 1945), 773-791.

The author claims Lincoln did more work for the Illinois Central Railroad than he did for any other client. He handled both large and small cases on behalf of the corporation. Smith provides details for some of the cases Lincoln appealed to the Supreme Court of Illinois for the railroad. He reviews the case in which Lincoln sued the Illinois Central Railroad to collect his fee. The article describes not only the work Lincoln did for the Illinois Central, but also his life as a circuit rider on the Eighth Judicial Circuit.

Issued also as a separate. Paper read at a meeting of the Western Conference of Railway Counsel, February 13, 1945. Chicago [1945?]. 23 p.

458
Smith, Len Young.
Abraham Lincoln as a Bar Examiner (Member of Illinois Board from 1858 until Election as President). 51 BAR EXAMINER (August 1982), 35-37.

In 1858 the Supreme Court of Illinois, by rule, appointed three-man examining committees in the Three Grand Division to examine prospective lawyers. Lincoln was appointed to the Second Grand Division Board in 1850. The article describes the procedure then used for one to quality for practice of law and Lincoln's involvement in such a procedure.

459
Snigg, John P.
The Great Prairie Lawyer. 37 ILLINOIS BAR JOURNAL (February 1949), 234-235.

Address delivered in Springfield, February 12, 1948, to members of the Sangamon County Bar Association.

Although Lincoln is regarded as a statesman and president by others, in the Illinois Bar he was the circuit rider and great prairie lawyer. He acquired his experience in human relationships in his old North Fifth Street law office. When he bade farewell to his partner, Herndon, he indicated that if he lived, he would return and they would go on practicing law. The speaker liked the simplicity of their shingle, "Lincoln and Herndon, Lawyers." Lincoln regretted leaving his profession and surely was nostalgic for riding the circuit. Snigg reminds Springfield lawyers that they practice in the town where Lincoln practiced.

460
Somers, W. H.
A New Light on Lincoln as an Advocate: Reminiscences of the clerk of the Circuit Court of Champagne [*sic*] County, Ill., for Several Years Following 1856. 40 CHICAGO LEGAL NEWS (February 22, 1908), 227-228; 20 GREEN BAG (February 1908), 78-80.

An interview by Allen Henry Wright, of W. H. Somers, clerk of the Circuit Court of Champaign County from 1856, where Lincoln frequently appeared as an advocate or counsel. Somers gives a physical description of Lincoln and fondly remembers his kindness, always having a pleasant word for everybody. Somers said Lincoln occupied the leading position at the bar and on the circuit, if not in the entire state. He claims Lincoln's advocacy was the best with a just cause and somewhat weaker when on the wrong side of a cause. "His love of justice and fair play was his predominant trait." Somers describes Lincoln's method of trying a case. "First, he would make as strong a showing as he could for the opposite side," but "later, turning to his own side, he would utterly demolish his previous arguments." "He was willing to concede to his opponent everything that justly belonged to them, and if he could not do that, and still win the case, he would not take it in the first place."

Lincoln was well known for his wit and humor. Attorneys considered it a "drawing card" to be associated with him. Lincoln sometimes filled in for Judge Davis on the bench. Somers never saw Lincoln or Judge Davis drinking alcoholic beverages at local taverns, where attorneys gathered.

461
Spencer, Omar C.
Abraham Lincoln: The Lawyer. 4 OREGON LAW REVIEW (April 1925), [177]-187; WASHINGTON STATE BAR ASSOCIATION REPORT OF PROCEEDINGS. 3rd Annual Convention, Spokane (June 1924), 133-140.

The author explains that little has been written about Lincoln dealing with that part of his life when he was a lawyer. History scarcely mentions his life as a lawyer, and biographers have largely skipped that phase of his life. His position as a lawyer seems to have been remembered only by lawyers, and they do not think of him as a great lawyer. Spencer proposes to look at that part of Lincoln's life at the bar, and believes that his years spent in learning and applying legal principles and associating with lawyers and judges deserve some credit in preparing him for his later presidential position.

He provides some biographical background, including the Blackstone's *Commentaries* story, meager law training, his passing the bar in 1837, and his move to Springfield. He mentioned Lincoln's preference for practicing in partnership, rather than by himself, and describes the trial lawyer, engaged in state circuit courts, including those on the old Eighth Judicial Circuit, comprised of fourteen counties. He tells of the judges, state's attorneys, and lawyers traveling to county seats during half of the year, writing in longhand and each "carrying his law in his head." The author provides some statistics on the number of cases in which Lincoln appeared as counsel, noting also that he was not to be judged by his trial work in state and federal courts but was a formidable lawyer in courts of appeal. He adapted himself to all forms of litigation.

He refers to Lincoln's representation of the Illinois Central Railroad Company, and tells of the *Hurd v. Rock Island Bridge Company*. In this particular article reference is made to *Averill v. Field*, because counsel for plaintiff later became an Oregon senator. Lincoln was counsel for defendant, with Justice Stephen A. Douglas writing the opinion, which was a decision against Lincoln's contention. Finally the author compares Lincoln to Chief Justice Marshall, quoting from Beveridge, and he lauds his ideals and ethics.

462
Sprecher, Robert A.
Lincoln as a Bar Examiner. 42 ILLINOIS BAR JOURNAL (August 1954), 918-922.

The writer describes how lawyers in Illinois were admitted to the bar prior to 1897 when the Supreme Court of Illinois instituted the Board of Law Examiners. During Lincoln's time permanent regular boards appointed by the supreme court examined applicants. Special committees were appointed by circuit court judges as needed. Lincoln served on both boards. The article describes some of the lawyers Lincoln interviewed as well as customs and practices of these boards.

463
Starr, John W.
Did Lincoln Decline an Offer to Become N.Y. Central's General Counsel? 8 NEW YORK CENTRAL LINES MAGAZINE (November 1927), 10-11.

When Lincoln was in New York in the spring of 1860 to give his Cooper Union address, Erastus Corning, president of the New York Central, was in the audience, and was impressed by the speech of this midwest lawyer. The story is that through James W. Merwin, he met Lincoln, and offered him the high position of general counsel for the railway at a salary of $10,000. Lincoln hesitated initially, thinking of himself and his family. Corning, not wishing a hasty decision, indicated that an offer through a letter would follow. When Lincoln was again in Springfield, he received the written offer and declined.

464
Stewart, Judd.
Law Partnerships of Abraham Lincoln: Letter from Mr. Judd Stewart. 9 JOURNAL OF THE ILLINOIS STATE HISTORICAL SOCIETY (July 1916), 209-210.

Stewart writes a letter to the journal to correct an earlier article concerning Lincoln's law partners. According to the letter, Lincoln was licensed to practice law in 1837 and from that time until 1841 he was a partner of John T. Stuart. Following that he was in partnership with Logan. In 1843 Herndon became his partner, continuing until Lincoln went to Washington.

The author claims that documents signed "Harlan and Lincoln," "Lincoln and Lamon," etc., were the result of the custom of that time; if two lawyers from different firms worked on a case they signed it as above. Lawyers do that today for a firm name. Thus he concludes that Stuart, Logan, and Herndon were the only partners Lincoln ever had.

(See Editorial, "Lincoln in Many Law Firms," 8 *Journal of the Illinois State Historical Society* [October 1915], 198.)

465
Stock, Leonard C.
Blackstone Commentaries: Where Did Lincoln Get Them? What Became of Them? 52 HOBBIES (February 1948), 129-131, 133.

The author acknowledges two distinct lines of thought pertaining to Lincoln's acquiring Blackstone's *Commentaries*. He quotes from the authors of biographies and other works. In favor of the "barrel" story were A. J. Conant, artist who painted Lincoln in Springfield, and authors McClure, Rankin, Rothchild, Tarbell, Sandburg, Hertz, Morgan, and Hill. William E. Barton presented both sides of the question. Herndon did not say where Lincoln obtained his copy, nor did Nicolay and Hay. Biographers who believed that he bought his Blackstone at auction included, J. C. Holland, Albert J. Beveridge, and Isaac N. Arnold. Ward H. Lamon thought that he borrowed a worn copy at Beardstown. The author, who did some research on the location, speculates as to where the volume or volumes were at the time of writing his article.

466
Stone, Claude U.
A. Lincoln: Attorney and Counsellor at Law. 55 LINCOLN HERALD (Spring 1953), 47-48.

This article shows Lincoln's purported business card "A. Lincoln: Attorney and Counsellor at Law," which was used by opponents as a handout with the message that Lincoln admits failure as president and will return to Springfield to practice.

467
Street, Arthur L. H.
Abraham Lincoln's Municipal Law Cases, 56 THE AMERICAN CITY (February 1941), 71, 73.

Abraham Lincoln appeared as counsel in lawsuits for or against municipalities. Cases reported in decisions of the Supreme Court of Illinois aid in appraising the character of Abraham Lincoln the lawyer.

He never refused to aid a poor person or one who was not influential. He was as ready to champion a cause for a small fee, such as *Byrne v. Stout* for a $3.00 hog, as he was for the important tax case of *Illinois Central Railroad Co. v. County of McLean*.

There is a brief review of cases in which Lincoln appeared as counsel for municipalities, such as *City of Springfield v. Hickox, Browning v. City of Springfield, Town of Petersburg v. Metzker*.

468
Stubbs, Roy St. George.
Lawyer Lincoln--A Canadian Estimate. 27 CONNECTICUT BAR JOURNAL (September 1953), 335-358.

Lincoln's greatness is attributed to the training he received as he practiced law. The author claims Lincoln was not a widely read man, but he knew intimately those books which he had read. He knew and used words of the Bible and Aesop's Fables to a large extent. Lincoln's own history is summarized, with several interesting stories about his life, including memorable quotations. Stubbs concludes, Lincoln's "first 52 years had been a preparation for the last four eventful years of his life."

469
Suppiger, Joseph E.
The Intimate Lincoln. Part 6: Life in Springfield, 1840-1847. 84 LINCOLN HERALD (Summer 1982), 114-125.

Suppiger tells of the decline in the professional relationship with Stuart, and of his joining Stephen T. Logan in partnership. He describes several of the cases argued. Logan remarked that he did not think Lincoln had studied very much but worked hard on any case at hand and was a "pretty good lawyer" without depth of legal knowledge. He mentions conflicting political goals of Lincoln and Logan, leading to conclusion of their partnership.

See also **Suppiger**, Monographs.

470
Suppiger, Joseph E.
The Intimate Lincoln. Part 8: Lawyer and Politician. 84 LINCOLN HERALD

(Winter 1982), 222-236. Part 9: The Making of a New President. 85 LINCOLN HERALD (Spring 1983), 7-20.

Lincoln tried a great variety of cases, and during 1853 he handled some 300 cases. There was usually a three-month stint on the legal circuit. The lawyer Lincoln was respected enough to have had the town of Lincoln, Illinois, named after him while he was a practicing attorney.

It was difficult for him to maintain his "honest" reputation when he was sued for misappropriation of Todd estate funds; the case was dismissed.

There is description of his office, discussion of his fees and principles with respect to his practice. Includes a facsimile of the check in the Illinois Central Railroad case.

"The Making of a New President" also tells of Lincoln's taking the study of law casually and hardly adding a book to the two-hundred volumes in the law-office collection. There is discussion of the Peachy Harrison case and information on lucrative federal cases.

See also **Suppiger**. Monographs.

471
Tarbell, Ida M. (Minerva)
Lincoln as a Lawyer. 7 MCCLURE'S MAGAZINE (July 1896), 171-181.

Contents as noted at head of article: reminiscences and anecdotes from men who practiced with him at the bar; his humor and persuasiveness; his manner of preparing cases, examining witnesses and addressing juries.

Tarbell tells of Lincoln's interest in reading the *Statutes of Indiana* and Blackstone's *Commentaries*. She notes that it took "a friend's" urging to persuade him to study law. Tarbell does not identify the "friend." From 1836, when he was admitted to the bar, until 1847 the law was secondary to Lincoln's public life. He did not plunge into the law as a full-time career until his return from Congress in 1849. Tarbell describes the judicial circuits in Illinois and how judges and lawyers rode the circuit by means of horse or buggy from town to town. Lincoln loved to ride the circuit where "he found humor and human interest on the route."

The author describes Lincoln's association with Judge Davis, the courthouses on the circuit, and Lincoln's interaction with other lawyers and clerks of the circuit.

She discusses the types of cases Lincoln took and his method of preparing a case by reducing it to its simplest element. She tells of his skills at examining witnesses and how he used common everyday stories to sway a jury to his line of reasoning.

The author concludes that Lincoln's real strength as a lawyer was his ability to present clearly the case to a jury, and she quotes from those who had heard him. "He never used a word which the dullest jury man could not understand." "His illustrations were almost always of the homeliest kind." "In making a speech . . . Mr. Lincoln was the plainest man I ever heard. He was not a speaker but a talker. He talked to jurors and to political gatherings plain, sensible, candid talk almost as in conversation, no effort whatever in oratory."

Tarbell draws heavily on an unpublished manuscript, "Lincoln on the Stump and at the Bar," by a member of the Illinois Bar.

472
Tarbell, Ida M. (Minerva)
Lincoln's Important Law Cases. 7 MCCLURE'S MAGAZINE (August 1896), 272-281.

This article, continued from the prior issue of the journal includes: Lincoln's defense of a slave girl; a five-thousand-dollar fee; the McCormick patent case and Lincoln's first meeting with Stanton; the Armstrong murder case and the almanac; the Rock Island Bridge case; the Harrison case.

473
Temple, Wayne C.
Lincoln Rides the Circuit. 62 LINCOLN HERALD (Winter 1960), 139-143.

The article concerns the horses Lincoln used and owned when he rode the circuit from 1839 to 1859. They were a necessity of the circuit before the advent of the railroads. When Lincoln first began to ride the Eighth Judicial Circuit, he rented or borrowed a horse. By the early 1840s he owned a horse, and by 1850 Lincoln had a horse named "Old Buck" with a buggy for his traveling. "Old Bob" was Lincoln's last horse in Springfield.

474
Temple, Wayne C.
Lincoln Witnesses a Will: A New Document. 91 LINCOLN HERALD (Spring 1989), 12.

Temple provides the verbatim text of the will of Elijah Utterback, dated June 12, 1859. Three prominent men, S[tephen] T. Logan, A[braham] Lincoln, and M[ilton] Hay witnessed the "X" of an illiterate man whose intention it was to keep the husband of one of his daughters from benefiting. The document itself was drawn up on blue paper in Sangamon County, and is presently located in the Illinois State Archives.

475
Temple, Wayne C.
Lincoln's First Step to Becoming a Lawyer. 70 LINCOLN HERALD (Winter 1968), 207-208.

"It is ordered by the Court that it be certified that Abraham Lincoln is a person of good moral character." This statement appeared by order of Judge Stephen Trigg Logan at Springfield in the Sangamon County Circuit Court Record, March 24, 1836. The next step in preparing for law practice was in passing the bar exam on September 9, 1836. Lincoln actually became a member of the bar in full standing in the supreme court office at Vandalia, March 1, 1837, when his name was written on the roll of attorneys.

476
Ten Lincoln Law Cases. 390 LINCOLN LORE (September 28, 1936), [1].

In celebration of the centennial of Lincoln's obtaining his license to practice law, ten cases are listed with summaries.

Includes *Hawthorne v. Wooldridge, Bailey v. Cromwell, People v. Harrison, Isaac Smith v. John H. Smith, Hurd v. Rock Island Bridge Co., Banet [sic] v. The Alton and Sangamon Railroad, McCormick v. Manny, Illinois Central Railroad v. County of McLean, People v. Armstrong, Jones v. Johnson [sic]*.

477
Thomas, Benjamin P. (Platt)
Abe Lincoln, Country Lawyer. 193 ATLANTIC MONTHLY (February 1954), 57-61.

In 1854 Lincoln set forth in his buggy on his round of the Eighth Judicial Circuit. It was evident that he loved circuit life, including its sociability, camaraderie, speechmaking, law, and politics.

He had not been popular with the people of his district while in Congress, and had little choice but to return to the routine of a country lawyer at Springfield. He resolved to become a better lawyer. Although Lincoln appreciated books, and gained knowledge from them, observation and experience were his best teachers. He longed to put his thoughts and expressions into understandable words.

Thomas quotes from his notes for a law lecture, acknowledges his honesty, and his enjoyment of storytelling and humor, which sometimes served a purpose.

The headnotes describe Thomas as author of the best single-volume biography of Lincoln.

478
Thomas, Benjamin P. (Platt)
Lincoln and the Courts, 1854-1861. ABRAHAM LINCOLN ASSOCIATION
PAPERS (1934), 46-103.

The author considers the time period of 1854-1861 in Lincoln's life
emphasizing his practice of law with particular reference to "the organization,
procedure and terms of the various courts in which Lincoln practiced, his legal
associates, and the changes that took place in legal practice."
He describes life on the Eighth Judicial Circuit, the country towns where
court was held, local politics, and local lawyers and judges with whom Lincoln
practiced or was associated. He wrote of the federal court and the state supreme
court at that period of time.

479
Thomas, Benjamin P. (Platt)
Lincoln's Earlier Practice in the Federal Courts, 1839-1854. No. 39 BULLETIN
OF THE ABRAHAM LINCOLN ASSOCIATION (June 1935),
[3]-9.

In 1855, the Federal Judicial District of Illinois was divided into a Northern
and Southern Judicial District. Files of pre-1855 cases that had been transferred
to Chicago were destroyed in the great 1871 fire. However, transcripts of many
pre-1855 cases remained in Springfield and the author based this article on
those. They do not contain all of Lincoln's earlier federal cases, but considerable
information of his federal practice is gleaned from the transcripts.
Lincoln was admitted to practice before the federal court, December 3,
1839. "In the Federal Courts, as on the Circuit, Lincoln was a favorite with the
bench." The transcripts reveal that Lincoln appeared in at least twenty-nine cases
before the federal court, pre-1855. Twenty-two of these involved collections of
debt. His first case, *Hooper, Martin, and Smith v. Haines,* was instituted in the
circuit court on October 19, 1839, six weeks before Lincoln was formally
admitted to practice in federal courts. Many of Lincoln's federal cases were
routine; however, he had several patent cases, and *Columbus Insurance Co. v.
Curtenius,* 1851, in which Lincoln represented a canal boat plaintiff who struck
a bridge on facts very similiar to the later famous case of "Effie Afton." The
author describes some of these cases, as well as others, all involving Lincoln's
pre-1855 practice in federal court.

480
Tilton, Clint Clay.
Lincoln and Lamon: Partners and Friends. 38 TRANSACTIONS OF THE
ILLINOIS STATE HISTORICAL SOCIETY (1931), 175-228.

Ward Hill Lamon, at nineteen years of age, arrived in Danville, Illinois, in
1847 to study law. Lamon was a Virginia gentleman fond of fine liquor, a
cavalier among the ladies, and known as the life of the party around town.

Lincoln took a liking to the "young Virginian" although "no two men ever
were more unlike than Lincoln and Lamon," and yet according to Judge David
Davis, "Abe trusted Lamon more than any other man."

There is a good discussion of life in Danville when the Eighth Circuit riders
came to town. Lincoln, when he traveled the circuit, began to team up with
Lamon, the ever-popular local attorney, in 1852. The partnership lasted until
1857 when Lamon was elected district prosecuting attorney. Yet they remained
close friends until Lincoln was killed. Lamon went with Lincoln to Washington
as marshal of the District of Columbia. It is the story of a true friendship.

Issued also as a separate. Danville, Ill.: Interstate Printing Co., 1932. 56 p.

481
Tilton, Clint Clay.
Ward Hill Lamon in Bloomington, Illinois. LINCOLN GROUP PAPERS 2nd
series (1945), 159-171.

Tilton tells of Lincoln's popularity as a circuit rider, following the traveling
judges semiannually. Lincoln showed some interest in young Lamon and
associated with him in several cases. Two years later "the Partnership of Lincoln
and Lamon" was formed, with the latter as the local member. The two men
were unlike, but became friends and associates.

482
Tipton, Virgil E.
Cass County, Site of Almanac Trial, Has Fascinating History. 71 ILLINOIS
BAR JOURNAL (January 1983), 326.

Cass County was the site of Lincoln's famous almanac trial. This article
deals with the thirty-year fight between the towns of Beardstown and Virginia
over which should be the county seat. Lincoln made numerous court
appearances in both towns. The almanac case was tried in 1850 at Beardstown,
where he used the almanac to prove that a witness could not have seen a
murder by the light of the moon.

483
Townsend, William H. (Henry)
Commonwealth of Kentucky v. Abraham Lincoln.   14 AMERICAN BAR
ASSOCIATION JOURNAL (February 1928), 80-82.

This article describes the only time Abe Lincoln was charged with the penal
offense of operating a ferry on the Ohio River without a license. The case was
tried before Squire Pate in Kentucky. Lincoln spoke in his behalf claiming he
did not know he violated any law and had not intended to encroach on a
licensed ferry. Lincoln was acquitted but received a lecture from Squire Pate in
which he stressed that everyone should be better acquainted with a knowledge
of the law. Lincoln on occasion would paddle the Ohio to attend sessions of
Pate's court. The author believes this occasion first inspired Lincoln to begin his
study of the law.

484
Townsend, William H. (Henry)
Lincoln on the Circuit.   12 AMERICAN BAR ASSOCATION JOURNAL
(February 1926), 91-95.

Townsend describes the Eighth Judicial Circuit of Illinois and what life was
like traveling the circuit as Lincoln did in the 1840s and 1850s. The article tells
several stories of Lincoln on the circuit, in the courtroom, and in dealing with
his clients, based on a number of quotations from Lincoln's contemporaries.

485
Townsend, William H. (Henry)
Lincoln the Lawyer. COURIER JOURNAL MAGAZINE [Louisville] (February
12, 1961), 21-24.

With little schooling, Lincoln considered becoming a blacksmith, but he
wanted to be a lawyer. He studied Blackstone, and through John T. Stuart
studied law in earnest. Townsend describes the partnerships as well as life of a
circuit rider on the Eighth Judicial Circuit. There is a glimpse of Lincoln's
appearance also. He was excellent at cross-examination of witnesses. He knew
the facts and rules of evidence and was direct and courteous. He had power of
analysis, logic, and a good grasp of subjects. Not only was he a popular lawyer
with the people, but he also represented powerful corporations. The only
criticism lawyers had of him was that he charged "picayune" fees, as exemplified
in his return of part of a fee to a Quincy client. There are quotations from
Lincoln's advice to law students, and a scene from his last day in Springfield.

486
Townsend, William H. (Henry)
Lincoln the Lawyer. 18 THE SUMMONS (Bancroft-Whitney) (May 1926), 3-12.

Reprinted from 12 AMERICAN BAR ASSOCIATION JOURNAL (February 1926). For annotation see **Townsend**, "Lincoln on the Circuit."

487
Townsend, William H. (Henry)
Lincoln the Litigant. 10 AMERICAN BAR ASSOCIATION JOURNAL (February 1924), 83-88.

Although Lincoln charged modest fees, he expected payment for his services, and was not afraid to use the courts to collect. ". . . Abraham Lincoln was a party to more lawsuits than was the average lawyer or citizen even of his own rather litigious day." The author describes some of the cases where Lincoln was a plaintiff, attempting to collect his fees, including the famous Illinois Central Railroad case, where Lincoln represented the railroad and later had to sue for his fee. Discussion continues on cases where Lincoln was the defendant himself.

488
Townsend, William H. (Henry)
Lincoln's Defense of Duff Armstrong. 11 AMERICAN BAR ASSOCATION JOURNAL (February 1925), 81-84.

This is the story of how Lincoln repaid the kindness of a poor farm couple in defending their son free of charge. Lincoln was befriended by the Armstrongs, a married couple in New Salem, Illinois, when he was just starting out as a young adult. He came to defend their son who was charged with murder some twenty-five years later. Townsend provides details of the trial in which Lincoln's "almanac" defense helped secure a not guilty verdict.

489
Townsend, William H. (Henry)
Lincoln's Law Books. 15 AMERICAN BAR ASSOCATION JOURNAL (March 1929), 125-126.

Townsend lists and describes the books that Lincoln borrowed and read during his study of law. There is information on Lincoln's law office and the law books it contained. The author notes that very few of Lincoln's books are still extant, and mentions some of those that remain.

490
Townsend, William H. (Henry)
Logan and Lincoln.   19 AMERICAN BAR ASSOCIATION JOURNAL
(February 1933), 87-90.

This piece concerns the law partnership of Lincoln and Stephen T. Logan
in Springfield, Illinois, from 1841-1844. The two men had contrasting styles. The
junior partner, Lincoln, learned a great deal of law from Logan and polished his
skills. Townsend includes a description of a murder trial, where Lincoln and
Logan defended three brothers. Lincoln adduced evidence to clear his clients.

491
Townsend, William H. (Henry)
"Old Abe" and the "Little Giant."   13 AMERICAN BAR ASSOCIATION
JOURNAL (February 1927), 99-104.

The article shows similarities and differences between Lincoln and Stephen
A. Douglas, known as the "Little Giant." Townsend discusses the Senate race of
1858 and the seven debates between the world-renowned, sophisticated Douglas
and the lesser known, yet able and honest Lincoln. Douglas remarked
concerning the debates that he "would rather meet any other man in the country
than Lincoln." The two men managed to remain friends despite their contests.

492
Townsend, William H. (Henry)
Stuart & Lincoln.   17 AMERICAN BAR ASSOCIATION JOURNAL
(February 1931), 82-85.

The author summarizes Lincoln's association with John T. Stuart. While the
article does not focus on any one aspect, it brings together various activities
during their partnershp and friendship from 1837 to 1841.

493
Tree, Lambert.
Side-Lights on Lincoln. II. Lincoln Among Lawyers. 81 CENTURY
MAGAZINE (February 1911), 591-593.

The author speaks of how he personally met Lincoln in his own law office
in Chicago in 1856. After describing his physical appearance, he tells how
Lincoln consulted the books on the library shelves, studied them for some time,
and asked to borrow *Littleton on Tenures*. Eventually, Lincoln returned the
volume with a new cover.

He shows in several ways how Lincoln was a moral person in accepting fees, and illustrated how he had to believe his client was in the right. Lincoln was highly respected by his peers.

See also **Tree**, "Lincoln Among Lawyers," in **Wilson**, Monographs.

494
Trent, Fred E.
The Will of Joshua Short. 15 THE ABRAHAM LINCOLN ASSOCIATION BULLETIN (June 1, 1929), 5-7.

Lincoln drew up this will seventeen days before he received his law license. It was simple, to the point, and stood all legal tests. The text of the will is quoted in full. The article continues with the filing of the will and property appraisal after the death of Short.

495
Wagner, Charles.
Lincoln as a Lawyer. 59 NEW JERSEY LAW JOURNAL (February 13, 1936), 57, 59-60.

Wagner points out the lack of writings on Lincoln as a lawyer; that phase of his life has been dwarfed by volumes devoted to his statesmanship. A few of the biographers, in describing his life as a lawyer, have spoken about him disparagingly. This article states that Lincoln was a capable lawyer, and the author believes that he would have left a reputation as a lawyer in Illinois, even if he had not ascended to the presidency. He quotes statistics on the number of cases in which he appeared, and mentions the diversity of his cases. He believes that Lincoln tried more cases than were recorded, due to laxity of legal reporting in that era. There is some description of court days.

496
Warner, H. H.
Abraham Lincoln, LL.D., a Professional Portrait. 27 MICHIGAN STATE BAR JOURNAL (February 1948), 5-11.

Warner outlines Lincoln's career as a lawyer, discussing some of the cases with which he was involved. He discusses several cases Lincoln tried that contributed to the law of tort liability in Illinois. He tells of several honorary doctor of laws degrees he received.

497

Weik, Jesse W. (William)
A Law Student's Recollection of Abraham Lincoln. 97 THE OUTLOOK
(February 11, 1911), 311-314.

The author, Jesse W. Weik, was the joint author with William H. Herndon
of *Life of Lincoln*. Weik was a friend of Jonathan Birch. Abraham Lincoln was
appointed to examine Birch for his admission to the bar in the late 1850s. At
that time an oral examination was required to obtain a license to practice in
Illinois. Weik published Birch's account of his meeting with Lincoln, found in
Birch's papers after his death, in which he describes the examination.

Birch remarked on how Lincoln would tell jovial and humorous stories in
his law office, and yet at other times would be withdrawn, solemn, and
uncommunicative.

498

Weik, Jesse W. (William)
Lincoln and the Matson Negroes: A Vista into the Fugitive-Slave Days. 17
ARENA (April 1897), 752-758.

Weik speaks of Illinois' Black Law, which said that no black shall reside in
Illinois unless he had a certificate to present to County Commissioner's Court.
If someone should harbor an illegal black in Illinois, there would be a $500 fine.
The article tells of Lincoln's involvement in the Matson slave case, and is not
very probative of Lincoln's skills as a lawyer, suggesting that he was halfhearted
in his prosecution.

499

Weik, Jesse W. (William)
Lincoln as a Lawyer: With an Account of His First Case. 68 CENTURY
MAGAZINE (June 1904), 279-289.

Weik describes Lincoln's borrowing law books to study, such as Blackstone,
Greenleaf, and Chitty. He quotes the entry in the records of the Circuit Court
of Sangamon County, and provides the facsimile of the certificate of character
for Lincoln, required as the first step in his legal career. He gives an example
of the type of examination for admission to the bar. A facsimile in Lincoln's
handwriting can be seen in the subsection "Papers Relating to Lincoln's First
Law Case." In this authentic account of the first law case, an action (actually
three) involving assumpsit, trespass, and replevin grew out of a transaction of
James P. Hawthorne against Wooldridge in the Circuit Court of Sangamon
County, declarations having been filed before Lincoln received his license to
practice.

An additional facsimile is furnished showing Lincoln's entries in a fee-book. Weik describes life on the circuit, and Lincoln's examination of a young man for admission to the bar.

500
Whelan, Frank.
A. Lincoln for the Railroads. 1 ILLINOIS REPRESENTATIVE (Spring 1975), 34-39, 42, 70.

Lincoln stands out as a leader of the Illinois bar with a reputation as one of the more skillful lawyers. Although historians have tended to ignore his role as a corporate attorney, he was one of the most successful railroad attorneys in the nation.

Alton and Sangamon Railroad v. James A. Banet [sic] in 1848 was actually Lincoln's first railroad case. It concerned the move of a direct route to Carlinville. (Lincoln held five shares in the Alton and Sangamon Railroad himself.) In the second case, *Alton and Sangamon Railroad v. Carpenter*, Lincoln argued that a landowner was wrong to consider his land devalued by presence of a railroad. In his third case, he argued successfully that a railroad was not responsible for livestock on the right-of-way.

His first case for the Illinois Central Railroad was a condemnation case in 1853. The company agent, James F. Joy, later called Lincoln to Chicago to act as arbiter between the Illinois Central and Northern Indiana railroads. In 1854 the McLean County suit was filed against the Illinois Central for failure to pay taxes. Lincoln had applied first to represent the county. When there was no response, he wrote to the railroad attorney and was assigned to the case. The article discusses his $5000 fee in *Lincoln v. Illinois Central*, 1857. Lincoln won by default when the railroad attorney did not arrive. Payment was forthcoming only after Lincoln had the sheriff of McLean County seize property. Later Lincoln battled State Auditor Dubois over the valuation of the Illinois Central Railroad property for tax purposes. This item includes details of Lincoln's confidential letter to Dubois.

501
Williamson, Glenn Yerk.
Lincoln, the Lawyer, Was Here. 9 BUICK MAGAZINE (February 1948), 5.

Lincoln was in the Metamora Courthouse many times. He, like other lawyers in the 1840s and 1850s, moved with an intinerant group from one county seat to another. The circuit riders gathered informally outside the courthouse, and stayed in the taverns and inns, such as the Metamora House. Lincoln had a distinct personality. His friendships and connections on the old Eighth Circuit later influenced his political career.

The history-shaping Eighth Judicial Circuit courtroom is basically the same today as it was when Lincoln tried cases there. A table with cut-out space to accommodate Lincoln's knees can be seen among other museum relics.

502
Wilson, Mitchell.
Abe Lincoln's First Big Fee. 68 READER'S DIGEST (February 1956), 21-25.

This article for the lay reader presents the *McCormick v. Manny* case in popular form. The author has based his story on Sandburg's *Abraham Lincoln: The Prairie Years*; Tarbell's *In the Footsteps of the Lincolns*; and Herndon's "letters and papers." He describes Lincoln's being retained as counsel, his intense preparation, and his rebuff when the suit was moved to Cincinnati. He describes Lincoln's humiliation, and also his being impressed with the logic of Edwin M. Stanton in his courtroom argument, which won the victory for Manny. Wilson suggests that Lincoln's own manner became more dignified and his speeches more polished after this courtroom observation. He informs readers that Lincoln returned his check. Only later did he accept it and share it with Herndon.

503
Wise, Stuart M.
For Sale: A Lincoln Landmark. 5 NATIONAL LAW JOURNAL (November 15, 1982), 47.

This brief article concerns the sale of the Springfield law office of Abraham Lincoln and William Herndon who occupied it from 1843-1852. The office was renovated and used as a tourist attraction. At the asking price of $750,000 for the real estate, the state with funding could acquire the historical site.

504
Woldman, Albert A.
Centennial of Lincoln's Admission to the Bar: An Historic Event.   23 AMERICAN BAR ASSOCIATION JOURNAL (March 1937), 167-171.

This article on Lincoln as a lawyer marks the one-hundredth anniversary of Lincoln's being admitted to the Illinois Bar. ". . . nearly every important and outstanding event in his public career was in one manner or another influenced by his training and experience as a lawyer." Woldman discusses how the practice of law taught Lincoln the talents and foresight he would use to become a great president and illustrates how Lincoln's presidential actions reflected the ideas of his training as a lawyer.

Wright, Allen Henry.
A New Light on Lincoln as an Advocate.
See **Somers,** W. H.

505
Wrone, David R.
Abraham Lincoln's Idea of Property. 33 SCIENCE AND SOCIETY (Winter 1969), 54-70.

Lincoln presented the view that this was not a closed society; upward mobility was possible. He owned little property and did not pursue wealth, although many others in his company on the Eighth Judicial Circuit did so. In the 1850s he acquired two lots in Bloomington, Illinois, apparently as part of a legal action. He owned a lot in Springfield and in Lincoln, Illinois, and had benefited from land grants in Iowa.

His public speeches did not touch on property. Judge David Davis summarized his attitude, "It did not seem to be one of the purposes of his life to accumulate a fortune." According to Lincoln, the property question rested on the character of the owners. The article mentions legislation that passed under his signature later in life, such as the Homestead Act, Morrill Land Grant Act, railroad land grants, and legal tender. It was suggested that his concept of property was formed while he was on the prairies of Illinois, where he matured and practiced law for twenty years.

A number of his friends, like Clifton H. Moore, were large land holders, some of whom were legal associates on the circuit. He saw the drive for power and land among landed aristocrats who often controlled the banks. Men of means, such as Lawyer Gridley of Bloomington, sought him as legal counsel; Attorney Coler later retired to Wall Street. These men held him in highest esteem, there being no question about his character, honesty, or ability. Later when he sought election, these people of the Eighth Judicial Circuit organized to assist in the campaign.

506
Younger, Irving.
Abraham Lincoln, Esq. 11 LITIGATION (Winter 1985), 37-38, 59.

The author notes that Lincoln "was a lawyer, one of the best and most successful of his time." Lincoln was at his best as a litigator. He was "unusually skillful at presenting complicated appellate issues simply and persuasively. . . ." "Lincoln's powers were at their most impressive before juries." Younger illustates this proposition with cases of a Revolutionary War widow and the Armstrong murder case. He talks briefly about how Illinois courts in 1841 came to decide that a promissory note was unenforceable when given for a black girl.

"The sale of a free person is illegal," thus consideration for the note unenforceable. Lincoln won the case.

A later case described by Younger is that of a captured Union soldier, Goff, imprisoned in the infamous Libby Prison. After exchange in a prisoner swap, Lincoln summoned him for an interview regarding prison conditions. Goff later became a noted West Virginia senator and judge.

507
Zane, Charles S.
Impressions of Herndon and Lincoln. Edited by James T. Hickey. 64 JOURNAL OF THE ILLINOIS STATE HISTORICAL SOCIETY (Summer 1971), 206-209.

Manuscripts presented to the Illinois State Historical Library contained "Some Reminiscences and Impressions of William H. Herndon As a Man and As a Lawyer With Reference to Abraham Lincoln, His Greatly Distinguished Partner," bearing the signature of Charles S. Zane. A facsimile of the full text, which was typewritten, appears in this article edited by James T. Hickey.

Zane can be considered an original source since he observed Herndon and Lincoln from his law office located above theirs. He indicated that they lent him books and advised him. He observed their ways, treatment of clients, and methods. He heard them examine witnesses and argue questions of law and fact. Generally Herndon and Lincoln did not engage in the same trial. Lincoln considered questions in the concrete, with great capacity for analysis and inference. He was methodical and systematic. Later Charles Zane became Herndon's law partner. Having observed Herndon's relationship with Lincoln, he believed that Herndon meant to be a friend of Lincoln. He believed that Herndon gave too much credence to exaggerated statements of some of Lincoln's earlier contemporaries.

508
Zane, Charles S.
Lincoln As I Knew Him. 14 JOURNAL OF THE ILLINOIS STATE HISTORICAL SOCIETY (April 1921), 74-84; 29 SUNSET MAGAZINE (October 1912), 430-538.

There were no openings in the law office of Lincoln and Herndon when Zane applied for a place as a law student. Later he practiced in the same courts at Springfield. He noted Lincoln's courtesy, and his ability in speechmaking, being able to gauge the difference between speeches in court and on the political platform. Zane reminisced on the day of Lincoln's death when members of the Springfield bar met at the old courthouse. Conkling, Logan, and Herndon spoke of his kindly disposition and moral qualities. Logan emphasized further that he was a great lawyer when he believed his client was in the right. Zane remarked, "Even his professional career has not received the credit to which his marvelous legal capacity entitled it."

509
Zane, John M. (Maxcy)
Lincoln, the Constitutional Lawyer. ABRAHAM LINCOLN ASSOCIATION PAPERS (1933), 25-108.

For Annotation, see **Zane**, Monographs.

Other Bibliographies

Index

Other Bibliographies

Angle, Paul M.
The Lincoln Collection of the Illinois State Historical Library. Springfield, Ill.:
The Library, 1940.
21 p.

The librarian of the Illinois State Historical Library in Springfield, Illinois,
describes the Lincoln collection as of 1940. The collection contains "more than
two hundred autograph letters and documents of Lincoln . . ." including many
early documents from when Lincoln was beginning his law practice. Collection
also contains over 4500 titles concerning works about Lincoln, as well as prints,
paintings, and photographs. Angle describes some of these works as well as
photocopies of certain items.

Angle, Paul M.
A Shelf of Lincoln Books: A Critical Selective Bibliography of Lincolniana. New
Brunswick: Rutgers University Press in Association with the Abraham Lincoln
Association of Springfield, Ill., 1946.
142 p.

Angle compiled a critical annotated bibliography of works about Lincoln
in an effort to separate worthy and useful works by knowledgeable Lincoln
scholars from the avalanche of numerous Lincoln works. Critics were
appreciative of his choice of items.
The work is divided into sections: I. Lincoln's writings and speeches,
biographies, monographs and special studies. II. Bibliography.

Baker Monty R.
Abraham Lincoln in Theses and Dissertations. 74 LINCOLN HERALD (1972),
107-111.

Barton, William E.
Abraham Lincoln and His Books. With Selections from the Writings of Lincoln and a Bibliography of Books in Print Relating to Abraham Lincoln. Chicago: Marshall Field, 1920.
108 p.

Booker, Richard.
Abraham Lincoln in Periodical Literature, 1860-1940. Written and compiled by Richard Booker.   Chicago: Fawley-Brost Co., 1941.

Fish, Daniel.
A Reprint of the List of Books and Pamphlets Relating to Abraham Lincoln. Compiled by Daniel Fish in 1906 [by] Joseph Benjamin Oakleaf. Rock Island, Ill.: Augustana Book Concern, 1926.
280 p.

Originally issued in Nicolay and Hay, *Complete Works of Abraham Lincoln,* 1905, volume 11, "Lincoln Bibliography."

Hall, Kermit.
A Comprehensive Bibliography of American Constitution and Legal History, 1896-1979. Millwood, N.Y.: Kraus International Publications, 1984.
5 v. and Supplement, 1980-1987.

Library of Congress.
A Catalog of the Alfred Whital Stern Collection of Lincolniana. Washington: The Library, 1960.
xi, 498 p.

Library of Congress.
A List of Lincolniana in the Library of Congress, by George Thomas Ritchie. Rev. ed., with Supplement. Washington: U.S. Government Printing Office, 1906.
86 p.

Monaghan, Jay.
Lincoln Bibliography, 1839-1939. Compiled by Jay Monaghan. With a foreword by James G. Randall. Springfield: Illinois State Historical Library, 1943-45.
2 v. (Illinois historical collections, v. 31-32; Bibliographical series; v. 4-5)

A two-volume bibliography of all the works written about Lincoln from 1839-1939 including speeches, reports, etc., made by Lincoln himself. A lengthy introduction describes the criteria necessary to be be included in the bibliography. Compiled chronologically then alphabetically by author within a particular year. Each work has a brief paragraph describing the work.

Includes Lincolniana in foreign-language titles, miscellaneous undated titles, and titles discovered during the early nineteen forties.

This bibliography superseded Fish and Oakleaf.

Oakleaf, Joseph Benjamin.
Lincoln Bibliography: A List of Books and Pamphlets Relating to Abraham Lincoln. Compiled by Joseph Benjamin Oakleaf. Cedar Rapids, Iowa: Torch Press, 1925.
424 p.

Searcher, Victor.
Lincoln Today: An Introduction to Modern Lincolniana. New York: T. Yoseloff, 1969.
342 p.

A bibliography of books about Abraham Lincoln. Part I concerns "Books about Lincoln"; Part II, "Lincoln in the Lively Arts" (plays, films, music). The book contains more than 600 annotated entries about Abraham Lincoln found in media up to 1969. The compiler has selected works covering different aspects of Lincoln. Annotations include explanation of why such a work should be read by the Lincoln reader.

It includes annotations of *Lincoln as a Lawyer*, by John P. Frank, and *A. Lincoln: Prairie Lawyer*, by John J. Duff, among others.

Books about the Literature

Basler, Roy P.
The Lincoln Legend: A Study in Changing Conceptions. New York: Octagon Books, 1969, ©1935.
viii, 335 p.

Includes a survey of Lincoln literature.

Fehrenbacher, Don E.
Lincoln in Text and Context: Collected Essays.   Stanford, Calif.: Stanford University Press, 1987.
x, 364 p.

Thomas, Benjamin P.
Portrait for Posterity: Lincoln and His Biographers. New Brunswick, N.J.: Rutgers University Press, 1947.
xvii, 329 p.

Index

Entries are cited by item number throughout.

Cases

Elizabeth W. Matthews is Librarian and Professor, School of Law Library, Southern Illinois University at Carbondale. Her masters degree is from the University of Illinois. The recipient of a Ph.D. degree from Southern Illinois University, she was awarded an LL.D. degree (honorary) by Randolph-Macon College, her alma mater. Her most recent previous books include *The Law Library Reference Shelf: Annotated Subject Guide* and *Seventeenth Century English Law Reports in Folio: Description of Selected Imprints*.

Cullom Davis is Director, The Lincoln Legal Papers, Illinois Historic Preservation Agency, Springfield. Professor at Sangamon State University previously, he is well-known for his oral and documentary histories. His graduate degrees are from the University of Illinois and his baccalaureate from Princeton University.